INTERMEDIATE

Language LEADER

COURSEBOOK
and CD-ROM

PEARSON
Longman

David Cotton   David Falvey   Simon Kent

Language Reference and Extra Practice by John Hughes

CONTENTS

Listening	Speaking / Pronunciation	Scenario	Study & Writing skills
Conversation about appearance and personality Radio interview with a psychologist	Discussing personalities Information gap Discussing charisma and personality *Pronunciation: word stress*	**Personality clash** **Key Language:** giving opinions, agreeing and disagreeing **Task:** choosing a new team member	Taking notes while reading Symbols and abbreviations A comparative essay Linkers
Talk about travelling abroad Interview Lecture	Discussing travel Discussing past life events Discussing jobs *Pronunciation: -ed endings* *Pronunciation: weak forms*	**A study trip** **Key Language:** discussing advantages and disadvantages, making suggestions **Task:** organising a study trip	Taking notes while listening A biographical profile Time linkers
Monologues describing jobs Monologues about homeworking Conversation with a careers advisor Monologues about writing CVs	Discussing jobs Discussing what is important in a job Discussing homeworking Asking killer questions *Pronunciation: correcting politely* *Pronunciation: contractions and weak forms*	**Situation vacant** **Key Language:** asking questions, giving answers **Task:** taking part in a job interview	Organising ideas Paragraphs Organising a paragraph Covering letter and curriculum vitae (CV)
Conversation between two students Radio interview about Gaelic	Discussing language Discussing texting and language in the future Debate – minority languages	**Language training** **Key Language:** accepting and rejecting ideas, considering consequences **Task:** selecting an English language programme	Describing tables and charts A report
Monologues about advertisements Conversation about advertising techniques TV debate about advertising	Talking about adverts Describing and discussing photos Discussing using different media to advertise products Roleplay	**B-Kool soft drinks** **Key Language:** the language of presentations **Task:** giving a formal presentation	Using your dictionary A formal letter Dependent prepositions
Radio interview about setting up a business Conversation about a business idea	Pairwork – planning a business idea Discussing business dilemmas Talking about famous people's achievements *Pronunciation: weak forms*	**Sunglasses after dark** **Key Language:** making offers, stating a position, bargaining **Task:** negotiating a deal	Recognising formal and informal language Beginning and ending letters and emails Writing emails

CONTENTS

LANGUAGE LEADER   INTERMEDIATE

UNITS 7–12

Listening	Speaking / Pronunciation	Scenario	Study & Writing skills
Discussion about a product Conversations at a design museum Conversation with a teacher about written work	Discussing objects in the home Discussing designs Designing a new product Pronunciation: word stress	**Martelli design competition** **Key Language:** describing qualities **Task:** evaluating designs	Editing and proofreading A report Linkers
Monologue about a teacher 'Call my bluff' Monologues about worth of university Conversation about a course	Discussing education Describing a teacher Talking about educational systems	**Trouble at Lakeside** **Key Language:** discussing possibilities and options **Task:** problem-solving	Reading strategies Skimming Scanning A formal letter Letter conventions
Radio interview with a woman engineer A talk	Discussing engineering achievements Passives quiz Discussing structures Designing a superstructure	**The Sky-High project** **Key Language:** discussing options, making decisions **Task:** assessing a project	Preparing for a talk Linkers Describing a process Using the passive
Conversation between manager and shop assistant Advice on learning vocabulary	Talking about trends Discussing fashion and clothes Discussing work, health and society Pronunciation: stress Pronunciation: numbers	**Belleview** **Key Language:** the language of meetings **Task:** participating in a meeting	Recording and learning vocabulary Describing a trend Avoiding repetition
Reviews Conversation about a job interview Beginnings of talks	Debate – how to spend an arts grant Discussing celebrities and the arts Describing a news event	**The silver screen** **Key Language:** comparing and contrasting **Task:** choosing a film to produce	Delivering a talk A report Making generalisations
Monologues by criminals Monologues about a robbery Lecture on home security Lecture on car security	Discussing crimes Discussing crimes and criminals Speculating about a crime	**You, the jury** **Key Language:** presenting a case and discussing a verdict **Task:** discussing court cases	Summarising A narrative using cause and effect Linkers

Audioscripts (p169–183)

Personality

1.1 PERSONALITY TYPES

When the personality of a man is not clear to you, look at his friends.
Japanese proverb

VOCABULARY: personality adjectives

1a Work with a partner to think of as many personality adjectives as you can, e.g. *friendly, happy, sad.*

1b Choose three adjectives which you think describe your own personality.

2 Look at these adjectives connected with personality. Which ones are positive, which are negative and which are neutral?

adventurous   ambitious   assertive   bossy
cautious   creative   energetic   generous   moody
organised   quiet   reliable   sensible   sensitive
serious   sociable   talkative   thoughtful

3a Match words 1–6 with words a–f to make compound adjectives connected with character.

1 easy-   a) willed
2 open-   b) confident
3 even-   c) going
4 hard-   d) minded
5 self-   e) tempered
6 strong-   f) working

pronunciation

3b **1.2** Word stress   On which part of the compound adjective in Exercise 3a does the stress fall? Listen and check, then repeat the words.

3c Match the meanings below with a compound adjective from Exercise 3a.

A person who …

1 does not easily become angry: *even-tempered*.
2 is determined to do what they want: _____.
3 is not easily upset or annoyed: _____.
4 accepts other ideas and opinions: _____.
5 makes a lot of effort: _____.
6 believes in their own success: _____.

4 Think of people you know and one or two adjectives to describe each person. Explain why you describe them like this. Give examples.

LISTENING

5a Look at the people in the photos below. What kind of personality do you think each person has?
I think A is nice. She looks very easy-going and relaxed …

5b **1.3** Listen to the three people talking. Was your description of them accurate? A speaks first.

READING

6 The psychiatrist Carl Jung described two personality types. Look at these adjectives and put them into two categories to show two different character types.

adventurous   cautious   quiet
self-confident   talkative   thoughtful

7a Read the encyclopedia entry about Jung quickly and check your answer to Exercise 6.

7b Are these statements true or false?

1 Jung studied medicine in Zürich.

2 He identified the following personality types: extroverts, introverts, balanced personality.

3 Extroverts like to be in large groups of people.

4 Introverts think carefully before they do things.

5 People are interested today in his theories on dreams.

7c Work with a partner to describe the qualities of extroverts and introverts. Do not look back at the text.

8 Which kind of personality do you think each of these jobs would attract? Why? Make notes about four of them, and then compare with a partner.

actor   artist   computer programmer
film director   inventor   journalist
librarian   musician   police officer
politician   tax inspector   teacher
writer

SPEAKING

9 Work with a partner to discuss the following.

1 What are the advantages and disadvantages of having a strong personality?

2 What is a 'personality clash'? Have you had a personality clash with someone? What happened?

3 What tells you more about a person's personality: their appearance, their voice, their attitude or something else?

OMN1PE∃1∃

| article | discussion | **edit this page** | history |

Carl Jung

Carl Jung (1875–1961) was a Swiss psychiatrist who had a lasting influence on psychology and society. He studied medicine at the University of Basel from 1894 to 1900, specialising in psychiatric medicine.

Jung developed ideas about personality types which still interest and influence people today. He identified two personality types which he called introverts and extroverts. According to Jung, extroverts find meaning outside themselves, in the surrounding world. However, introverts are introspective. They look into themselves and find meaning in themselves.

Extroverts seem to like other people. It is easy for them to form close relationships. They enjoy the excitement of crowds. They tend to be assertive, self-confident, and are often leaders in groups. They are energetic and lead busy lives. In general, they are talkative, adventurous and sociable. Introverts, on the other hand, feel comfortable alone. They avoid large crowds. They are relaxed, thoughtful and reflect before they act. They are often quiet, cautious and have good powers of concentration. They often have creative ideas.

Jung's influence on our society and culture has been enormous. Two well-known tests (Myers-Briggs and David Keirsey) are based on his theory of personality types. His ideas have influenced writers as well as film-makers like Fellini and Kubrick. Jung's ideas have even influenced video games and rock music groups. There is still great interest in his theories on the interpretations of dreams.

[edit]

LISTENING AND SPEAKING

1 How useful do you think the following are for judging a person's character?

personality tests   handwriting analysis
star signs / horoscopes   interviews

2 Have you ever done a personality test? If so, why?

3a 1.4 Listen to an interview with Dr Frank Partridge, an expert in psychometrics (the measurement of intelligence and personal qualities). Tick (✓) the topics covered in the interview.

1 things that psychometric tests measure
2 the first tests
3 problems with personality tests
4 the Myers-Briggs test
5 the future of personality tests

3b Listen again and complete the questions that the interviewer asks.

1 What exactly _____ psychometrics _____?
2 How _____ psychometric testing _____?
3 _____ useful _____ the tests?
4 _____ they reliable?
5 What _____ personality tests _____ you about a person?
6 _____ you _____ any of these tests yourself?
7 What _____ you _____ on at the moment?

GRAMMAR: question forms

4 Look at the questions you completed in Exercise 3b. Which tense is used in each question?

5 Are these statements about question formation true or false?

1 In questions with the verb *to be*, we put the verb before the subject.
2 In present simple questions (except with *to be*), we use the auxiliary verb *do/does*.
3 In past simple questions, we use the auxiliary verb *has/have*.
4 In present continuous questions, we put *do/does* before the subject.
5 In present perfect questions, we put *has/have* before the subject.

6 Look at these sentences and answer the questions.

a) Who designed the Stanford-Binet test?
 – Alfred Binet designed it.
b) What did Alfred Binet design?
 – Alfred Binet designed the first usable intelligence test.

1 In which question is the *wh-* word the *subject*? This is a subject question.
2 In which question is the *wh-* word the *object*? This is an object question.
3 In which type of question do we form the question with *do/does*?

➡ Language reference and extra practice pages 134–135

7a Put the words in the right order to make questions from a psychometric test.

1 do   ever   you   get   worried   ?
2 you   are   a   confident   person   ?
3 you   do   make   easily   friends   ?
4 happy   were   you   were   when   you   child   a   ?
5 friends   did   many   at   you   your   have   first school   ?
6 in your life   influenced   most   what   you   has   ?
7 test   you   a   ever   have   personality   taken   ?
8 succeeding in   aims   achieving   your   you   are   ?

7b Work with a partner to ask and answer the questions.

SPEAKING

8 Work with a partner to complete a text about Sigmund Freud. Take turns to ask and answer questions. Prepare your questions first.

Student A: turn to page 158.
Student B: turn to page 160.
A: Who was born on 6th May 1856?
B: Sigmund Freud.

READING

9a Read the introduction to the article. Who or what are the following?

1 Hideo Nakata   3 Reiko Asakawa
2 *Ring* and *Ring 2*   4 Suzuki Koji

9b Read the rest of the interview. Fill the gaps 1–8 with these questions.

1 What's your biggest regret?

2 What was the last movie you walked out of?

3 ~~Why did you become a director?~~

4 There are five minutes left till the end of the world – what do you do?

5 How seriously do you take reviews?

6 What was the last movie that you paid to see?

7 And which film-maker do you consider the most overrated?

8 What film-maker do you consider the most underrated?

9c Why do you think he changed the main character from male to female?

WRITING

10 Imagine you are going to meet a famous person, dead or alive (e.g. a famous leader in history, a film star, a pop star, a character in a book). Write down five questions you would like to ask them. Compare your questions with a partner.

Director of the Month

Hideo Nakata

This month we talk to **Hideo Nakata**, the Japanese film-maker, who became internationally famous when he directed two films, *Ring* and *Ring 2* (both 1998). Both films were the most successful horror films ever produced in Japan. Part of the reason for this is that the stories are very original and creative.

The *Ring* films are about a videotape that kills everyone exactly one week after they view it. In the first film a reporter, Reiko Asakawa, tries to solve the mystery, but she also has only one week left to live after watching the film. *Ring* was a huge success because it showed the psychology and personalities of its main characters and it created an atmosphere of tension and anticipation. Asakawa's character transformation is astonishing – from a curious reporter investigating a story to a human being living in terror as she approaches almost certain death.

Nakata wants to create dramas with a touch of humanity. For him, films

▲ Hideo Nakata

▲ Nanako Matsushima as Reiko Asakawa in *Ring*.

should be about the essential human emotions such as tears, laughter and fear.

The film is based on a book written by Koji Suzuki. In the book, the main character is male, but in the film she is female. Nakata likes to make movies that focus on female personalities.

[1]*Why did you become a director?*
I began as a real movie fan and I just wanted to go on the other side of the screen. I became an assistant director at a film studio and then of course I gradually wanted to become a film director.

2 _____
Ring 2 because I wanted to see it with a real audience.

3 _____
Oh ... Walked out? No, I usually watch everything until the end.

4 _____
Very difficult. Can I name a Japanese director? It's Makino Masahiro. He made a lot of Yakuza movies.

5 _____
Hmm. No comment.

6 _____
I can't read them all, but for Japanese movies, I'll read as many as I possibly can. But for American movies, like , I have to say reviews don't matter that much – especially for horror movies. It's because the majority of my audience don't read reviews.

7 _____
I try my best in terms of my professional life. I always try to do my best so I don't have to regret. So I have no regrets.

8 _____
Try to contact all my old friends.

Adapted from an interview by Stella Papamichael on www.bbc.co.uk

READING

1 Look at the photos of famous people. Work with a partner to discuss the following.

1 What do you know about the people in the photos on this page?

2 Think of three qualities which you associate with each person.

2a Read the article quickly and answer the questions.

1 Which people are mentioned in the article?

2 What do (or did) they do to earn a living?

2b Read the article again and answer the questions.

1 Why is Bill Clinton so good at giving talks?

2 What mistake do people make about charisma?

3 Why is Oprah Winfrey famous?

4 What kind of relationship does she have with people who attend her shows?

5 How did Joe DiMaggio feel about Marilyn Monroe's charisma?

An Indefinable Quality

>> Most people will recognise the man in this photograph. He is, of course, Bill Clinton, ex-President of the United States. Bill Clinton is a very popular speech giver and ¹regularly gives talks
5 all over the world, to many different audiences. He is so effective at giving talks because he has a special quality which we call 'charisma'.

Nowadays, psychologists are becoming very interested in charisma and want to redefine its
10 meaning. People often misunderstand what charisma is and think of it as a kind of fame, but it is not the same as fame. Charisma is a kind of magic and is relatively rare. A well-known American psychologist thinks that charismatic people are
15 basically brilliant communicators. However, they have other qualities such as sensitivity, self-confidence, eloquence and vision.

Charismatic personalities are able to draw people to them, and people feel happy in their company.
20 There is a sense of 'togetherness' when a charismatic person is with other people. A good example of this ability, some say, is the famous American, Oprah Winfrey. She is a highly-successful businesswoman and is probably best known as the presenter of
25 a very popular talk show. Oprah is able to relate to audiences at her shows and they respond well to her. Her charismatic personality has made her one of the richest women in the world. ²She owns several houses and publishes her own magazines.
30 ³Currently, she is presenting a new series of the *Oprah Winfrey show*. She also runs a book club, which influences the nation's reading habits and may be one of the reasons why ⁴people are reading more these days in the USA.

35 A woman who had extraordinary charisma was the film star, Marilyn Monroe. A beautiful woman and a talented but underrated actress, she was always the centre of attention wherever she went. She married an ex-baseball player, Joe DiMaggio,
40 and later a famous writer, Arthur Miller. Marilyn Monroe's charisma was so great that DiMaggio was overshadowed by her. As he put it so well, 'It's no fun being married to an electric light.'

Unlike fame, charisma doesn't fade and disappear
45 over time. Even now, nearly fifty years after her death, when young people see Monroe in her films, her charisma seems as fresh and powerful as ever.

VOCABULARY: prefixes

3a Find words in the article that mean the following.

1 a former leader and head of state (line 3)

2 describe something again, and in a better way (line 9)

3 not understand correctly (line 10)

4 better than people think or say (line 37)

5 a former baseball player (line 39)

6 less important and successful than another person (line 42)

3b Underline the prefixes in the words you found. Match each prefix with one of these meanings.

incorrect	before	again
too much	not enough	

4a Look at the words below. What do the underlined prefixes mean in each?

a) <u>bi</u>cycle   d) <u>out</u>perform

b) <u>anti</u>social   e) <u>semi</u>circle

c) <u>mono</u>rail   f) <u>dis</u>comfort

4b Think of a word with a prefix that means the same as the underlined phrase in these sentences.

1 He was always <u>too confident</u>.

2 He <u>ran faster than</u> the police officers and escaped.

3 She asked her <u>former boss</u> for advice.

4 His mum's French and his father's Italian, so he's <u>able to speak two languages</u>.

5 He told me to <u>do the essay again</u>.

6 Her expertise was <u>not used enough</u>.

7 When children <u>behave badly</u>, parents should stop them.

8 We <u>don't like</u> that kind of music.

SPEAKING

5 Work with a partner to discuss the following.

1 If you were choosing photographs of people for an article about charismatic people, who would you choose?

2 Is charisma the most important quality to possess if you want to be successful in your career? If not, what other qualities are important?

GRAMMAR: present simple and present continuous

6a Look at the highlighted phases in the text. Mark them *PS* for present simple and *PC* for present continuous.

6b Look at the uses a–d of the present simple and present continuous. Match each use to one of the highlighted sentences in the text. Then write the correct tense in the gaps.

a) an action happening around now (often temporary): _____

b) a regular or habitual action: _____

c) a fact or general truth: _____

d) a trend or a changing situation: _____

GRAMMAR TIP

We also use the present continuous to talk about photographs.
In the photograph, Bill Clinton is talking to a group of people.

➡ Language reference and extra practice, pages 134–135

7a Look at these sentences and choose the correct answer.

1 Dr Partridge *regularly gives / is regularly giving* talks about personality.

2 The professor *interviews / is interviewing* a candidate at the moment and can't come to the phone.

3 The number of companies using personality tests *grows / is growing*.

4 I do lots of different research but today *I carry out / I'm carrying out* research into the personalities of twins.

5 He *drives / is driving* to work every day.

6 People *become / are becoming* very interested in how personalities develop over time.

7 A psychologist *studies / is studying* the way people's minds work.

8 The doctor's practice *is / is being* in Harley Street.

7b Match the sentences in Exercise 7a with the uses in Exercise 6b.

8a Use the following prompts to write questions in the present simple or continuous.

1 make friends / easily?

2 what / usually / do / weekend?

3 what / read / at the moment?

4 enjoy / art and music?

5 prefer / extroverts or introverts?

6 work / on any new projects now?

7 do / anything interesting / at the moment?

8 lose temper / easily?

8b With a partner, take turns to ask and answer the questions. Then tell the class one interesting fact about your partner.

SITUATION

Pacific Television, a US company, has a small office in Vancouver which sells the company's television and radio programmes to Canadian broadcasting stations. The office staff consists of Ben Jackson (television), Sylvia Webb (radio) and two secretaries Donna and Susan. The office needs to hire a new assistant who will work for both Ben and Sylvia.

1 Read the situation. Can you think of any problems the new assistant might have working for two bosses? What other problems could there be?

2a **1.5** Listen to Ben and Sylvia talking. What is the problem? Did you think of it in Exercise 1?

2b Listen again and note the good and bad points about Ben and Sylvia's personalities. Compare your answers with a partner.

Ben		Sylvia	
+	–	+	–
ambitious		sociable	

KEY LANGUAGE: giving opinions, agreeing and disagreeing

3a Listen again and complete the extracts.

1 BEN: It's not our fault, is it?
SYLVIA: _____ _____ _____, Ben, maybe it is.

2 BEN: … But Barbara didn't seem to mind.
SYLVIA: I don't know, _____ _____ it really upset her.

3 BEN: I pay people to work 9.00 to 5.00, not to leave the office …
SYLVIA: _____ _____ Ben, an hour off, just before Christmas?

4 BEN: I got on all right with Louise but she didn't like you or your secretary much, did she?
SYLVIA: _____, _____ _____, Louise and I didn't get on.

5 SYLVIA: She just couldn't take a joke – she was far too serious.
BEN: _____ _____ _____, Sylvia. Actually I thought Louise was quite nice …

6 BEN: What we need is someone who'll be a good match for us. I suggest we contact the agency again …
SYLVIA: _____ _____. Let's do it.

3b Look at the words/phrases you put in the gaps in Exercise 3a. In each case was the speaker:

a) giving an opinion?   c) disagreeing?
b) agreeing?

4 Ben and Sylvia send an email to Recruitment Associates, an employment agency in Vancouver. Read the email and answer the questions.

1 Discuss the most important qualities that the new assistant must have, according to the email.

2 What other qualities, not mentioned in the email, do you think the assistant needs?

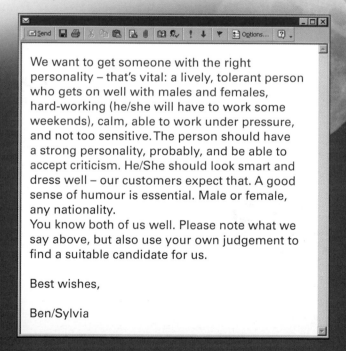

We want to get someone with the right personality – that's vital: a lively, tolerant person who gets on well with males and females, hard-working (he/she will have to work some weekends), calm, able to work under pressure, and not too sensitive. The person should have a strong personality, probably, and be able to accept criticism. He/She should look smart and dress well – our customers expect that. A good sense of humour is essential. Male or female, any nationality.
You know both of us well. Please note what we say above, but also use your own judgement to find a suitable candidate for us.

Best wishes,

Ben/Sylvia

Personality clash

TASK: choosing a new team member

5a Work with a partner. You work for Recruitment Associates. You are going to choose a suitable candidate for the job.

Student A: read the profiles of May Lin and Céline.
Student B: read the profiles of Richard and Anil on page 160.

Underline the good points of your two candidates and put a cross against the bad points.

5b Share information about the personalities of the candidates you studied. Discuss the good and bad points of each one. Use the Other Useful Phrases to help you.

5c Rank the candidates in order of suitability (1 = most suitable, 4 = least suitable).

6 As a class, choose the best candidate for the position of Ben and Sylvia's assistant.

OTHER USEFUL PHRASES
Making a suggestion
I suggest we/you [+ infinitive].
Why don't we [+ infinitive]?
How about [+ -ing]?

May Lin: Chinese, aged 22

A happy person. Smiles a lot. Comes from a large family (three older brothers, two sisters). Speaks in a soft voice. Quiet but confident.
Your three best qualities? 'hard-working, responsible, energetic'
Your worst quality? 'I want people to like me and get upset if they don't.'
Your ideal boss? 'I prefer a male boss. They are less emotional than women and, in my opinion, better managers.'
Why choose her? 'I get on well with people. I'm a caring person.'
Doesn't smoke. Thinks smoking should be banned in public places.
Elegantly dressed in a black business suit.
Interests: reads, paints, enjoys classical music.

Céline: French Canadian, aged 28

A strong personality. Very self-confident. An only child. A good sense of humour. Laughs a lot. Speaks English with a strong French accent.
Your three best qualities? 'charismatic, assertive, open-minded'
Your worst quality? 'I'm rather moody at times.'
Your ideal boss? 'I definitely prefer working for a woman, but will work for a man if necessary.'
Why choose her? 'I am the best candidate.'
Smokes a lot. Life-long vegetarian. Has strong views about people who eat meat.
Dressed casually in white jumper and black skirt.
Interests: goes to the gym, plays for a women's ice hockey team at weekends, dances (rock and jive).

STUDY SKILLS: taking notes while reading

1 Work with a partner to discuss the following.

1 When do *you* need to make notes?

2 What techniques do you use when you make notes?

2a **Note-taking** Read the essay and complete the notes.

PARAGRAPH 2 NOTES

WOMEN DRIVERS

– patient and ¹_____ to others on the road like ²_____ and ³_____

– stay ⁴_____ in ⁵_____ situations

– road ⁶_____ incidents fewer

– cautious

– take fewer ⁷_____ when ⁸_____

– more ⁹_____, less likely to ¹⁰_____ when ¹¹_____ or after drinking

PARAGRAPH 3 NOTES
WOMEN DRIVERS

indecisive   react ¹²_____

(Accidents)

lack¹³_____   ¹⁴_____ distracted

for example by ¹⁵_____

map ¹⁶_____ more difficult   ¹⁷_____ with left and ¹⁸_____

(Research)

poor spatial ¹⁹_____   more ²⁰_____ accidents

2b Which style of note-taking do you prefer? Why?

Are women better drivers than men?

1 Some people believe that women are better drivers than men. However, others think that women make worse drivers. The idea that women make worse drivers is a stereotype. It comes from a time when women drove less than men, and driving was seen as a man's responsibility. There are certainly different views on this controversial question, although there are a number of reasons why a woman's personality makes her a more competent driver.

2 Firstly, women are more patient and polite towards other road users, such as pedestrians and cyclists. In stressful situations they are more likely to stay calm, and less likely to be involved in 'road rage' incidents. Secondly, female drivers are more cautious and therefore take fewer risks, for instance when overtaking. Thirdly, they are more responsible so they tend not to drive when tired or after drinking alcohol.

3 On the other hand, many people argue that women cause accidents because they can be indecisive or react slowly because they lack confidence. In addition, they are easily distracted, for example, by children in the car. Research also shows that women find map reading more difficult than men, and can have problems with the difference between left and right. Despite the fact that women have more accidents, insurance is often cheaper for them because the accidents tend to be minor. In particular, women have accidents when parking. This is because women often have poor spatial awareness. In contrast, men tend to have more serious accidents.

4 To sum up, it can be seen that women make safer drivers than men because of their personality. This is supported by the fact that women have fewer accidents in general and pay lower insurance premiums than men. On balance, it is clear that women are less competitive and aggressive than men behind the wheel and therefore better drivers.

3a Symbols and abbreviations Have you thought about using symbols and abbreviations? Match the common symbols and abbreviations below with their meaning.

1	&	a)	this leads to / causes
2	+	b)	male/man
3	>	c)	greater / more than / better than
4	<	d)	female/woman
5	e.g.	e)	smaller / less than
6	♂	f)	is not equal to / the opposite
7	♀	g)	that is / this means
8	→	h)	and
9	=	i)	is the same as / equals
10	∴	j)	for example
11	i.e.	k)	plus / in addition to
12	≠	l)	therefore

3b Look again at the notes in Exercise 2a and change them using some of the above symbols and abbreviations.

**WRITING SKILLS:
a comparative essay**

4 Look again at the essay *Are women better drivers than men?* Match ideas a–d with each paragraph.

a) conclusion

b) arguments for

c) introduce the topic / state the proposition

d) arguments against

5a Linkers Look at the phrases highlighted in the text. Decide which of them are used to do the following.

1 list/add points

2 introduce examples

3 show contrast

4 introduce a conclusion

5b Look at the structures that are used with the linkers for contrast. Which linkers need a new sentence? Which linkers always need two clauses?

6a Combine these two sentences using the five phrases for showing contrast in Exercise 5a.

He is patient and careful at work. He is impatient and aggressive when he drives.

He is patient and careful at work. However, he is impatient and aggressive when he drives.

6b Complete the sentences in an appropriate way.

1 He was slow and often late for work. However, …

2 Although the twins looked the same, …

3 Despite the fact that he was shy …

4 Children find learning languages easy. Adults, on the other hand, …

7a Work in groups. Choose an essay title from the following.

Are men/women better …	managers	than women/men?
	politicians	
	teachers	
	doctors	

7b In your groups, brainstorm the qualities you think apply to men and women.

7c Look at the statements 1–13 below and do the following tasks.

1 Decide which of the statements below apply more to men or women.

2 Add two more statements of your own.

3 Select some to include in your essay. Remember to have some to show the other side of the argument.

4 Think of examples to support your statements.

1 _____ are good at listening.

2 _____ find it easier to deal with people.

3 _____ have more authority.

4 _____ are more sympathetic to others.

5 _____ are better organisers.

6 _____ pay more attention to detail.

7 _____ stay calm in stressful situations.

8 _____ are good at getting the best out of people.

9 _____ are energetic and enthusiastic.

10 _____ work better in a single-sex team.

11 _____ are better at public speaking.

12 _____ are more inspiring.

13 _____ take decisions quickly.

8 Write your essay. Use the structure of the essay on page 14 as a model.

9a Read your partner's essay and take notes.

9b Tell another student about your partner's essay, using your notes.

2 Travel

In this unit

Grammar
- past simple
- present perfect and past simple

Vocabulary
- travel expressions
- phrasal verbs (1)

Scenario
- A study trip

Study skills
- taking notes while listening

Writing skills
- a biographical profile

2.1 TOURISM AND TRAVELLING

A man travels the world in search of what he needs and returns home to find it.
George Moore, 1852–1933, Irish novelist

LISTENING AND VOCABULARY: travel expressions

1a Complete the questions with the words in the box.

> destinations   travel   journey
> abroad   trip   package   ~~home~~

1 What's the furthest you have travelled from _home_?
2 Have you ever been _____? Where did you go to?
3 Have you ever been on a business _____? Where to?
4 Do you like _____ holidays where everything is arranged for you? Why / Why not?
5 What is the longest _____ you have been on?
6 Do you think that _____ broadens the mind? Why / Why not?
7 What are the most popular _____ for people from your country?

1b In pairs or small groups, ask each other the questions.

2a [1.6] Listen to Nadia, a Swedish student who has travelled a lot. Tick (✓) the questions in Exercise 1 which she answers.

2b Listen again and make notes on her answers to the questions she answers from Exercise 1. Are they similar to your answers?

3a Complete the reasons for travelling with the words in the box. Look at Track 1.6 on page 169 and check your answers.

> broaden   experience   explore   find
> get   meet   learn (x2)   ~~see~~   become

People travel in order to …

1 _see_ new sights.
2 _____ different cultures.
3 _____ a new language.
4 _____ themselves.
5 _____ more independent.
6 _____ away from it all.
7 _____ new people.
8 _____ new places.
9 _____ new skills.
10 _____ their horizons.

3b Work with a partner. How important are the different reasons, do you think? What are the three most important? Why?

THINK FOR A MINUTE
TRAVEL AND TOURISM

Getting away from it all?

1

What's the difference between travel and tourism? Well, being a traveller is more than just being a holidaymaker. A holiday is just a short time away, and it normally involves relaxation. Tourists stay in holiday resorts, not travellers. Travellers go for the experience and their journeys are usually much longer and more challenging. For example, travellers tend to avoid tourist traps and like to go off the beaten track to discover new places. Travel is an age-old phenomenon, but tourism is a relatively recent invention. Thomas Cook is often described as the first travel agent because he arranged the first 'package tour': a 19-kilometre trip for 500 people, in 1841.

2

Going overseas in order to experience a different way of life is what many people think of as travel, but travel does not necessarily mean going abroad. How many people can say they have visited every part of their own country? Many people who live in vast countries such as Russia and the USA have only visited a small part of their own country, and so domestic travel is also very exciting. It's a surprising fact that about 75 percent of US citizens do not own a passport, so travelling does not mean leaving the country for them.

3

Some people can't travel or don't like the physical reality of travelling to faraway destinations. These days it is easy to be an 'armchair traveller'. People can visit distant corners of the world or even little known parts of their own country without leaving their living rooms. Television documentaries make the world a small place and some people argue that travel is no longer necessary. Perhaps soon people will use interactive computer programmes and virtual travel will become common. Enthusiasts argue that by doing this we will have all the benefits of travel without the inconvenience.

Next week: water

> **'How many people can say they have visited every part of their own country?'**

READING

4 Work with a partner to discuss the following.

1 What's the difference between a tourist and a traveller?

2 How much of your own country have you visited?

3 Is it possible to travel without leaving home?

5a Read the article quickly and choose the most suitable heading for each paragraph. (There are two extra headings.)

a) Virtual tourism   d) Holiday at home

b) Tourist or traveller?   e) Holiday problems

c) Most popular destinations

5b Read the article again and answer the questions.

1 How is a traveller different from a tourist? Give three examples.

2 How did tourism start?

3 What does the text say about people who live in large countries?

4 What is an 'armchair traveller'?

5 How has television affected attitudes to travel?

6 How could travel develop in the future?

SPEAKING AND WRITING

6 What are the most interesting places you have visited in your own country and abroad? Where else would you like to visit?

7 Complete these travel tips with the words in the box.

> accommodation be customs documents
> find out inoculations insurance ~~read~~
> respect take

1 *Read* about local laws and customs.

2 _____ aware of people acting suspiciously.

3 Obtain comprehensive travel _____.

4 Check what _____ and healthcare you need.

5 Make copies of _____ , e.g. tickets, passport, insurance policy, and leave one copy at home.

6 _____ enough money.

7 _____ about local tricks used on tourists.

8 Never carry packages through _____ for others.

9 _____ local dress codes; think about what you wear.

10 Stay in locally owned _____ and try to eat in locally owned restaurants.

8 Work with a partner. Think of as many travel tips for visitors to your country as you can, and write the five most important.

Marco Polo

Marco Polo was born in Italy in 1254. A traveller and merchant, he was one of the first Europeans to travel across Asia and into China. His journey lasted 24 years.

He set out, aged 17, with his father Nicolo and his uncle Maffeo on their great journey to China. They sailed south from Venice, Italy and stopped off in the Middle East. They then carried on overland to Persia (now Iran), through the Pamir Mountains and the Gobi Desert before they got to Beijing, China.

At that time, China was more advanced than Europe. They already had paper, so large numbers of books were available. They also used paper money in many parts of the empire.

After he got back to Italy, Marco Polo talked about his experiences in China, and he wrote a book describing the riches of Asia. His written account was the first Western record of porcelain, coal, gunpowder, printing and silk. Unfortunately, not many people believed Polo's stories and he became known as 'the man of a million lies'. He died in 1324.

Jacques Cousteau
underwater explorer

Jacques Cousteau was a French undersea explorer, environmentalist and inventor. He was born in France in 1910. When he was young, he became fascinated by the sea, machines and film-making. In the French navy, Cousteau began exploring underwater and worked on a special breathing machine which allowed divers to stay underwater for several hours. This gave them time to really look around under the ocean. In 1943, he and engineer Emile Gagnan invented the aqualung – the very first scuba diving equipment. In 1948, Cousteau began travelling the world's oceans in his research ship *Calypso*. Cousteau produced many films and books about his underwater adventures, including the TV series *The Undersea World of Jacques Cousteau*, which introduced the public to the world of sharks, whales, dolphins, treasure and coral reefs. Cousteau started the Cousteau Society to protect ocean life. In 1989, he received a great honour: he was made a member of the French Academy. Finally, after a long and varied life, Cousteau died on 25th June 1997.

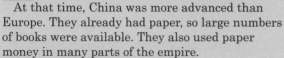

READING

1 What do you know about the people in the pictures? Who are they? What did they do?

2a Work in groups of three. Read about one explorer each and complete the chart for that explorer. Tell the rest of your group about your explorer and complete the rest of the chart.

	Marco Polo	Cousteau	Tereshkova
Nationality			
When born			
Job/work			
Where travelled to			
Length of journey			
Greatest achievement			
What they were called			
When died			

2b According to the texts, which explorer:

1 became interested in the sea at an early age?

2 was particularly interested in the Far East?

3 was accused of not telling the truth about their achievements?

4 had a name related to a seabird?

5 received an important award?

6 had a relationship with someone who did the same job?

7 travelled with members of their family?

8 cared for the environment?

Valentina Tereshkova
space pioneer

Valentina Tereshkova parachuted out of over 125 aircraft before she jumped out of the spacecraft *Vostok 6*. This unusual hobby led to her selection for cosmonaut training and her achievement of becoming the first woman in space. Tereshkova was born on 6th March 1937, in western Russia. As a teenager she worked in a textile plant and took up parachuting in her spare time. When Tereshkova was selected for the Soviet space programme in 1962, she became the first recruit without experience as a test pilot. Her selection was based on her parachuting skills. Tereshkova was chosen to be the pilot of the *Vostok 6* mission. She was given the name Chaika, Russian for 'seagull'. The craft lifted off from Tyuratam Launch Centre on 16th June 1963. It re-entered the Earth's atmosphere on 19th June and Tereshkova parachuted to the ground, landing near Kazakhstan, in central Asia. On 3rd November 1963, Tereshkova married another cosmonaut. They had a daughter, Elena – the first child born to parents who both went into space.

VOCABULARY: phrasal verbs (1)

3a Look at the phrasal verbs highlighted in the texts and match them with their meanings below.

leave   break a journey   return
arrive   explore   continue

3b Complete the text with the phrasal verbs.

We ¹_____ very early, before dawn, and drove south. We ²_____ at a service station for petrol and a coffee. After this we ³_____ on driving for another three hours. There were a lot of delays and hold ups. We finally ⁴_____ our destination at 2 p.m., and ⁵_____ the main sights. We didn't ⁶_____ until midnight. It was a very tiring day.

GRAMMAR: past simple

4a Look at the text you read in Exercise 2a again. Find six examples of regular past simple verbs.

4b Write the infinitives of the verbs. What spelling changes are there when we form the past simple of regular verbs?

4c Find the past simple forms of the following verbs in the texts. They are all irregular.

become   begin   write   lead   take   go

5 Which one of these statements about the past simple is not true?

1 We use the past simple for finished actions that are in the past.
2 We use the past simple with the following time expressions: *never, all my life, ever, yet*.
3 We often say the exact time of the action.
4 We use time expressions like: *yesterday, last week, in 1999, ago, when I was young*.

➡ Language reference and extra practice, pages 136–137

pronunciation

6a 1.7 *-ed* endings Listen to the sentences containing these words. Do the words end in the sounds /d/, /t/ or /ɪd/?

invented   produced   lasted   sailed
talked   worked   lifted

6b Listen again and practise saying the words.

7 Complete the facts below with the past simple of the verbs in the box.

| photograph   lead   hit   pilot   die   fly (x 2) |
| sail   bring   explore   find   discover |

1 Louise Boyd (1887–1972) *explored* and *photographed* the Arctic Ocean. She also _____ over the North Pole.
2 Ferdinand Magellan _____ the first expedition that _____ around the Earth, between 1519 and 1522.
3 Sir Walter Raleigh (1554–1618) _____ potatoes and tobacco from America to Europe.
4 In 1992 Ranulph Fiennes _____ the legendary Lost City of Ubor in the desert of Oman.
5 Vasco da Gama _____ in India in 1524. He _____ an ocean route from Portugal to the East.
6 Alan Shepard _____ America's first manned space mission. He briefly _____ into space on 5th May 1961. In a later mission he _____ golf balls on the moon.

SPEAKING

8 Write down the dates or years of six important events in your past. Give your list to a partner. Ask each other questions to find out what the dates represent.

2001

Did you start primary school then?

Wilfred Thesiger

Explorer of the 'Empty Quarter'

Wilfred Thesiger was one of the greatest explorers and travel writers of the 20th century. He died in 2003. His books, which describe his journeys in Africa, Asia and the Middle East,

5 have won many literary prizes. His best known book is *Arabian Sands*, which is about two journeys through Arabia. People have praised his description in the book of the 'Empty Quarter', a vast, waterless desert stretching between Saudi Arabia, Yemen and

10 Oman. He spent five years travelling in the 'Empty Quarter', often accompanied by the Bedu, the fierce tribespeople living in the area.

Thesiger fell in love with the desert. He enjoyed the 'sense of space, the silence, and the crisp clearness

15 of the sand'. It was a place where he found peace and friendship. He also learned to love the Bedu, and they learned to respect him. He shot lions to protect them, and he became a competent amateur doctor. He chose the 'Empty Quarter' for his

20 journeys because it was 'one of the very few places where I could satisfy an urge to go where others had not been'.

READING

1 Work with a partner to discuss the following.

1 Make a list of six words you associate with deserts. Compare your list with another pair.

2 What might attract people to life in a desert?

2a Read the article about the explorer Wilfred Thesiger. What attracted him to life in a desert?

2b Find expressions in the first two paragraphs which tell you:

1 that Thesiger was well-known in the 20th century.

2 that his books were popular.

3 that it was difficult to travel in the 'Empty Quarter'.

4 who the Bedu were.

5 what kind of relationship Thesiger had with the Bedu.

3 Read an extract from *Arabian Sands*. Are these statements true or false?

1 The camels began to rest at sunset.

2 Thesiger was happy because he thought the difficult journey was over.

3 The most difficult journey was the one for the next day.

4 When the travellers stopped the first time, they were near Uruq al Shaiba.

5 The Uruq al Shaiba are bigger and higher than the Himalayas.

To rest the camels we stopped for four hours in the late afternoon on a long gentle slope which stretched down to another salt-flat. There was no vegetation on it and no salt-bushes bordered the

5 plain below us. Al Auf announced that we would go on again at sunset. While we were feeding I said to him cheerfully, 'Anyway the worst should be over now that we are across the Uruq al Shaiba.' He looked at me for a moment and then answered, 'If

10 we go well tonight we should reach them tomorrow.' I said, 'Reach what?' and he replied, 'The Uruq al Shaiba. Did you think what we crossed today was the Uruq al Shaiba? That was only a dune. You will see them tomorrow.' For a moment I thought he was

15 joking, and then I realised that he was serious, that the worst of the journey which I had thought was behind us was still ahead.

It was midnight when at last al Auf said, 'Let's stop here. We will get some sleep and give the camels a

20 rest. The Uruq al Shaiba are not far away now.' In my dreams that night they towered above us higher than the Himalayas.

4 Find words in the texts that mean the following.

1 said good things about something (article, line 7)

2 extremely large (article, line 8)

3 looking very aggressive or violent (article, line 11)

4 have a good opinion of (article, line 17)

5 strong wish (article, line 21)

6 formed the edge of (extract, line 4)

7 mountain of sand (extract, line 13)

5 Would you like to read *Arabian Sands*?

LISTENING

6a **1.8** Listen to Alice Harker having an interview. What kind of expedition does she want to join?

6b Listen to the interview again. Tick (✓) the things that Alice has done.

1 been to most continents in the world
2 done something for charity
3 climbed in the Alps
4 been to the Himalayas
5 climbed to the top of Mount Everest
6 worked for a management consultancy firm

pronunciation

7a **1.9** **Weak forms** Listen to the sentences and underline what the speaker says.

1 *I travelled / I've travelled* up by train yesterday.
2 *I stayed / I've stayed* in a hotel last night.
3 *I visited / I've visited* nearly every continent in the world.
4 *I climbed / I've climbed* extensively in the Alps.
5 *You had / You've had* the right mountaineering experience.
6 *I worked / I've worked* as a consultant last year.

7b Listen again and repeat the sentences.

GRAMMAR: present perfect and past simple

8a Look at Track 1.8 on page 170. Underline the following.

1 three examples of the past simple + a time expression, e.g. *this week*
2 three examples of the present perfect + a time adverb
3 two examples of the present perfect + a time expression

8b Complete the rules with *present perfect* or *past simple*.

1 We use the _____ to talk about finished actions in a time period that continues up to now (with time expressions such as *this week*, *this year*).
2 We use the _____ to talk about finished actions at a specific past time (with time expressions such as *yesterday, last night, last year, in 1999*).
3 We use the _____ to talk about experiences in our lives, but we don't say when they happened (with adverbs such as *never, ever, already, yet*).

9a Underline the sentences in Track 1.8 on page 170 that contain *already* and *yet*. Answer the questions.

1 Which adverb (*already* or *yet*) do we use in negative sentences?
2 Does *already* come before or after the main verb?
3 Where does *yet* come in the sentence?
➡ Language reference and extra practice, pages 136–137

9b Look at the sentences below. Each has a mistake with an adverb or time expression. Replace the wrong word/phrase with words from the box.

already	before	never	this week	yet

1 Martin has yet climbed Mont Blanc twice.
2 We've interviewed five people for this expedition so far last week.
3 We've ever been to the Himalayas.
4 The students haven't passed the climbing course already.
5 Mark and Susanna have been on a climbing expedition once yet.

10a Choose the correct tense.

1 *I've never been / I didn't go* in hospital before.
2 *I left / have left* school when I was 16.
3 *I already visited / have already visited* a foreign country.
4 *I finished / haven't finished* my university studies yet.
5 *I've known / I knew* my best friend for the last ten years.
6 *I've never been / I never went* on a plane.

10b Change the sentences to questions. Work with a partner to ask and answer the questions.

Have you ever been in hospital?
– Yes, I went to hospital when I was ten.

SPEAKING

11a Look at these jobs. What would you have to do in each one?

1 Tour assistant – Paris, London, Rome
2 Mountain expedition assistant – Himalayas
3 Field trip volunteer – Amazon
4 Assistant travel agent – busy travel agency

11b Work with a partner. You are going to see if you are suitable for the jobs in Exercise 11a.

Student A: turn to page 158.

Student B: turn to page 161.

Which of the four jobs would suit you best?

SITUATION

Arcadia is an American university. Two years ago, the History Department organised a ten-day educational trip for students to Poland and the Czech Republic. Because of mistakes made by the organisers, the trip was unsuccessful and was not repeated the following year. This year, however, they will take a similar group of students (aged 18–21) to the same area, but the organisers plan to avoid the mistakes which they made in the past.

1 Read the situation. What kind of things can go wrong on a trip like this, do you think?

2a Read an extract from the report written by one of the organisers. How many of the mistakes mentioned in the report did you discuss in Exercise 1?

2b Match each problem in the report with one of these categories. You can use each category more than once.

theft   money   transport   language
feedback   violence   organisation

3 In small groups, discuss the questions. Compare your answers with another group.

1 Which were the most serious mistakes? Rank them in order of seriousness (1 = most serious, 6 = least serious).

2 Which of the following do you blame for each mistake?

the organisers   the students   other people
bad luck

4a [1.10] Listen to a conversation between Ingrid and Harry, two organisers of the previous trip. Which problems from the report do they talk about?

4b Listen again. Make notes on the other three problems they talk about. Use these headings.

• Relations with students
• Hotels
• Free time

The students complained about the following:

1 Three visits to historical sites were set up. The students lost interest because there was not enough information about the sites in English.

2 Some students couldn't find their way back to the hotel in the evening after a concert. They returned very late, so a visit next day was cancelled.

3 One Saturday night, a group of our students went to a club in Prague. One of our students got involved in a fight and ended up in hospital.

4 Students took different amounts of money, so some had to borrow from friends and this led to arguments.

5 Cameras were stolen from students while they travelled on the underground. One student lost all his documents, and had to spend a day at the embassy.

6 Students were unhappy because we changed the programme several times.

7 A visit to a college outside Prague was a disaster. The bus was too small and the seats were uncomfortable. The air conditioning didn't work properly and water dripped onto the passengers. Because of traffic, we arrived three hours late at the college.

8 Students said that on visits to rural areas they couldn't understand the menus in the restaurants, as they were not in English.

Velehrad Monastery and Church, Czech Republic

A study trip

5 Listen again and complete the two extracts.

Extract 1

HARRY: Well, we talked about that before we went,
how much free time to give them. There are
¹_____ _____ and ²_____, aren't there? On
the one hand, giving them a lot of free time is
good – they have a chance to explore places
they visit. ³_____ _____ _____ _____, if they
have too much time, they say we haven't
organised enough trips. You can't win, can
you?

INGRID: True, and don't forget Harry, ⁴_____ _____ of
giving them a lot of free time is that they get
into trouble.

Extract 2

HARRY: Don't remind me! Actually I've got a few
suggestions for this next trip.

INGRID: Me too.

HARRY: Good. Well, I think ⁵_____ _____ have more
meetings with the students before they leave.
An advantage of this is they'd get to know
each other a lot better.

INGRID: Yeah. That's true. Also, it'd be a ⁶_____ _____
to give the students maps of the cities they
visit. I suggest ⁷_____ _____ to the tourist
boards and ask them to send us some.

HARRY: Yeah, why not? And ⁸_____ _____ asking
the students where they want to stay? Do
they want to share a room in a cheap hotel,
or stay in a youth hostel? There are lots of
possibilities.

The astrological clock in Prague, Czech Republic

Rynek Glowny Square, Krakow, Poland

6 Do you think it is a good idea to give young
people a lot of free time when they are on an
educational trip? Why / Why not?

7a You are a member of the organising committee
for the next trip to Poland and the Czech Republic.
Discuss the advantages and disadvantages of these
suggestions for the next trip.

* the group of students should meet many times
before they go on their trip
* students should all take the same amount of money
* they should keep a diary each day and show it to
the organisers at the end of each day
* an organiser should always accompany the group
during the evenings

7b Add five suggestions of your own which will
make the next trip more successful. Think about the
problems in the report and conversation.

7c Compare your suggestions with another group.
Decide on the best five.

STUDY SKILLS: taking notes while listening

1a Work with a partner. Discuss these ideas for how to take notes while listening. Which do you agree with? Why?

- Before you start, have some key questions you want the answers to, for example *Who? What? When? Why?*
- Listen for structuring language, e.g. *firstly, secondly,* etc.
- Listen carefully for phrases which tell you important information is coming, e.g. *Now, let's move on to …*
- Wait until the end and write down what you can remember.
- Use a numbering system for your notes.
- Try to write down as much as you can.
- Use abbreviations where possible.
- Focus on verbs and nouns – leave out articles/pronouns/conjunctions, etc.
- Write in complete sentences.
- Use diagrams / mind maps.

1b Can you add any other ideas that work for you?

2a When you take notes it is important to focus on the most important words – these are generally nouns and verbs, and sometimes adjectives. Look at the extract from the article on page 20, and the notes below it. What differences are there?

Wilfred Thesiger was one of the greatest explorers and travel writers of the 20th century. He died in 2003. His books, which describe his journeys in Africa, Asia and the Middle East, have won many literary prizes.

Thesiger – greatest explorers / trav. writer 20C. Died 2003. Books – journeys Africa, Asia & Mid. East – prizes.

2b You are going to listen to a talk about the famous explorer Thor Heyerdahl. Look at the notes and try to predict what type of information goes in each gap.

2c 1.11 Note-taking Listen to the talk and complete as many of gaps 1–30 in the notes as you can. Use one or two words or a number in each gap. Compare your answers with a partner.

THOR HEYERDAHL

i) _____
- born Larvik, [1]_____ [2]19_____
- [3]_____ Zoology & Geography @ [4]_____ Uni
- 1st [5]_____ → Polynesia 1937– [6]_____
- was interested in how [7]_____ 1st inhabited

ii) _____
- [8]19_____ – built raft (Kon-Tiki) – crossed Peru → Polynesia in [9]_____ days
- wanted to prove ancient cultures connected by [10]_____ who crossed [11]_____
- [12]_____ Norwegian archaeological expedition → Galapagos Islands 19 [13]_____
- led Easter [14]_____ 1955–56
- 1969–70 [15]_____ 2 rafts (Ra 1 & Ra 2) across [16]_____ to show ancient Egyptian contact with S. [17]_____

iii) _____
- most people [18]_____ Kon-Tiki was most important work
- all [19]_____ and [20]_____ had great influence on anthropology & archaeology

iv) _____
- most famous publications: Kon-Tiki Expedition ([21]_____), The Ra Expeditions (1970), The Tigris Expedition ([22]_____)
- many [23]_____: elected to Norwegian Academy of [24]_____ in 1958 & [25]_____ Academy of Science in [26]_____; [27]_____ of Kon-Tiki expedition [28]_____ Oscar for [29]_____ feature

v) _____
- died 2002 at home in [30]_____

Kon-Tiki raft

2d Choose the most suitable headings for sections i–v in the notes. (There are two extra headings.)

a) Career
b) Travels in Polynesia
c) Publications and awards
d) End of his life
e) Greatest achievement
f) Early life and education
g) Books

Amelia Earhart
(1897–1937)

1 Amelia Earhart was born in Kansas, USA, in 1897 and moved to Chicago in 1914 when her father was fired from the Rock Island Railroad. After graduating from high school in 1915, she went to Canada where she trained as a nurse's aide. In 1919 she attended Columbia University but gave up after a year to join her parents in California.

2 In 1920 Earhart went to her first air show and was hooked. She took flying lessons and bought her first plane, which she flew to a height of 14,000 feet in October 1922, a women's world record. In 1925 she moved to Boston and got a job as a social worker. During that time, she also wrote local newspaper columns on flying.

3 Earhart will be principally remembered for being the first woman to fly solo non-stop across the Atlantic. On May 20 1932, she took off from New Brunswick. She wanted to fly to Paris, but poor weather conditions and mechanical problems forced her to land in Derry, Northern Ireland.

4 It was inevitable that Earhart would attempt a round-the-world flight and she left Miami on June 1 1937. After stopping in South America, Africa, the Indian subcontinent and south-east Asia, she arrived in New Guinea on June 29. She left on July 27, but while she was crossing the Pacific, contact was lost. The US government spent $4m looking for her, but she was never found.

5 Earhart published two books about her flying experiences: *20 Hours 40 Minutes* and *The Fun of It*, but she went missing before her third book was published. She was awarded the Distinguished Flying Cross by Congress and the Cross of Knight of the Legion of Honour by the French government.

WRITING SKILLS: a biographical profile

3 Read a biography of Amelia Earhart. Match each paragraph with one of these topics.

a) the end of her life

b) her early life and education

c) her early career

d) publications, awards and prizes

e) her greatest achievement

4 Find verbs in the text that mean the following.

1 be dismissed from a job (paragraph 1)

2 finish high school or university (para. 1)

3 learn a particular job (para. 1)

4 go to (school or university) (para. 1)

5 stop doing something (para. 1)

6 go to a new place to live (para. 2)

7 write and print something for sale (para. 5)

8 receive a prize, honour or money (para. 5)

5a Time linkers Look at the time linkers highlighted in the text: *before, after, when, during, while*. Which structures follow each linker?

5b What is the difference in use between *during* and *while* in the examples in the text?

6 Match these sentence halves and join them in an appropriate way using the time linkers. Look at Track 1.11 on page 170 to check your ideas.

1 Heyerdahl received a number of awards

2 Heyerdahl went to the Galapagos Islands

3 Heyerdahl became curious about how the islands were inhabited

4 He set out to prove his theories

a) leading an expedition to Easter Island.

b) his lifetime.

c) he was staying in Polynesia.

d) giving up his study of geography.

7 Write a biographical profile of Thor Heyerdahl. Use the notes you completed in Exercises 2c and 2d. Use the text about Amelia Earhart and the time linkers from Exercise 5a to help you.

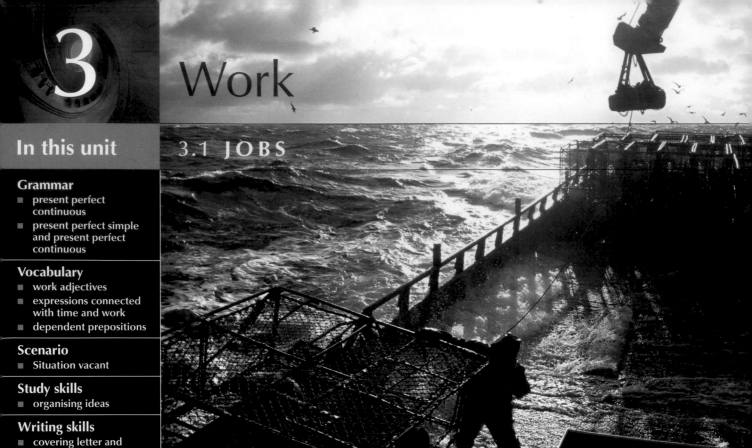

3 Work

In this unit

3.1 JOBS

Grammar
- present perfect continuous
- present perfect simple and present perfect continuous

Vocabulary
- work adjectives
- expressions connected with time and work
- dependent prepositions

Scenario
- Situation vacant

Study skills
- organising ideas

Writing skills
- covering letter and curriculum vitae (CV)

I worked myself up from nothing to a state of extreme poverty.
Groucho Marx, 1890–1977, US comedian

SPEAKING

1 Look at the jobs below and discuss the questions.

nurse   politician   model   journalist   firefighter
lawyer   professional footballer   teacher
shop assistant   police officer   TV presenter
personal assistant   sales manager

1 How important/useful do you think they are?
2 How much status do these jobs have in your country?
3 Approximately how much are people paid for these jobs in your country?
4 Do you think they should be paid more or less money? Why?

LISTENING

2a 1.12 Listen to five people talking about their jobs. Match each speaker to a job from Exercise 1.

2b What are the key words which tell you the jobs?

1 shifts, patients, …

2c Listen again. What aspects of their jobs does each person say they like/dislike?

VOCABULARY: work adjectives

3a Add the missing letters to the adjectives below. Which adjectives would you use to describe the jobs from Exercise 1?

1 r_w_rd_ng   4 str_ssf_l   7 s_t_sfy_ng
2 ch_ll_ng_ng   5 b_r_ng   8 _xc_t_ng
3 gl_m_r_ _s   6 r_p_t_t_v_   9 fl_x_bl_

3b Which of the jobs in Exercise 1 would you like to do? Which wouldn't you like to do? Why?

READING

4 Read the job advertisements opposite and match them with statements 1–8 below.

1 The company is the most important one in its area of business.
2 You will need to work by yourself.
3 You will work for more than one boss.
4 The company offers the chance to work abroad.
5 You will need to work some anti-social hours.
6 The company offers extra money once a year for good work.
7 There are opportunities for promotion.
8 You will be in charge of a number of staff.

A

Marketing Executive
Competitive Salary + Pension Scheme

Jakarta, the country's leading sports shoe manufacturer, is looking for an ambitious marketing executive to join our busy marketing department. You will have experience of designing and coordinating large advertising campaigns. Candidates should be prepared to spend time at our overseas branches in Rome and Berlin. Fluency in a European language would be an advantage. This is a very exciting opportunity for the right candidate. Salary will depend on experience.

Jakarta

C

Assistant to Finance Director

Foxtree is an IT company supplying software to the engineering sector. We are currently seeking an assistant to the finance director. The ideal candidate will be both flexible and ambitious. Candidates should have experience of preparing budgets, preferably in the IT industry. Although you will report to the Finance Director, you will also be responsible for assisting the Chief Executive when she travels abroad. There are excellent prospects for rapid career progress in the company for the right candidate.

Excellent Salary + Share Options

Foxtreee

B

Sales Manager
Excellent Benefits + Annual Bonus

Broadgate PLC is one of the largest suppliers of office equipment in the country. The successful candidate will be a dynamic person with excellent organisational skills. You will be responsible for leading and motivating a large sales team. You will also be expected to develop new market opportunities as part of Broadgate's continuing programme of expansion. A knowledge of the office equipment market is desirable, but not essential. This is a challenging opportunity with one of the country's most respected employers.

D

Frontline

Chief Administrator

Frontline is a national charity that has been working with disadvantaged young people for over 50 years. The administrator will be based in our new London office. Duties will include providing support to the team and keeping our database up to date. The post will suit a self-confident and organised person who is used to working under pressure and alone. Although the hours are flexible, the post will involve some evening and weekend work. This is a very satisfying and rewarding job for the right person.

Competitive Salary + Car

5 Match the words with the correct preposition from the box. Check your answers in the adverts.

| on   to   for   of   in |

1 looking
2 experience
3 depend
4 responsible
5 knowledge
6 fluency
7 report
8 prospects

6 Which job in the above adverts would you apply for? Why?

WRITING

7 Work with a partner. Write a short job advertisement using some of the word combinations above. Include the job title, salary and details of the positions.

SPEAKING

8a Which of the following are important to you in a job?

long holidays   friendly colleagues   travelling time   competitive salary   pleasant working environment   regular bonus   good pension   prestigious company   opportunity for promotion   flexible hours   foreign travel   other perks (e.g. company car)

8b What would your dream job be?

1a Do you work at home or do you know anyone who does? Do you/they enjoy it?

1b Homeworking is generally on the increase. Why do you think that is?

2a Read the article and check your answer to Exercise 1b.

2b Read the article again and find the following information.

1 how long Sunjit has lived in England

2 how long Sunjit has been working at home

3 how many people work from home in Britain nowadays

4 a reason why employers might encourage homeworking

5 a disadvantage for an employee of working from home

6 three methods of communication mentioned by Sunjit

VOCABULARY: expressions connected with time and work

3a Match the expressions with their meanings.

1	time-consuming	a)	organising your time effectively
2	time management	b)	taking up a lot of time
3	workstation	c)	how much time you spend at work and home
4	work-life balance	d)	use time doing something
5	spend time	e)	the place in an office where a person works, especially with a computer

3b Complete the text with the words and expressions from Exercise 3a.

I've got a full-time job and I'm tired all the time. I don't need to improve my ¹_____ skills as I organise my time efficiently. But I do have to ²_____ (a lot of) _____ commuting to work and it's very ³_____. One way I could save time would be to look at homeworking. My boss might like that as she could reduce the number of ⁴_____. I could stay in touch with the office by email and phone. I'm not a workaholic. What I want is a better ⁵_____ so I can be with my family more of the time.

Working-from-home dream now a reality

Sunjit Patel is a graphic designer with a well-known publishing company. He has lived in England since he was five. He lives in South London, and for the last three years he has been working from home. He prefers working from home because he can spend more time with his family and have a better work-life balance. Sunjit isn't alone: in Britain, there are 2.1 million people who work from home at present. In addition, about eight million people spend some time working in the home rather than in an office. This is almost twice as many as ten years ago.

This rapidly-growing trend towards working from home is the same in many countries. But what are the reasons for it? The main reason is technological: easy access to broadband and the availability of phone and video-conferencing. These enable people to use their home as an office in an efficient and cost-effective way.

Other reasons for homeworking are the benefits to both employers and employees: office space is costly, so if an organisation can reduce its workstations, it may be able to move to a smaller site. Employees often work better at home: travelling to work can be very time-consuming and tiring. Many homeworkers save a lot of time if they don't commute and they can start the day fresher and therefore work more efficiently; parents with young children appreciate the flexibility that homeworking allows and are more relaxed.

Sunjit Patel says, 'I have been working from home since my son was born and have been really enjoying it. But, I can tell you that homeworking requires special skills like self-discipline and time management. I've known my boss and colleagues for a long time now, which really helps because you've got to trust each other. You also need to have regular contact, by phone, email or video conferences, and you need to make regular trips to your office. Otherwise you really miss out on the gossip and on the social side of work.'

Not everyone agrees with Sunjit though. This response to a query about homeworking was recently posted on the Internet: 'The only people who can work from home are those who do an unnecessary job. Can surgeons work from home? Ambulance drivers? Firefighters? If you can work from home full-time, you have a pointless job.' Fortunately for Sunjit and the 2.1 million like him, not many people think that way!

SPEAKING

4 Work with a partner to discuss the following.

1 What are the disadvantages of homeworking from the employer's point of view?

2 Would you like to work from home? What would be the advantages/disadvantages for you?

3 Do you agree with the opinion in the last paragraph of the article?

GRAMMAR: present perfect continuous

5a Look at the two highlighted sentences in the text. Which of these statements about the present perfect continuous are true?

1 It is formed with *have/has* + *been* + *-ing*.

2 It is used to talk about an action that finished a long time ago.

3 It is used to talk about an action that continues to the present.

4 It is often used with the time expressions *since* and *for*.

5b Look again at the highlighted sentences. Complete the rule with *for* or *since*.

We use ____ + a point in time (when the activity started) and ____ + a period of time.

GRAMMAR TIP

Remember that we do not usually use state verbs in the continuous form, e.g.

be   know   understand

Language reference and extra practice, pages 138–139

5c Write sentences using the present perfect continuous, unless it is not possible to use the verb in the continuous. Use *since* and *for* when appropriate.

1 Cristina / work as a designer / she graduated.

Cristina has been working as a designer since she graduated.

2 I / know Yukiyo / six months.

3 How long / Mohamed / study engineering at university?

4 Fuat / live in Istanbul / he got a job there.

5 Marianna / work at home / two years.

6 I / not live here / very long.

7 Ji Hyun / understand the problem / yesterday morning

8 Mark and Julie / teach / same college / a year?

LISTENING

6a 📻 1.13 Listen to five people talking about working from home. What is each person's job?

6b Listen again. How long has each person been working from home? Do they like it? What reasons do they give?

7 Complete the extracts with the present perfect simple or present perfect continuous of the verbs in the box.

| be   take   learn   live |
| work (x2)   translate   pay |

1 ____ from Italian to English for most of my career.

2 ____ from home for 12 years, since my first child was born.

3 ____ a lot more for heating.

4 ____ from home as a website designer since I left my last job in 2004.

5 ____ guitar lessons for the last six months.

6 ____ a new language since January.

7 ____ abroad for five years.

8 ____ (never) ____ a morning person.

pronunciation

8a 📻 1.14 **Correcting politely** Listen to this short dialogue. Underline the main stress in what B says.

A: So you've been working in Shanghai for six months?

B: No, actually I've been working in Shanghai for two months.

8b Listen again and repeat the dialogue with a partner. Then practise some more dialogues.

Student A: turn to page 158.

Student B: turn to page 161.

SPEAKING

9 Work with a partner. Talk about things you've been doing for some time, using *since* and *for*.

I've been revising for my exams since Monday and I haven't been sleeping properly. I'm really tired at the moment. So far, I've revised English and Arabic.

READING

1a Have you ever had an interview? What was it for? How did you feel? What was the result?

1b What kind of difficult questions have you been asked at an interview? Rank the following questions in order of difficulty (1 = most difficult).

a) What are your strengths and weaknesses?

b) How would your colleagues/friends describe you?

c) What can you offer our organisation?

d) Why do you want the job?

e) Would you ever lie to get what you want?

2a Read a leaflet from a recruitment agency giving advice about interviews. Choose the most suitable headings for paragraphs A–E. There are three extra headings.

1 contact details	5	survey results
2 shock tactics	6	hypothetical questions
3 attitude	7	one person's experience
4 appearance	8	advice

2b Read the leaflet again. Which of the following ideas are mentioned?

1 Your answers to killer questions are extremely important.

2 An interviewee left the interview before it was meant to finish.

3 The way candidates look and dress was one area which bosses thought could have improved.

4 Difficult questions often come at the end of an interview.

5 Some experts prefer candidates to talk about things they have done rather than answer hypothetical questions.

6 You should not hesitate when answering killer questions.

3 Find words in the leaflet for someone who:

1 is applying for a job.

2 asks questions at an interview.

3 has other people working for him/her.

4 is attending an interview.

5 is paid to work for an organisation or another person.

6 has special knowledge of a subject.

4 In groups, discuss the following.

1 Do you think it is fair to ask killer questions?

2 Do you think hypothetical questions are useful?

3 How do you react under pressure?

A _____

When it comes to interview questions, it pays to expect the unexpected. This is a true story of one candidate's experience. This is how his interviewers greeted him:
'We've been interviewing candidates all morning and we're getting bored. Do something to impress us.' Then the interviewers got out their newspapers and started reading them.
The candidate said, 'Well, I've been waiting in this office for more than two hours because you've been running late. Actually I'm not impressed by your organisation and not sure I want to work for you. Goodbye.'
The interviewee walked out, was invited back the next day and was offered the job.

B _____

How would you act in a situation like this?
That interview was rather extreme, but a lot of employers have turned to using 'killer questions' or 'shock tactics', such as these:
'Tell me something about yourself that you have never told anyone.'
'Which three famous people would you invite to a dinner party and why?'
'We have employed people from your university, and they haven't been good. Can you tell us why you think you'd do better?'
Killer questions often come early in the interview and are aimed at throwing the candidate off guard. By surprising the candidate with an original or difficult question, interviewers can get an honest reaction and an unplanned response. They also want to see candidates think through their responses calmly.

GRAMMAR: present perfect simple and present perfect continuous

5 Look at the examples from the leaflet, and then complete the rules with *present perfect simple* or *present perfect continuous*.

1 JOBS4U have prepared three other leaflets …

2 We've been interviewing candidates all morning and we're getting bored.

3 An interviewer has asked you a 'killer question'…

4 I've been waiting in this office for more than two hours …

C _____

Interviewers also ask candidates other kinds of difficult questions to see how they react under pressure. For example, they may ask a hypothetical question related to work, such as:
'Imagine you are an employee in customer services. What would you do if an important customer was very rude to you?'
However, some experts think that hypothetical questions are not useful because they only generate hypothetical answers. They prefer candidates to talk about their past experience.

D _____

So, what should you do in these circumstances? Imagine: an interviewer has asked you a 'killer question' and you just don't know how to answer it – your mind is blank. Remember, the interviewer isn't interested in your response as much as the way you respond. So, stay calm, take a few deep breaths and buy some time, e.g. 'Actually, that's interesting. I haven't thought about it, but maybe I'd ...' It's a good idea to practise asking and answering some of these questions with friends. You can find some typical 'killer questions' on the front of this factsheet.

E _____

JOBS4U have prepared three other leaflets, full of hints and tips about interviews. We can be reached in the following ways:
Telephone 01865 701813
Email   info@jobs4u.com

JOBS4U

We use the:

a) _____ to emphasise that an action started in the past and is still continuing.

b) _____ to emphasise that an action started in the past and is completed.

GRAMMAR TIP

The present perfect simple emphasises the result of the activity.

I've written six reports. (focus on number)

The present perfect continuous emphasises the activity and its duration.

I've been writing reports since 2 p.m. (focus on time)

➡ Language reference and extra practice, pages 138–139

6 Complete the sentences with the present perfect simple or present perfect continuous of the verbs in the box. Use each verb twice.

watch   learn   write   ask

1 I _____ emails all day.
2 I _____ 20 emails today.
3 He _____ Polish for six months.
4 He _____ six new words today.
5 I _____ dozens of killer questions over the years.
6 Interviewers _____ killer questions for years.
7 Shizuka _____ TV all afternoon.
8 Shizuka _____ five TV programmes this afternoon.

pronunciation

7 1.15 **Contractions and weak forms** How do you say the words in bold? Listen and check, then repeat the sentences.

1 **We've** employed people from your university.
2 **We've been** interviewing candidates all morning.
3 **I've been** waiting in this office for more than two hours.
4 **He's** interviewed 14 candidates.

8a Complete the chart with information about things you did or started in the past. Follow the example. Use ideas from your home and family life, work or studies, leisure activities and hobbies.

activity	when
moved to the city	*two years ago*
started piano lessons	*three months ago*

8b Write about your activities using the present perfect. Compare your sentences with a partner.

We've been living in the city for two years.

I've been having piano lessons for three months. I've had about ten lessons.

SPEAKING

9 Work in groups to think of some killer questions. Then work with a partner from another group and ask each other the questions. Did your partner give good answers?

SITUATION

Shape-Shifters Inc., a famous New York health club chain, is opening a new London branch. The club will be in the City, the financial area of London, so customers will be mostly business people, such as employees of international banks and companies.

The club is about to invite applications for the position of Manager. The job will be challenging and rewarding, and it could also be glamorous and exciting as some well-known people are likely to join the club.

At present, the management are discussing the advertisement for the job. They know what the role of the successful candidate will be. However, they are still considering what skills and personal qualities that person should have.

1 Read the situation. Do you think you would like this job?

2 The manager will be responsible for the five areas of work below. Match them with the typical tasks from each area a–e.

1 Customer service
2 Finance
3 Strategy
4 Personnel management
5 Marketing

a) lead and motivate a team and recruit new staff
b) introduce a customer care programme and deal with complaints
c) develop advertising campaigns and research new markets
d) set objectives for growth and put together a five-year plan
e) prepare budgets and look at ways of reducing costs

3 List the skills and personal qualities you think the ideal candidate should have.

4a **1.16** Listen to two senior managers from Shape-Shifters, Harry and Marta. Which qualities and skills do they say are important?

4b Compare the skills/qualities they have chosen with the ones you discussed in Exercise 3. Are they the same?

KEY LANGUAGE: asking questions, giving answers

During interviews, framing expressions can be very helpful. Framing expressions for questions help to show another question is coming. Framing expressions before answers help to avoid silence and give candidates time to think.

5a **1.17** Listen and complete the extracts from the interviewer at a job interview.

1 Now, looking at your CV. I _____ like to know what you learned in your last job.

2 I'm also interested _____ knowing your reasons for leaving the job.

3 Now, a question we like to ask all our _____. What are your strong points?

4 I _____ wondering what you feel you can bring to this job.

5 OK. Thank you. A _____ now about your computer skills. What software are you familiar with?

6 Let me _____ that up with another question. How do you feel about working abroad?

7 Right, thank you. Moving on, _____ you tell me what you think the growth areas in the leisure industry are?

8 OK. Just one _____ question. Where do you think you'll be in five years' time?

Situation vacant

7 Think about the new position of Manager for Shape-Shifters. Write down three questions the interviewer might ask. With a partner, practise asking and answering the questions using framing language. You may invent any information you wish. You could ask about:

- foreign languages
- education
- good/bad qualities
- skills
- opinions about travel for work

TASK: taking part in a job interview

8a Work with a partner. You are going to take part in a job interview.

Student A (interviewer): turn to page 158 and prepare for the interview.

Student B (candidate): turn to page 161 and prepare for the interview.

8b Now do the interview with your partner. Allow around 15 minutes.

9 Turn to page 167 and complete the evaluation sheet about your partner. Discuss the results and if necessary explain the scores to your partner.

> **OTHER USEFUL PHRASES**
> Thank you for coming in today.
> Please take a seat.
> Are there any questions you'd like to ask us?
> It's been a pleasure meeting you.
> We'll let you know shortly.

5b Listen again and complete the extracts from the candidate at the interview.

1 I'm _____ you asked me that because I developed some important skills while I was there.

2 That's a very _____ question. Basically it was no longer challenging enough.

3 Well, without going into too much _____, I have very good people skills.

4 Let me just _____ about that for a moment. Well, my sales and marketing experience should be very useful to you.

5 I thought you might _____ me something about that. Well, what I can say is, I have a good knowledge of Excel and Word, and can prepare excellent Powerpoint presentations.

6 I haven't really _____ about that, to be honest, but I think it'd be really interesting.

7 Well, I'm not an _____, but I think the boom in fitness centres will continue in the next few years.

8 I'm _____ I don't know the answer to that, but I hope to be working for your company in a senior position.

5c Look at Track 1.17 on page 171 and check your answers.

6 Work with a partner to practise the questions and answers in Exercise 5.

STUDY SKILLS: organising ideas

1a Paragraphs Complete the text about paragraphing with the words in the box.

| information | link | texts | logically | main |

It is common to divide writing into paragraphs. A paragraph contains sentences, and these all ¹_____ to the ²_____ idea contained in the key sentence. This is called the topic sentence. It is usually the first one but can come later in the paragraph. The other sentences support it by giving more ³_____ or examples. A paragraph will have a final sentence which often signals what will come next. Most written ⁴_____ have several paragraphs which connect ⁵_____ to each other.

1b Why do we divide texts into paragraphs?

2 Organising a paragraph Read this paragraph from an application letter. It was sent by a candidate who applied to Shape-Shifters Inc. for a job. Work with a partner to discuss the following.

1 Which is the topic sentence?
2 Which sentences support the main idea?
3 Why is the final sentence not suitable for this paragraph?

I have been interested in healthy living and fitness for many years. This is why I chose to study for a degree in Sports Management at my local university. I have had excellent grades throughout my studies and expect to graduate in a few weeks' time. After this, I am thinking of going on to do a part-time Masters degree in Business Administration. I am a member of the university debating society and enjoy dancing to South American music.

3 The following sentences are from another paragraph in the letter. Put the sentences in the right order and underline the topic sentence.

a) For example, I am captain of the university debating team.

b) One of my strongest points is my personality. I am a confident person, very outgoing and sociable.

c) I believe the qualities that I have mentioned are important for a fitness instructor.

d) Because of this, I have many friends and am a member of several clubs.

4a Imagine you have seen an advertisement for a position in an organisation which interests you. Think about these questions:

1 Why do you want to apply for the position?
2 What skills and qualities do you have to offer the organisation?

4b Complete the first paragraph of an application letter. Then write two more paragraphs, explaining your reasons for applying and describing your skills and qualities.

I am writing to apply for the position of _____, which you advertised in today's *Daily Informer*. I am very excited by the opportunity you offer and believe that I have the personality and qualifications you are looking for.

WRITING SKILLS: covering letter and curriculum vitae (CV)

5a **1.18** **Covering letter** Listen to a careers counsellor answering questions from a student about covering letters. What three things does the student ask about?

5b Listen again. What are the counsellor's answers to the questions? Make notes next to the questions you wrote in Exercise 5a.

6 Denise Martin is applying for a job as an instructor at the London branch of Shape-Shifters (see page 32). Read her covering letter and complete it with the words and phrases in the box.

| work placement | available for interview | skills |
| look forward | degree | delighted | position |

Dear Ms Khan,   August 15, 2007

Re: Fitness Instructor

I am a student studying Sports Management at the University of Surrey. I am writing to apply for the ¹_____ of Fitness Instructor, which you advertised in today's *Sporting News*.

I have been interested in healthy living and fitness for many years, which is why I chose to study for a ²_____ in Sports Science at my local university. I graduate in three months' time and would like to work in a Health and Fitness club. I was ³_____ to see your advertisement because your clubs have an excellent reputation.

I am an outgoing, confident person and believe that I have good communication ⁴_____. I speak French fluently and German to an intermediate level. Last summer, I worked with a dietician at a hospital and gained useful knowledge of health foods. I also had a two-month ⁵_____ with a sports goods company. In my spare time, I run an aerobics class every Monday evening.

I am ⁶_____ at any time convenient to you. I ⁷_____ to meeting you to discuss my application.

Yours sincerely,

Denise Martin

Denise Martin

7 Curriculum Vitae (CV) Work with a partner to discuss the following.

1 What is the purpose of a CV?

2 Is there a standard format for a CV?

3 Should you use the same CV for all job applications?

4 What headings do you normally find in a CV?

5 Should you always tell the truth when writing your CV?

8a ▪1.19 Listen to six people giving their opinion about writing CVs. Make notes about what they say.

8b Discuss what each person said with your partner. Do you agree with them?

9 Look at part of a CV of Françoise Luneau. Fill the gaps with these extracts.

a) Cycle regularly. Play tennis in a local club.

b) Masters in Business Administration (MBA), Nanterre University

c) Work placement

d) Graduate trainee

e) leadership qualities

f) Good at teamwork

10 Shape-Shifters have vacancies in administration, sales, personnel and finance. Apply to their Head Office in London for any position. Write a covering letter and a CV.

Curriculum Vitae:
Françoise Luneau

Profile
I am a highly-motivated graduate in Commerce with over three years' experience in the retail clothing and food industries. I am interested in working for a fast-expanding company in the leisure industry, which will appreciate my dynamism, 1_____ and sales ability.

Education
1996–1998	2_____
1992–1995	Diploma in Commerce, University of Provence
1990 (June)	Baccalauréat Series B (Economics)

Work Experience
2004–present	Euromarché, Paris: Manager
2002–2004	Lee Cooper, Paris: Sales assistant
1999–2001	Clairefontaine, Paris: Assistant
1998–1999	Clairefontaine, Paris: 3_____
1997 (summer)	Kopcea, Paris: 4_____ (two months)

Key skills
Fluent in English, French and German

IT-literate; working knowledge of Microsoft Office package

5_____

Fast typing – 80 words a minute

Interests
Enjoy music. Play in a local jazz band.

6_____

REVIEW

Career Profiles

When most of us think of a career in film, we think of being an actor or becoming the next Steven Spielberg. But this week we take a look at three of the many careers open to people who are ambitious, energetic and prepared to work very hard.

The cameraman

'People usually ¹*think / are thinking* my job is exciting and involves meeting lots of famous people. In fact I ²*spend / am spending* most of my day hiding behind the camera and listening to instructions from the director. Take my current project in New York, where we ³*film / 're filming* a spy movie. Yesterday, I⁴*'ve been / was* on the top of a skyscraper all day trying to film a car crash below. It ⁵*'s taken / took* seven hours to make five seconds of film ...'

The runner

'The "runner" ⁶*doesn't have / isn't having* a normal job description. I can do anything from cleaning the floor to buying lunch for Jack Nicholson. I've always ⁷*known / been knowing* that I wanted to work in films and every day I ⁸*learn / 'm learning* so much from watching professionals.
I ⁹*graduated / 've graduated* from university last year with a degree in media studies and I ¹⁰*'ve sent / sent* my CV to over 100 film companies before I got this job!'

The stunt double

Nikki Berwick ¹¹*is working / has been working* as a stunt double for the past six and a half years. It's a glamorous job but you need to be tough. For example, Berwick ¹²*has become / became* a world champion in the Korean martial art Tang Soo Do at the age of 16, but to qualify as a stunt double you also ¹³*take / are taking* tests in five other sports.

GRAMMAR

1 Read the text and choose the correct answer.

2 Complete some questions that the journalist asked the people in Exercise 1. Use between one and three words.

1 What _____ do in your job?

2 What qualifications _____ have for your job?

3 How long _____ doing this kind of work?

4 What _____ working on at the moment?

5 _____ you always _____ to work in film?

3a Work with a partner. One of you is the journalist, the other is one of the people from Exercise 1. Ask and answer the questions from Exercise 2.

3b Now swap roles and ask and answer questions about a different person from Exercise 1.

4 With your partner, use the questions in Exercise 2 to ask and answer questions about your real job, or a job you'd like to do. Afterwards, write a short article about your partner's career.

VOCABUARY

5a Complete the job advertisement with words from the box. There is one extra word.

| easy even self mono hard |

A ¹_____-confident person with an ²_____-going manner is required to join our ³_____-working customer service department. An ⁴_____-tempered attitude to stressful situations is essential.

5b Replace the words in *italics* in the job advertisement with the adjectives below. There are two extra adjectives.

a) ambitious   c) assertive   e) bossy   g) serious
b) organised   d) reliable   f) creative

Trainee Manager

We are currently interviewing for a Trainee Manager at a famous high street store. The successful candidate will be ¹*someone who wants to achieve* and is ²*able to make decisions confidently*. You will demonstrate that you are ³*someone who can plan carefully* and can approach problems in a ⁴*new and original* way where necessary. Your team of ten will need you to lead and inspire rather than simply be ⁵*someone who tells everyone what to do.*

5c Complete the job advertisement with prepositions from the box. There are two extra prepositions.

| to | for | in | of | for | about | of |

FREELANCE JOURNALIST

••••••••••••••••••••••••••••••••

A financial news website is looking ¹_____ a freelance journalist with a knowledge ²_____ economics and the stock markets. You will be responsible ³_____ investigating the latest trends and investment opportunities for a highly-specialised readership. You will report ⁴_____ an editor and there are long-term prospects ⁵_____ a full-time permanent position.

KEY LANGUAGE

6 [1.20] Listen to two students, Kris and Piotr, talking about where to travel during their summer break. Are these statements true, false or not given?

1 Piotr and Kris have been to Greece before.

2 Piotr prefers travelling in order to learn about a country.

3 Kris agrees that they should spend all their time sightseeing and travelling.

4 Piotr doesn't want Pavel to come because of his personality.

5 Kris has stayed in hostels before but didn't like it.

6 Piotr finally agrees to let Pavel come.

7a Complete the words in the extracts.

K: I think we ¹s_____ head for Greece, Piotr. For one thing it's cheap to fly there.

P: I don't ²k_____. It's a bit too hot for me. Besides, what will we do?

K: Well, on the ³o_____ hand you've got loads of historical sites so that's interesting and on the ⁴o_____ hand you can always spend a few days by the sea relaxing.

P: Yes, well it's ⁵t_____ about the history and broadening the mind but sitting on the beach isn't my idea of real travelling!

P: Yes, you're right. OK then. It'd be a ⁶g_____ idea to go to an island, get a tan and then after about a week we can go to Athens and travel on the mainland.

K: Great ⁷i_____. Oh, by the way, I was ⁸w_____ if Pavel could come with us?

P: That's true, but another ⁹d_____ of Pavel coming is ¹⁰t_____ there'll be three of us, which always makes it harder to come to decisions about what to visit – you know, one person wants to do one thing and someone else doesn't want to.

K: OK. He doesn't have to be with us all the time but how ¹¹a_____ saying to him that he can meet up with us somewhere?

P: Let me just think about that for a ¹²m_____.

7b Listen again and check your answers.

8 Write in the missing adverbs or prepositions in sentences 1–10. Look at the pages to check your answers.

1 My idea of a holiday is to get from it all with a good book on a beach. (page 16)

2 Did you find from the travel agent which flight we're on? (page 17)

3 Let's stop here for a few days and take a really good look at the temples. (page 19)

4 There's nothing interesting here so why don't we carry driving until we reach the capital? (page 18)

5 I've been living here I was 13 years old. (page 29)

6 They've been talking on the phone two hours. (page 29)

7 Without going too much detail, I left my last job because I wanted to try something new. (page 33)

8 Let me just think that for a moment. (page 33)

9 I am writing to apply the position of office assistant. (page 34)

10 We need someone who is fluent Spanish. (page 35)

LOOK BACK

9 Find the exercises in Units 1–3 where you …

• learn 24 new adjectives for describing personality and character. (U1)

• practise forming questions. (U1)

• read an article about charisma. (U1)

• compare being a traveller with being a tourist. (U2)

• learn phrasal verbs for talking about a journey. (U2)

• write a profile of someone's life. (U2)

• talk about what is important when choosing a job. (U3)

• ask some killer questions. (U3)

4 Language

In this unit

Grammar
- future forms
- first conditional

Vocabulary
- language learning
- phrasal verbs (2)
- *allow, permit, let*

Scenario
- Language training

Study skills
- describing tables and charts

Writing skills
- a report

4.1 LEARNING LANGUAGES

A different language is a different vision of life.
Federico Fellini, 1920–1992, Italian film-maker

VOCABULARY: language learning

1 Work with a partner. Discuss how similar you think these activities are to learning a language.

driving a car   playing a musical instrument
playing/doing a dangerous sport   painting/drawing
dancing the tango, waltz, etc.   playing a board game
(e.g. backgammon, chess, Monopoly)

Learning to drive a car is similar because you need to practise a lot.

2 What sort of people do you think make the best language learners?

3 Complete the statements with the words in the box. Which ideas do you agree with?

> bilingual   native   slang   accent
> foreign   grammar   dialects

1 Organised and logical people find it easy to learn _____ rules.

2 Musical people find it easy to develop a good _____.

3 Extroverts find it easy to communicate in their _____ language and so often find it easy to learn to speak a _____ language fluently.

4 Flexible people can adapt to different _____ (the way a language is spoken in different areas).

5 People who are _____ already know two languages so learning one more is very easy.

6 Learners of languages should make an effort to learn informal phrases, everyday expressions and even _____.

READING

4a Look at the text opposite about language learning. Where does it come from? What is its purpose?

4b Read the text quickly. Who is it aimed at?

a) foreign language speakers

b) native English speakers

c) people who want to speak English as a foreign language

d) business people

4c Read the text again. Are these sentences true, false or not given?

1 You will receive a certificate at the end of the course.

2 There are exams to check your progress during the course.

3 English is one of the languages offered.

4 You will become fluent in six weeks.

5 There are support materials in English.

VOCABULARY: phrasal verbs (2)

5a Look at the phrasal verbs highlighted in the text and match them with their meanings below.

1 make as much progress as others
2 learn easily
3 understand
4 make less progress than other people
5 survive
6 disappoint/fail
7 start doing something, e.g. a new activity

5b Complete the sentences about your English studies. Compare your answers with a partner.

1 I can get by in _____ (language) when I am abroad.
2 I would like to stop learning English and take up _____.
3 I catch on quickly when my teacher _____.
4 It took me _____ (weeks/months/years) to pick up the basics of _____.
5 I find it difficult to keep up with my work/ homework because _____.
6 The aspect of my English which lets me down is _____.
7 I'm falling behind in _____. I'm going to have to work hard to catch up.

SPEAKING

6 Work with a partner to discuss the following.

1 English is an international language because it is easy to learn.
2 Language is the most important part of cultural identity.
3 Everyone should learn at least one foreign language.
4 A government has a duty to protect its country's language.
5 The world would be a better place if everyone spoke the same language.

not only English Spoken Here!

■ *Do your foreign language skills let you down when you travel abroad?*

■ *Are you falling behind in your career?*

■ *Would you like to make new friends?*

■ *Do you want to learn about other cultures?*

If you answered 'yes' to any of the above, then you need 'Learn fast', the all-inclusive foreign language course.

At school you may have found foreign language learning confusing, but don't worry – our fully-supported courses will teach you the language you need for every situation. Our accelerated learning system means that we can guarantee that within six weeks you will pick up the basics of any language you choose. Pretty soon you will be able to do much more than just get by. You will become fluent and able to hold intelligent conversations with native speakers.

All aspects of the language are covered – reading and listening, grammar and vocabulary development and pronunciation work to perfect your accent. A printed workbook will answer your grammar questions and there are also regular online tests as part of the course.

Slow to catch on? Not with our special system which is designed with the non-language learner in mind. We offer a series of DVDs and CDs for in-car or at home practice with a writing skills support package. Extensive notes in English make learning easier and faster.

Now, more than ever is the time to take up a new language. It will open up a new world for you and help you keep up with the bilingual high flyers.

Don't delay … Do it today!

Choose from the following:
French, Spanish, German, Italian, Portuguese, Polish, Russian, Arabic, Japanese, Chinese.

All levels from beginner to advanced.

LEARN FAST

For more information visit our website at: www.learnfast.edu.

LISTENING

1 Do you text? If yes, why and how often? If not, why not?

2a [1.21] Listen to two friends at university, Howard and Fred, talking on the phone. What is the reason for the phone call?

2b Listen again and complete the sentences. Use the word in brackets to help you.

1 Fred is going to finish his essay _____. (when?)

2 Howard is going to finish his essay _____. (when?)

3 Fred is going to the cinema with _____. (who?)

4 Fred is going to the cinema on _____. (when?)

5 Howard's presentation is on _____. (when?)

6 Howard and Fred will see each other at the lecture _____. (when?)

2c Fred sends Howard a text message after the phone call. Which of these three text messages is the one that Fred sent?

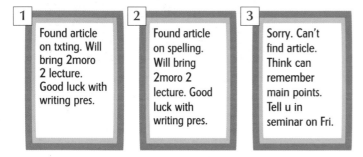

1
Found article on txting. Will bring 2moro 2 lecture. Good luck with writing pres.

2
Found article on spelling. Will bring 2moro 2 lecture. Good luck with writing pres.

3
Sorry. Can't find article. Think can remember main points. Tell u in seminar on Fri.

GRAMMAR: future forms

3a Look at Track 1.21 on page 172. Underline all the ways of expressing the future that you can find.

3b Look at your underlined examples in the audioscript and find an example of:

1 a prediction about the future

2 a decision made at the time of speaking

3 an intention for the future

4 a fixed arrangement, plan or programme

3c Complete the rules with *will, going to* or *the present continuous*.

1 We use _____ to talk about unplanned decisions and promises that we make at the time of speaking, and to make predictions about the future.

2 We use _____ to talk about fixed future arrangements, usually involving other people.

3 We use _____ to talk about plans or intentions (something which you have already decided).

➡ Language reference and extra practice, pages 140–141

4 Work with a partner. Look at part of another conversation between Howard and Fred. Choose the best answer and discuss the reasons for your choice.

F: I've made a decision. ¹*I'm going to take / I'll take* a Masters Course in Communication. The course ²*will challenge / is challenging* me but I think I can manage it. What about you?

H: Not sure. I haven't made any arrangements yet but I think ³*I'm taking / I'll take* a postgraduate course. ⁴*I'm not knowing / I won't know* my exam results till the end of August. ⁵*I'm probably deciding / I'll probably decide* then.

F: Sounds good. Oh, I've arranged to meet Richard on Wednesday for a band practice. ⁶*We're meeting / We'll meet* at 5 p.m. Do you want to join us?

H: Sorry, but ⁷*I'm playing / I'm going to play* tennis with Fran then.

F: OK, how about going for a coffee now?

H: Sorry, I'm so tired. I think ⁸*I'll go /I'm going* home now.

READING

5 How important is correct spelling in a language? What about correct grammar? Are you good at spelling and grammar in your language?

6a Read the website opposite. Underline the arguments for and against texting.

6b Complete the summary below using the words in the box. There are more words than you need to fill the gaps.

affected	listening	increasing	teachers
literacy	improve	means	understanding
students	allowed		

It is clear that the use of SMS is ¹_____. But some teachers believe that the ²_____ skills of young people may be ³_____ if they use text for everything. These teachers believe that good grammar, spelling and sentence structure will suffer if texting is ⁴_____ in class. Other teachers disagree and say that texting is just another modern ⁵_____ of communication. Young people have different points of view. One person argued that education will suffer if we keep using text language instead of correct English. However, another view was that text is just a new type of language, and that the first people to learn SMS should be ⁶_____.

VOCABULARY: *allow, permit, let*

7 Look up the words *allow, permit* and *let* in a good dictionary and answer the questions below.

1 Which is the most formal of the words? Which is the most informal?

2 Which of the following sentences is/are incorrect?
   a) The visa permits you to study for two months.
   b) My father would never allow me to study English
   c) Let me to go. You're hurting me.

SPEAKING

8 Work with a partner to discuss the following.

1 Texting seriously affects young people's ability to write good English.

2 Texting will be permitted in exams within five years.

3 Students will soon prefer to study British English rather than American English.

4 In twenty years' time, nobody will write letters.

Is SMS good for young people?

Does SMS seriously affect young people's ability to write good English?

Recently, a Scottish teenager wrote her entire English exam in text language. Should she be allowed to do that?

SMS is on the increase but is it sending the right message to young people and teachers? Some teachers believe that SMS is having a negative effect on young people's literacy skills.

They say that texting is preventing young people from writing properly. Because texting is fast and users have to be brief, good grammar, spelling and sentence structure is forgotten. As a result, young SMS users are not able to write correct English.

Other teachers, however, say that young people should be permitted to express themselves and that texting is just a modern means of communication. Teachers who want to ban it are 'old-fashioned'. One educational expert commented: 'Children need to learn to communicate in a range of ways.'

A lot of teachers and lecturers refer to the story of the teenager who wrote an entire English essay in text language. Her essay started: 'My summr hols wr CWOT. B4, we used 2go2 NY 2C my bro. ILNY, it's a gr8 plc.' The translation of this is: 'My summer holidays were a complete waste of time. Before, we used to go to New York to see my brother. I love New York. It's a great place.'

About us

Portfolio

Student list
Case studies
Students say
Partnerships

Services

Join us

Contact us

➔ Text language should only be used for texting! (That's why it's called TEXT language.) We'll never get a good education if we keep using text language instead of correct English.
Lucy, 17, Oxford

➔ I don't think that students should be allowed to text because it will create problems for the teachers. Most of them simply don't understand text language.
Chris, 18, Leeds

➔ No way! I think it's OK for emails and texts, but NOT for schoolwork, because it will affect your spelling when you're older.
Jordan, 16, London

➔ I think teachers should let us use text in classes. Over thousands of years our language has changed a lot. Text is a new type of the language and teachers should learn it.
Ahmed, 17, Bradford

O **Click here to add a comment.**

READING

1 What is a dead language? Why do languages die out, do you think?

2a Answer the questions. Read the first two paragraphs of the article to check your answers.

1 Which of these languages is more than 2,000 years old?
a) French   b) English   c) Greek

2 What percentage of languages have died out in the last 500 years?
a) 1.3%   b) 1.9%   c) 4.5%

3 How many languages are in danger of disappearing now?
a) over 3,000   b) over 300   c) over 1,300

2b Read the rest of the article and answer the questions.

1 What four reasons are given in the text for languages disappearing?

2 Why do some people think there is no reason to worry about the death of languages?

3 According to the author, why should we care about languages dying out?

4 What do the following, mentioned in the text, claim about languages?
a) Steve Sutherland
b) The Ethnologue
c) Ani Rauhihi

3 Read the article again and find the following.

1 a verb and a phrasal verb meaning 'to stop existing' (lines 5 and 10)

2 a noun used for when something stops existing, usually used with plants, animals or volcanoes (line 7)

3 the noun related to one of the verbs in 1 (line 16)

4 the adjective related to the noun in 2 (line 21)

5 a verb meaning 'to damage something very badly' (line 30)

6 an adjective meaning 'very bad' or 'ending in failure', often used with the words *consequences*, *results* and *effects* (line 39)

LAST WORDS

There are around 6,000 living languages in the world – and at least half of those are in danger. In every part of the world,
5 languages are disappearing. In fact, one scientist has said that languages are in more danger of extinction than birds or mammals. Professor Steve Sutherland of the University of East Anglia calculated that in the past 500 years 4.5 percent
10 of languages have died out – compared with 1.3 percent of birds, and 1.9 percent of mammals.

Languages come and go, and thousands have done exactly that without leaving any trace. Only a very few – Basque, Greek and Latin among
15 them – have lasted more than 2,000 years. But it seems that the pace of their disappearance is becoming quicker.

The Ethnologue, a database of all the languages spoken in the world, claims that 417 languages
20 are spoken by so few people that they are in the final stages of becoming extinct. There is one living speaker of Luo in Cameroon, and a handful of people that speak the Saami Pite language in Sweden and Norway. If very few people speak a
25 language, it will probably die out.

Languages may be lost through migration, as people move from small rural communities to urban centres, or when environments are destroyed by the search for oil or wood. Natural
30 disasters can also devastate populations, and along with them, their language – like the speakers of the Paulohi language in Maluku, Indonesia: only 50 survived after an earthquake and tidal wave some years ago. Governments
35 also play a role in the extinction of languages. The need to establish 'official languages', for a country to educate its children, conduct its political affairs and carry out its business, had a disastrous effect on many small languages.

40 What is lost if a language is lost? Some people argue that languages die as the human race evolves. Obviously there could be great benefits if everyone in the world spoke the same language – some industries already reflect this,
45 with English essential for pilots and air traffic controllers. But there are more important things than convenience. As languages are lost, whole ways of life and knowledge may be lost along with them.

50 Put simply, language expresses something about identity, about our place in the world. Ani Rauhihi, a Maori teacher in New Zealand's North Island, sums it up: 'If you grow up not speaking your language, you won't know who you are.'

From '50 facts that should change the world'
by Jessica Williams

LISTENING

4 Work with a partner to discuss the following.

1 What languages are spoken in Scotland?

2 What could you do to prevent a language from disappearing?

5a 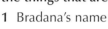 Listen to a radio interview with Bradana MacKinnon, spokesperson for the Society for the Promotion of Gaelic. Tick (✓) the things that are mentioned.

1 Bradana's name

2 statistics about people speaking Gaelic

3 the differences between Gaelic in Scotland and Ireland

4 the economy of the Gaelic-speaking community

5 investment in cultural events and festivals of Gaelic arts

6 training teachers of Gaelic

5b Listen again and complete the sentences.

1 If we _____ Gaelic-medium education at all levels, more people will speak Gaelic.

2 If we _____ more TV and radio programmes in Gaelic, more people may listen to the language.

3 Unless we all _____ to promote Gaelic, there might not be a significant increase in speakers.

4 When we _____ our targets, we'll invest in more Gaelic books in public libraries.

5 As soon as we _____ more Gaelic speakers involved, we'll run more Gaelic language classes.

GRAMMAR: first conditional

6 Look at the examples in Exercise 5b and choose the correct answer.

1 We use *if + present simple / past simple* in the *if*-clause, and *will (may, might, should,* etc.) in the main clause.

2 We use *unless* in the *if*-clause + affirmative verb to mean *if not / if*.

3 After time expressions like *when* and *as soon as*, we use *will / the present simple*.

4 We use the first conditional to talk about *real possibilities / unreal situations* in the future.

➡ Language reference and extra practice, pages 140–141

7a Match the beginnings and endings to make conditional sentences.

1 If languages die out,

2 You will never learn a language well

3 If foreign words enter a language,

4 Languages will die out

5 If I study French more,

6 I'll go home

7 I'll revise

a) I might make fewer mistakes.

b) unless you know its grammar.

c) unless we protect them.

d) the world will be less interesting.

e) when I get home.

f) as soon as the class finishes.

g) they will damage it.

7b Work with a partner to discuss the first four statements from Exercise 7a.

SPEAKING

8a You are going to hold a debate about language. This is the motion:

The government should spend more money on promoting languages used by a minority of the population.

Divide into two groups to prepare the arguments.

Group A (for the motion): turn to page 158.

Group B (against the motion): turn to page 161.

8b Now hold the debate. Follow the debate procedure.

1 The spokesperson from Group A speaks for the motion.

2 The spokesperson for Group B speaks against the motion.

3 Other people from both groups can speak and give their opinions for or against.

4 The groups vote on the motion. You can change your mind at this stage.

A bilingual road sign in Ireland

SITUATION

International Medi-Aid (IMA) is a large independent charity which provides medical aid to over 80 countries. Based in Nice, France, it has a staff of approximately 300, including about 200 volunteers. The volunteers have always been encouraged to use English, so a few months ago IMA decided that English will now be the working language within the whole organisation. The Human Resources Department of IMA, therefore, must organise English language training for its staff at head office who need to improve their command of the language.

1 Read the situation and answer the questions.

1 Why does IMA need an English language programme?

2 Which department is responsible for planning the programme?

2a Read the email opposite from a member of the HR department at IMA. What are the two problems concerning the language programme?

2b In small groups, discuss and make notes on the advantages and disadvantages of each proposal, from the point of view of both the staff and the agency.

3a 1.23 Listen to three members of the HR department, Sven, Don and Delphine, talking about how to improve the English of some groups in the agency. Do they agree on each point?

3b Listen again. What does each member say about these things? Make notes.

1 the English language training of the directors and senior staff

2 the choice of British or American English

3 the language training of the volunteers

Here are the results of the survey of the staff's English language ability that I carried out recently.

Number	English Language Ability			
	Excellent	Good	Fair	Poor
Directors	4	2	2	6
Senior staff	8	2	3	7
Fundraisers	8	2	6	12
Medical staff	12	8	6	14
Volunteers	38	15	23	122

As you all know, we need to keep any training costs low: the budget for language training for the first year is only €150,000. During a recent meeting, we identified five possible ways of providing English language training. However, we were unable to agree on the best proposal. Below is an outline of each proposal, together with the estimated costs of each.

Proposal 1: Send staff to a language school.

Cost: for a four-week course for ten participants close to the head office for 20 hours a week, the total cost will be €10,000.

Proposal 2: Hire two English language instructors.

Cost: €50 per teaching hour (to give courses at the office).

Proposal 3: Hire a language expert to set up courses online for staff.

Cost: no information at present, but this option could be expensive – at least €30,000.

Proposal 4: Send groups of staff to the UK or the US for a crash course.

Cost: for a four-week course with 20 hours' teaching per week + air fare and accommodation, the total cost will be €5,000 for the UK or €6,000 for the US.

Proposal 5: Provide one-to-one English language training in the office.

Cost: €100 per teaching hour.

OTHER USEFUL PHRASES

That's an excellent idea.
I don't think that's a good idea.
If we do that, what will happen?
Let's look at the consequences. If we …

KEY LANGUAGE:
accepting and rejecting ideas,
considering consequences

---

4 Listen again and complete the extracts.

DON: Mmm, I don't ¹_____ _____ that. I can see a problem right away. If we send them to England, it ²_____ _____ a bad effect on our work.

DON: … who'd run the charity?

SVEN: Yeah, I think ³_____ right. That would create problems for us. Well, how about this? Why don't we …?

DON: Yes, I think that ⁴_____ _____. Good idea, Sven. What do you think, Delphine?

DELPHINE: Well, I'm afraid I don't ⁵_____ the ⁶_____.

DELPHINE: Well, we could hire two teachers … one could be British and the other American. I think that would solve the problem.

SVEN: Mmm, ⁷_____ _____, Delphine.

DON: Yeah, I like that idea. It's definitely ⁸_____ _____.

DON: … And we'll need to set up a programme very soon.

SVEN: I'm not ⁹_____ _____ that, Don.

TASK: selecting an English language programme

5a Work in groups of four. You are members of the Human Resources department of IMA and are going to decide on the English language programme.

Student A: turn to page 158.

Student B: turn to page 161.

Student C: turn to page 166.

Student D: turn to page 166.

Follow this procedure. Use the Other Useful Phrases to help you.

1 Discuss the four options for English language training. Try to persuade the members of your group that your option is the best and that the agency should spend most of the budget on your option.

2 Listen to the suggestions of other members of your group. Accept the suggestions which you like. Reject the other suggestions.

3 Share your suggestions with another group.

5b Present your suggestions to the class. Vote on the best.

STUDY SKILLS: describing tables and charts

1 Match the percentages and the fractions.

1 67%	a) just under a quarter
2 32%	b) just over two thirds
3 75%	c) slightly less than a third
4 23%	d) just over half
5 52%	e) (exactly) three quarters
6 48%	f) more than three quarters
7 80%	g) approximately three quarters
8 74.5%	h) almost half

2 Answer the questions.

1 Which of the following is a *majority*?
   a) 32%   b) 24%   c) 77%

2 Which of the following is a *minority*?
   a) 21%   b) 83%   c) 91%

3 Look at the table showing results from 100 student questionnaires at a university language centre last year and this year on student satisfaction in two areas: teaching and facilities (buildings, rooms, equipment).

	Teaching		Facilities	
	Last year	This year	Last year	This year
Very satisfied	51	65	32	10
Satisfied	24	24	38	52
Quite satisfied	10	6	20	25
Not satisfied	12	2	8	12
No opinion	3	3	2	1

Look at the results for last year. Are these statements true or false? Correct the false statements.

1 Approximately half the students were very satisfied with the teaching.

2 Ten percent of the students were quite satisfied with the facilities.

3 Just under two thirds of the students were very satisfied with the facilities.

4 Almost a quarter of the students were satisfied with the facilities.

5 The majority was very satisfied or satisfied with teaching and facilities.

6 A small minority had no opinion about teaching and facilities.

7 More than a quarter weren't satisfied with the teaching and facilities.

4 Look at the results for this year. Work with a partner to make statements about the results. Discuss your statements with another pair.

This year almost two thirds of students were very satisfied with the teaching.

5 Look at the chart below and complete the report with the words and phrases a–g.

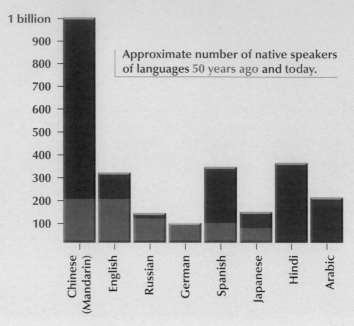

Approximate number of native speakers of languages 50 years ago and today.

a) the approximate number	e) however
b) approximately	f) over the period
c) a significant increase	g) overall
d) there were no figures given	

The bar chart shows [1]_____ of speakers of different languages in the world now and 50 years ago. [2]_____, the chart demonstrates that the greatest increase over the period has been in the number of people speaking Chinese.

Fifty years ago there were [3]_____ 200 million speakers of Chinese. This has increased to the present figure of one billion. There were also 200 million speakers of English 50 years ago, but this figure has only increased to 309 million.

In addition, there has been [4]_____ in the number of Spanish speakers from 100 million 50 years ago to 322 million today. Similarly, there were increases in the number of Russian and Japanese speakers. On the contrary, there were 100 million speakers of German 50 years ago, but this figure has remained almost the same [5]_____.

[6]_____ for speakers of Hindi and Arabic 50 years ago. [7]_____, at present there are 364 million speakers of Hindi and 206 million speakers of Arabic.

6a You have been asked to write a report for a university lecturer describing the information shown in the chart below. In pairs or small groups, discuss the following.

1 What percentage of the population of Australia uses English as a first language?
2 Which country has the highest percentage that uses English as a second language?
3 Only one country in the chart has a population that uses English entirely as a first language. Which one?

6b Discuss the other countries in the chart. Try to make statements about their use of English as a first and second language.

7a Look at the chart again and complete the sentences.

Percentage of population using English as a first or second language.

■ English as a first language.
■ English as a second language.

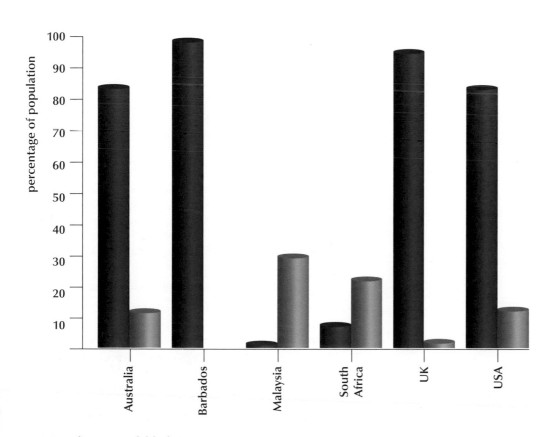

Note: no figures available for Nigeria

☐ In Malaysia almost a third of the population …
7 There were no figures given for …
☐ Overall, the chart demonstrates that four countries in the chart have a majority of …
1 This chart shows the percentage of people from a number of countries who …
☐ The country with the lowest percentage of speakers of English as a first language …
☐ In South Africa, just under a quarter of …
☐ It is also interesting that in Barbados …

7b Put the sentences in a logical order. The first and last have been numbered.

8 Look back at the report in Exercise 5. Underline the linkers (e.g. *However*).

9 Write a report about the information in the chart in Exercise 6. Use your sentences from Exercise 7 and link them where you can. Use the report in Exercise 5 as a model.

Advertising

In this unit

Grammar
- second conditional
- comparison

Vocabulary
- adjectives, advertising
- advertising methods
- word combinations

Scenario
- B-Kool soft drinks

Study skills
- using your dictionary

Writing skills
- a formal letter

5.1 WHAT MAKES A GOOD ADVERT?

Many a small thing has been made large by the right kind of advertising.
Mark Twain, 1835–1910, US writer and humorist

SPEAKING

1 Work with a partner to discuss the following.

1 Think of a memorable advert. Describe it.

2 Have you ever bought something just because of an advert? When?

3 Have any adverts impressed you? Which one(s)? Why?

READING

2a Read three opinions about advertising. Are these statements true or false?

1 Michael Hamilton says that adverts must attract attention and be persuasive.

2 He also states that an advert should encourage us to buy the product it is advertising.

3 Miranda Hoyles states that adverts nowadays are different from years ago.

4 Hoyles also says people like adverts that reflect everyday life.

5 Christie Peterson focuses on slogans and logos.

6 She says that excitement is more important than the image of the company.

First of all, an advert has to be attention-grabbing and powerful. You need a strong image that is eye-catching, a catchy slogan, a joke or something shocking. In advertising, we talk about the AIDA formula. A is for attention. I is for interest. D is for desire. A is for action. An ad needs to do more than get our attention. It also has to be effective and persuasive. It must get us interested, make us want the product and motivate us to go out and buy it.

Michael Hamilton, advertising executive

Advertising has changed over the years. Adverts are no longer purely informative and focused on the product. Many of the adverts that we see today are short stories telling inspirational tales that are often witty, humorous and sophisticated. People do not want to remember that life can be dull. They want to see something original and creative. The adverts take away the ordinariness of everyday life and take us to somewhere exotic or romantic.

Miranda Hoyles, head of US advertising agency

Many people talk about advertisements that are exciting and intriguing. But for me, an instantly recognisable logo is really important. Good logos have been built up so they are recognisable. Part of what makes a good advert is a clear symbol that people immediately identify with the company. A good slogan also helps you make a connection. 'The real thing' makes you think of Coca-Cola immediately. It's also important that your slogan does not become irritating.

Christie Peterson, illustrator

2b Work with a partner to discuss the following.

1 Which opinion do you agree with the most?

2 Which opinion mentions an advert for a soft drink?

3 Which opinion(s) might these ideas for adverts illustrate?

   a) a fast car chase with lots of action

   b) an advert with a clever use of a few words

   c) an advert set on a beautiful island

VOCABULARY:
adjectives, advertising

---

3 Find adjectives in the first two texts in Exercise 2a which mean the following.

1 attracting your attention because it is easily remembered

2 very noticeable

3 amusing and enjoyable, easy to remember

4 very bad, upsetting

5 works well and produces the results you want

6 able to make people do or believe something

7 funny and clever

8 not interesting or exciting

9 imaginative, using completely new and different ideas

10 unusual and exciting because it comes from a distant country

4 Match the words connected with advertising with their meanings.

> sponsorship   commercial (n)   promote
> misleading   slogan   endorse   logo

1 an advert on TV or radio

2 financial support a company gives in order to get publicity for themselves

3 a short phrase that is easy to remember

4 to say publicly that you support or approve of something

5 giving the wrong idea or impression

6 special design/symbol that a company puts on all its products or adverts

7 to try to sell a product, e.g. by special advertising

5a Choose the correct answer.

A: OK, let's brainstorm how we're going to ¹*promote* / *endorse* this product.

B: Well, we could get a famous celebrity like David Beckham to endorse it.

A: I think that would be much too expensive. ²*Commercial* / *Sponsorship* of a TV programme would also cost a lot. And a TV ³*logo* / *commercial* is out for the same reason. I've seen some great TV shots which are visually beautiful and really ⁴*eye-catching* / *shocking*, often set in romantic or ⁵*dull* / *exotic* locations. But I don't think they've been very ⁶*effective* / *witty* as people can't remember the product they're advertising.

B: I agree, but we don't want something ⁷*catchy* / *dull* and boring. How about advertising on the radio – would the budget run to that?

A: Yes, we could stretch to that.

B: And would you like something witty and ⁸*eye-catching* / *catchy*?

A: Maybe. I want something new and ⁹*dull* / *original*. But most importantly, it must be ¹⁰*persuasive* / *misleading*. It must get people to buy the product.

5b 1.24 Listen and check your answers.

LISTENING

6a 1.25 Listen to three people talking about different adverts. What type of product is advertised in each one?

6b Listen again and answer the questions below about each advert.

1 Which brand was advertised?

2 Did the speaker enjoy the advert?

3 What adjectives did the speaker use to describe the advert?

6c Which advert was the most effective? Why?

SPEAKING

7a You are going to discuss some photos for use in adverts. Look at your photos and describe them to your partner.

Student A: Look at the two photos on page 159.

Student B: Look at the two photos on page 162.

7b Look at all the photos together. Choose one and discuss:

a) which product you could use it for.

b) how you would use it for advertising.

c) what slogan you would choose.

READING

1 Work with a partner to discuss the following.

1 What are the most common ways of advertising products and services today?

2 What ways of advertising do you think people used before paper was invented?

2a Read the article and underline the different ways of advertising mentioned.

2b Answer the questions about the first three paragraphs of the article.

1 What sort of things were advertised in ancient times?

2 What effect did printing have on advertising?

3 Which statements are true about the 1960s?
   a) People used more imagination when making advertisements.
   b) Advertisements gave much more information.
   c) Advertisements focused more on the special features of products.

4 What is a USP? Why is it important for a new product to have a USP?

2c Complete the summary of paragraphs 4–7 of the article with no more than three words in each gap.

Three ways of advertising nowadays are product placement, TV commercials and using famous personalities to ¹_____. In the film, *Minority Report,* two ²_____, Nokia and Bulgari, used product placement to advertise their brands. During the Superbowl game in the US, advertisers pay $2.5 million for a ³_____. Endorsements are also a good way of advertising because they usually ⁴_____ but they can be expensive.

VOCABULARY: advertising methods

3 Find words and phrases in the text that mean the following.

1 passing messages from one person to another orally

2 a large notice or picture to advertise something

3 a colourful image on stone

4 small notices and advertisements

5 a small advert in a newspaper to buy or sell something

6 buying goods from a company that sends them by post

7 advertising a product by putting it in a film or a television programme

8 use of a product by a well-known person who says they like it

ADVERTISING

Then

1   **M**ost advertising in ancient times was word-of-mouth, that is, people liked something and told others about it. But even then, people advertised by putting inscriptions on walls, for example to display political slogans and to offer household goods for sale. Also, in Rome and Greece, in ancient times, it was common for people to use papyrus, a kind of paper, to advertise things they had lost or found. Papyrus was also used for posters to advertise political campaigns. Many traces of these advertisements have been found in the ruins of Pompeii, a city destroyed by a volcano which erupted in 79AD. The tradition of wall or rock painting as a way of advertising goods is even more ancient and examples can still be found in parts of Asia, Africa and South America.

2   Printing developed in the 15th and 16th centuries, and this increased the forms of advertising. Handbills – small printed notices and advertisements – became common. Then, by the 17th century, advertisements started appearing in weekly newspapers in England, including classified adverts for personal goods and services. In the 19th century mail order catalogues appeared, promoting all kinds of goods.

3   Finally, the 1960s were a key period in the development of advertising. Advertisements became more creative and more interesting. Also, they began to draw attention to the 'unique selling points', the USPs of products. These are the qualities that make a product different from competitors' products.

4   These days, advertisers have come up with new ways of promoting their products. For example, product placement is now common. This is advertising in TV programmes or films by

LISTENING

4a ▌1.26▐ Listen to the conversation between a manufacturer and a marketing consultant. What kind of product are they talking about? Which group of consumers is it aimed at?

4b Listen again and complete the sentences.

1 If we _____ a bigger budget, we'd get someone well-known to endorse the product.

2 If I _____ you, I'd look for a cheaper way of doing it.

3 If you ran a series of short TV commercials, you _____ reach a younger audience …

4 Yes, if we got the right people, it _____ be a lot cheaper than using a film star.

5 If you got a young director to do the films, you _____ have to pay them too much.

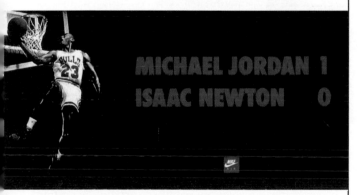

AND **Now**

MICHAEL JORDAN 1
ISAAC NEWTON 0

having a character, preferably played by a famous actor, use a particular product. For example, Tom Cruise's character in the movie, Minority Report, had a computer with the Nokia logo on it, and his watch was clearly made by Bulgari.

5 TV commercials are a very effective medium for advertisers, though these are very expensive. If an organisation wants to have a 30-second TV advert during the annual Superbowl game in the United States, they have to pay about $2.5 million.

6 Perhaps the most interesting development is the use of famous personalities to endorse a product. The basketball player, Michael Jordan, endorsed Nike products and wore them while playing. David Beckham, the footballer, endorsed Police sunglasses.

7 Getting well-known personalities to endorse a product can be very expensive, but endorsements certainly increase a product's sales, especially if the personality has a positive image in the eyes of the public.

GRAMMAR: second conditional

5 Look at the sentences from Exercise 4b and choose the correct answer.

In the second conditional …

1 we use the *past simple / present simple* in the *if*-clause, and the *past simple / would ('d)* + infinitive without *to* in the main clause.

2 we can use a modal verb, e.g. *could* or *might*, in the *if*-clause / *the main clause.*

3 we talk about *an unreal / a real* situation in the present or future.

4 We can say *If I were you / If I would you* to give advice.

➡ **Language reference and extra practice, pages 142–143**

6 Complete the sentences in the second conditional, using the verbs in brackets.

1 If I _____ the agency's number, I _____ them. (know, phone)

2 If we _____ the choice, we _____ on the radio. (have, advertise)

3 If you _____ in charge of the advertising campaign, what _____? (be, you do)

4 What _____ if we _____ before 9 p.m.? (happen, advertise)

5 If he _____ for a job in our agency, he probably _____ it. (apply, not get)

SPEAKING AND WRITING

7 In small groups, say which of the media in the box you would use to advertise the products and services below. You can only choose one medium for each product. Give reasons for your choices.

If I wanted to advertise an expensive ring, I'd put it on the Internet.

TV commercials   radio spots   newspapers   magazines   billboards   the Internet   leaflets   sides of buses/taxis   telephone calls

- an expensive ring
- a new range of computers
- raising money for a charity
- a lost wallet
- an unwanted new mobile phone
- financial advice
- a request for information about a crime
- a household item, e.g. a carpet
- a valuable antique chair

8 Choose one of the products/services from above and write a brief description of how you would advertise it. Include a slogan if necessary.

Advertisers targeting young people

■ **Paul Johnson** reports

A NEW report has concluded that advertising managers are becoming increasingly interested in children. Studies show that children influence
5 about 50 percent of things that families buy, so they are an attractive target for advertisers.

John Taylor, the author of the report and a lecturer at the Department of
10 Media and Communications at the University of West London, says: 'Advertisers can reach their target in many ways. They can, for example, show an ad many times during
15 school holidays, they can make the TV commercials a little louder than the programmes to attract attention, or they can sponsor programmes and show their commercials just before
20 the programme begins.'

Most advertisements aimed at children are short, imaginative and often in the form of animated cartoons. 'Children love the adverts
25 and watch them in the same way as any entertainment programme,' Taylor says.

There are concerns about advertising aimed at young people.
30 The concerns are shared by Sarah Durham, a writer and journalist specialising in media analysis. 'The most worrying thing is that children do not think carefully when they see
35 television advertisements. They are less critical than adults and do not usually realise that the advertisement has a persuasive message, to encourage them or their parents to
40 spend as much money as possible on the product or service,' she says.

There are also concerns over the vast sums of money that junk food manufacturers spend on advertising
45 to persuade children to buy their food products. Many advertisements, argues Durham, promote food that is a lot higher in fat, salt and sugar than healthier alternatives. 'Many
50 companies target children with offers of free toys, models of cartoon characters, gimmicky packaging and interactive websites. In most western countries, there are a lot more
55 advertisements during children's TV for food than any other type of product, and these are mainly for confectionery, sweetened breakfast cereals and fast food restaurants.'
60 Government approaches to controlling advertising to children vary. In Sweden, one of the strictest countries where advertising is concerned, TV advertising to children
65 under the age of 12 is banned. Greece bans television advertisements for children's toys between 7 a.m. and 10 p.m. Other countries, such as Denmark and the Netherlands,
70 also have legal controls whereas France, Britain and Germany prefer self-regulation, arguing that the television industry should regulate itself and bring out a 'code of good
75 conduct'.

Some countries are not as certain as the Swedes that advertising to children is harmful. The French argue that children need to see many
80 advertisements so that they can develop their ability to think as they grow up. The belief is that advertising will help children to be more aware of its persuasive power.
85 This all means that there is little hope that the situation will be resolved by any kind of cross-European regulations. 'Because some countries are much more relaxed than others
90 about advertising to children, the European Union is unable at present to have a common approach to the problem. Until the majority of member states are as sure as the
95 Swedes of the harmful nature of advertising, the current indecision will continue,' concludes Taylor.

READING

1 What products are most commonly featured in adverts for children? How are they advertised?

2a Read the article quickly and say which of the following are NOT mentioned in the text.

1 the time children spend watching television
2 the ways in which advertisers can reach children
3 the problems of advertising to children
4 how different countries control advertising
5 products that are not allowed to be advertised in different countries

2b Read the article again and find the following.

1 three examples of ways in which advertisers reach children
2 three serious problems with advertising for children
3 four countries that impose controls on advertising for children
4 three countries that don't impose controls
5 three examples of how countries approach the control of advertising to children differently

VOCABULARY: word combinations

3 Look at the article again and find the words below. Which other words do they combine with? Is each combination adjective + noun or noun + noun?

a) managers (line 2)   e) sums (line 43)
b) target (linc 6)   f) food ×2 (lines 43 and 59)
c) commercial (line 16)   g) websites (line 53)
d) message (line 38)   h) advertisements (line 66)

4 Complete the sentences so they are true for you.

1 I think advertising managers should …
2 I think junk food is …
3 I like / don't like TV commercials that …
4 Companies should not spend vast sums of money on …

5 Work with a partner to discuss the following.

1 Do you agree that advertising should be aimed at children? Why / Why not?
2 In the text there are a number of approaches to controlling advertising for children. Which is the best?
3 In your opinion should some products not be advertised? If so, which?

GRAMMAR: comparison

6a Look at the comparative and superlative adjectives highlighted in the article and complete the rules.

1 We make the comparative of one-syllable adjectives by adding _____ to the adjective. With most longer adjectives we put _____ before the adjective.
2 We make the superlative of one-syllable adjectives by adding _____ to the adjective. With most longer adjectives we put _____ before the adjective.

6b Find the comparative forms of *loud* (line 16), *critical* (line 36), *high* (line 48), *relaxed* (line 89) and *sure* (line 94) and complete the rules.

1 We use _____ or _____ to emphasise a large difference.
2 We use _____ to emphasise a small difference.
3 We use _____ + adjective + _____ to say there is no difference.
4 We use _____ to make an adjective weaker.
➡ Language reference and extra practice, pages 142–143

7 Correct the mistakes in the sentences.

1 Coca-Cola is the most biggest seller of soft drinks to children.
2 Children's teeth are a much more bad than they were ten years ago.
3 This computer game is so expensive as that one.
4 These trainers are much more better than those ones.
5 The new ZX radio-controlled car is lot faster that the 2007 version.
6 Coffee is just as tastier as tea.
7 When it comes to children, health is the more important thing in the world.

SPEAKING

8a Work in groups of three. You are a family (mother, father, son) and you want to buy a quad bike (a motorbike with four wheels) for the 16-year-old son.

Student A (father): turn to page 159.
Student B (mother): turn to page 162.
Student C (son): turn to page 166.

8b Look at the table on page 167, which has information about four different quad bikes. As a family, compare and discuss the four bikes, talking about small and big differences, and things that are the same. Try to agree on which bike to buy.

SITUATION

B-Kool is a soft drinks manufacturer, based in Chicago. The company is going to introduce a new drink to the market soon, which will appeal to the 8–14-year-old age group. The drink has a high sugar content and an unusual taste because it is made from a mixture of exotic fruits. When it was tested with young people, the children used three words to describe it: fresh, delicious, healthy. The drink will be sold all over the world, so there will be an international advertising campaign.

The marketing department still have several decisions to make before they decide on the advertising campaign. To help them, they have contacted three agencies and asked them to present their ideas to the department. B-Kool will probably offer a contract to the agency which makes the best presentation and has the most creative ideas.

1 Read the situation. Work with a partner to discuss the following.

If you were Marketing Director of B-Kool:

1 which quality of the new drink would you like to emphasise?

2 what do you think would be a good name for the drink?

3 would you sell the drink in a can, bottle or carton, or in all three containers?

2a ▮1.27▮ Listen to the Marketing Director, Amy Chen, talking to Larissa Klein, head of an advertising agency. What five points does Amy Chen want the agency to cover in their presentation?

2b Look at the ways of advertising the new drink. Which two ways does Amy Chen NOT mention?

TV commercials   magazines   posters   the Internet
radio spots   newspapers   special promotions

2c Listen again. Complete the notes that Larissa Klein made during the conversation. Use one or two words in each gap.

Points to cover in the presentation:

- Name of drink?

- Slogan?

- Packaging: can or bottle? Design,
  ¹_____ and ²_____?

- How to advertise? ³_____ during
  children's television? Children's
  magazines? Use the ⁴_____? One TV
  commercial or ⁵_____ for each country?
  ⁶_____ spots? If yes, what time of
  day? What sort of programmes
  to ⁷_____?

- Ideas for promoting the drink,
  e.g. ⁸_____ in schools or offer ⁹_____
  with the logo on them?

---

3 Work in small groups. Each group represents an advertising agency which will make a presentation to the marketing department of B-Kool.

1 Choose a name for your agency.

2 Discuss the points mentioned in the notes in Exercise 2c. Prepare for your presentation by noting down your ideas for each point.

KEY LANGUAGE: the language of presentations

4a ▮1.28▮ Larissa Klein and two colleagues make a presentation to the marketing department of B-Kool. Listen to the beginning of the presentation and complete the gaps.

Beginning a presentation:

1 I'd like to _____ _____ _____, Emilio Sanchez on my left, and next to him, Karl Reiner.

2 Our _____ _____ is to present some ideas for your new product.

3 Our presentation _____ _____ _____ three parts.

4 If you _____ _____ _____, we'll be pleased to answer them at the end of our presentation.

4b ▮1.29▮ Listen to the next part of the presentation. Complete the phrases Emilio uses to:

1 talk about a different subject:
_____ _____ _____ to the design of the can.

2 refer to an illustration:
Please _____ _____ _____ _____.

4c ▮1.30▮ Listen to the end of the presentation and complete the gaps.

Ending a presentation:

1 Now, let me _____ _____ _____ points.

2 Thank you very much _____ _____ _____ _____.

3 Are there _____ _____?

TASK: giving a formal presentation

5a Work in your groups from Exercise 3. Prepare your presentation for the marketing department of B-Kool. Each person in your group presents one part of the presentation. Use the following structure for the presentation. Make notes.

name of drink   slogan   design of the packaging
suggestions for advertising   special promotions

5b Make your presentation to the other groups.

6 As a class, discuss the presentations. Which one was the most interesting/creative/persuasive?

OTHER USEFUL PHRASES

I'm going to talk to you about …
This is how I'd like to organise my talk.
That's all I have to say. X will now talk about …
This brings me to my next point.
Now I'll sum up …

STUDY SKILLS: using your dictionary

1 Read the text about a road safety advertisement published by Transport for London. What is the aim of the writer?

2a What do you think the following words mean?

1 hard-hitting
  a) using difficult language
  b) using frightening images
  c) using many actors

2 theme
  a) main image   b) main commercial   c) main idea

2b Now look up *theme* in a dictionary. What other information can you find apart from the definition?

3a Most dictionaries have a section at the beginning entitled *Guide to the dictionary*. What kind of information do you usually find in the guide?

3b Look at the entries from the *Longman Active Study Dictionary*. In groups, discuss the questions.

1 How do you pronounce *advertisement* and *advertising*? Use the phonetic symbols to help you.

2 What part of speech is *advertising*?

3 What does the abbreviation *BrE* mean in the entry for *advertisement*?

4 If you found the abbreviation *AmE* after a word, what do you think it would mean?

5 What preposition usually follows the word *advertisement*? How do we know this?

6 How do you know that you cannot add *-s* to *advertising* to make it plural?

7 What examples are there to show you how you can use *advertising*?

3c Look at the entry for *campaign*. Are these statements true or false?

1 The word *campaign* rhymes with the word *foreign*.

2 It is a noun and you can make it plural by adding *-s*.

3 It is always followed by the preposition *for*.

4 *Campaign* has more than one meaning.

4a Work with a partner. Each of you chooses three words from the vocabulary sections of this unit. Note down information about the words from your dictionary. Check the guide to the dictionary so that you understand all the information.

4b Show each word to your partner. He/She asks questions about the word. Take turns asking and answering questions about the words.

How do you pronounce it? What part of speech is it? What preposition usually follows it?

Transport for London

TEEN Road Safety Campaign: Introduction

Transport for London has launched a new hard-hitting TV advertisement in support of their advertising campaign to reduce the number of teenagers killed or seriously injured on London's roads.

The overall theme for the campaign is 'don't die before you've lived'.

advertisement /əd'vɜːtɪsmənt $ ˌædvər'taɪz-/ also **ad** *informal*, **advert** *BrE n* [C] a picture, set of words, or a short film, which is intended to persuade people to buy a product or use a service, or that gives information about a job that is available, an event that is going to happen etc.: **+for** *The Sunday papers are full of advertisements for cars.*

advertising /'ædvətaɪzɪŋ $ -ər-/ *n* [U] the business of advertising things on television, in newspapers etc.: *a career in advertising | advertising executives*

cam·paign¹ campaign /kæm'peɪn/ *n* [C] **1** a series of actions intended to get a particular social or political result: *an election campaign* / *an advertising campaign* | **+for/against** *a campaign for equal rights* **2** a series of military attacks

WRITING SKILLS: a formal letter

5 Read this description of a recent television advert for road safety, which some people complained strongly about. Why do you think they complained?

The advert is shot entirely on a mobile phone. It starts by showing a group of friends having a good time walking along a suburban street. One of them begins to cross the road, but is distracted by his friends. He looks one way as he steps into the road, but a car comes from the other direction and knocks him down.

6a **1.31** Listen to three people, Eric, Lisa and Rebecca, talking about the advert described above on a television debate programme. Answer the questions.

1 Which person is *for* the advert? Why?
2 Which person is *against* it? Why?
3 Which person wants more information about the effect of the advert? Why?

6b Listen again. Complete the extracts with the correct prepositions.

1 Tonight we're focusing _____ road safety.
2 How do you feel _____ this?
3 I couldn't sleep all night thinking _____ it.
4 I'm really worried _____ this advertising trend.
5 Do you agree _____ Eric …?
6 I think we need more research _____ the effects of this type of advertising.
7 I mean, will shock advertisements result _____ fewer deaths of young people?

7 **Dependent prepositions** Read the letter to a newspaper about the television road safety advert. Underline all the examples in the text of the following.

1 verb + preposition
2 adjective + preposition
3 noun + preposition

Letters *to the Editor*

DEAR SIR – I'm writing to complain about the advertisement for road safety currently being shown on television. I think the advertiser should be banned from showing it.

Most people have seen the commercial and are horrified by it. It really is in very bad taste. Who could ever forget the awful image of that boy lying on the road, with blood pouring from his head? I simply do not believe the advertisement will discourage people from driving fast – nothing seems to do that.

I think the Government should prevent any advertiser from using images which shock or frighten people. There should be a law against such advertising methods. I intend to launch a campaign against this kind of advertising. Anyone interested in joining me can contact me on my website. I very much hope we will succeed in persuading advertisers to use less shocking methods to communicate their message.

Marina Warner

8 As a representative of the Department of Transport, write an open letter to the editor of the newspaper defending the use of the television advertisement. The following information may be useful to you to include in your letter.

Young teenagers (boys 13–16) are most likely to have accidents.

Almost one in five (18 percent) teenagers have been involved in road accidents or 'near misses' on their way to and from school.

Almost 65 percent of teenagers report that a friend prevented them from having an accident when they were crossing a road.

Mobile phones are particularly distracting. Other distractions include personal stereos, texting on phones, ball games and rollerblading.

Start the letter like this.

Sir,
I cannot agree with the opinion of Marina Warner. I think this kind of advertising will have a strong effect on road safety …

6 Business

In this unit

Grammar
- past continuous
- past perfect

Vocabulary
- business terms and roles
- business word combinations

Scenario
- Sunglasses after dark

Study skills
- recognising formal and informal language

Writing skills
- writing emails

6.1 IN BUSINESS

Eat and drink with your relatives; do business with strangers.
Greek proverb

VOCABULARY: business terms and roles

1a Complete the statements with the words in the box.

community	competitors	customer	law
loss	prices	profit	~~staff~~	taxes	wages

To succeed in business you should:

1 value your *staff*.
2 focus only on making a big _____.
3 pay employees low _____.
4 charge high _____.
5 never break the _____.
6 avoid paying _____ to the government.
7 believe the _____ is always right.
8 invest in the local _____.
9 put your _____ out of business.
10 be prepared to make a _____ for at least the first year.

1b Work with a partner to discuss the statements.

2 Match the people in the box with their job role.

customer	entrepreneur	manufacturer
partner	retailer	supplier	wholesaler

1 sells directly to the public
2 makes goods
3 starts new businesses
4 is one of the owners of a business
5 buys large quantities of goods from producers and sells them to shops and businesses
6 buys directly from a shop or a company
7 provides goods/parts to shops and businesses

3 Work with a partner to discuss the following.
1 Which are your favourite retailers?
2 Name three large manufacturers.
3 What services can a wholesaler offer a retailer?
4 Give an example of good/bad customer service you have experienced.
5 What problems can a business have with its suppliers?
6 Can you name a famous entrepreneur?
7 If you started a business, who would your partner be? Why?

READING

4 Read the leaflet about business plans and choose the most suitable heading for each paragraph.

a) Financial information

b) Management plan

c) Business description

d) Market analysis

5 Find words or phrases in the leaflet that mean the following.

1 the buildings that a company uses (paragraph 1)

2 goals for the long and short term (para. 1)

3 finance for the business (para. 1)

4 businesses/products which sell the most (para. 2)

5 a reduction in the usual price (para. 4)

6 predictions of how much money you will make or lose (para. 6)

LISTENING

6a ▮1.32▮ Allan Smith appears regularly on the radio giving advice on starting a business. Listen to Part 1 of an interview with him and answer the questions.

1 In his first tip, Allan mentions four areas of business. What are they?

2 Which of the following does Allan mention in his second tip?

advertising   price   costs   promotion
competitors   tax

3 What does Allan think the 'key to success' might be?

6b ▮1.33▮ Listen to Part 2 of the interview and complete the summary.

Firstly, some failed because the market had
¹____ ____, and the business was left behind.
The second reason is over-dependence on one
²____ ____. Other reasons are poor ³____, cash flow problems, bad debts and firms not dealing with ⁴____ properly.

6c ▮1.34▮ Listen to Part 3 of the interview. Are these statements true, false or not given?

1 Business plans are very important.

2 Business plans help to improve sales.

3 You should keep your business plans in your head.

4 At the beginning, you may make mistakes when you forecast.

Writing a BUSINESS PLAN

What to include ...

1 _____

The name of the business – what it is called. You should make sure this is not used by another business

The location of the business – where it is, e.g. your home or a business premises

Products or services you offer

Management and technical skills which you possess

Business objectives – what the aims of the business are

Funding – where the money will come from

2 _____

The market for your product or service

Industry trends – what is happening in the market at the moment

The target market – the sort of people you want to sell to

Your main competitors

The market leaders – the most successful companies and products

3 *Product or service*

Full description of products/services

Comparison of your products/services with the competition for quality/price

4 *Market strategy*

Pricing policy, e.g. discounts/opening offers, etc.

Distribution – how you will get your goods/services to your customers, e.g. mail order, retail outlets

After-sales service

5 _____

Structure of the business – how the business is organised, e.g. self-employed/partnership

Staff – description of jobs and CVs of key staff

Operating plan – details of how you are going to run the business

6 _____

Figures for the first two years

Profit and loss forecast

Capital expenditure forecast – money you will spend on, e.g. equipment

SPEAKING

7 ▮1.35▮ Listen to two people talking about an idea for a business in their home town. Answer the questions.

1 What type of business is it?

2 What is the name of the business?

3 What advantages of the business are mentioned?

4 Do you think it is a good idea? Why / Why not?

8 You have ten minutes to plan a business idea to start in your home town. Work with a partner and choose an idea from below or think of your own.

a garden care service   selling second-hand books
a mobile hairdressing service   selling fresh flowers

Think about the name and location of the business, the goods or services you will offer and your target market.

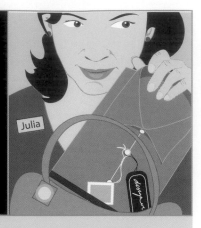

1

You work in the clothing department of a store.

Your friend, Julia, works in the same department. She is a good friend, who supported you when the two of you didn't get a good bonus at the end of last year. There was a lot of shoplifting in the clothing department then: people were stealing a lot of expensive items like designer shirts and silk ties. Your boss said that you weren't paying enough attention to your work and didn't deserve a good bonus.

Yesterday, you were having a drink with Julia after work in a local café and you noticed that Julia had two new men's shirts in her bag. 'Wow! They look expensive,' you commented. Julia laughed. 'You don't think I paid for them, do you? I take a few things from time to time to make up for our rotten bonuses.'

2

You are an environmental manager for a chemical firm.

All last year, the company was looking for ways of reducing costs because it was making a loss. It decided, therefore, to cut back on investment in technology.

As a result, the company did not spend money on buying some expensive new equipment. This reduces a special toxin in waste water. At present, scientists don't know exactly how poisonous this toxin is, and your waste is within legal limits. However, the polluted waste from the factory flows into a nearby lake and river. It seems to be affecting fish and wildlife, and a local scientist has warned that people should not eat fish caught in the river.

If you tell the press or the local authorities about the waste water, the firm will have to buy the expensive equipment. The company could go bankrupt and everyone, including yourself, would lose their jobs.

READING

1a Work with a partner to discuss the following ethical dilemmas.

1 Your best friend gives you an expensive birthday present. You do not like it. What do you do?

2 Your friend's husband has lost his job – you've seen him at the job centre. His wife doesn't know this. Would you tell her?

1b What ethical problems do people experience in business?

2a Read the three texts above quickly and match them with the following ethical problems.

a) You have information that could damage the company you work for.

b) A company that gave you an expensive present is trying to become a supplier for your company.

c) You have a colleague who is not honest.

2b Read the texts again. Are these statements true or false?

Text 1

1 Your manager complained that you (Julia's friend) were not paying enough attention to him.

2 Julia said she stole things because she did not get a decent bonus.

Text 2

3 The company was acting illegally.

4 The expensive equipment could stop the company going bankrupt.

Text 3

5 You did not tell your colleagues about the expensive watch.

6 You were given an expensive watch, an antique clock and some radios as gifts.

3 What do the following words highlighted in the text refer to?

1 them	3 This	5 their	7 It
2 it	4 It	6 he	8 those

SPEAKING

4a In groups, discuss the questions.

1 What would you do in the situations described in the texts if you were:
a) Julia's friend?
b) the environmental manager?
c) the Chief Executive?

2 What punishment, if any, do you think Julia should receive?

3 Is there a difference between a gift and a bribe?

3

You are *Chief* **Executive of** *a car manufacturer.*

You visited an overseas supplier some time ago, and when you left, he gave you an expensive watch as a present. On returning, you were planning to tell your colleagues about the present, but forgot.

Last week, you were sitting in your office when another present from the same supplier arrived. It was a magnificent antique clock! At the time, you were considering three competing offers to supply radios for a new range of cars. Your generous supplier had made one of the offers. His firm's radios were more expensive than those of another supplier, while the quality of the products was similar. You have never done business before with the supplier of the cheaper radios.

4b Work with a partner. Talk about a time when you, or a person/company that you know had to make a difficult ethical decision.

GRAMMAR: past continuous

5 Look at the examples of the past continuous from the texts and match them with their uses. Look at the context in the text to help you.

1 People were stealing a lot of expensive items like designer shirts.

2 Yesterday, you were having a drink with Julia after work …

3 All last year, the company was looking for ways of reducing costs …

4 You were sitting in your office when another present … arrived.

a) for a longer background action in the past when a shorter action interrupts it or happens during it

b) for repeated actions in the past that take place over a temporary period of time

c) for a background action

d) to emphasise the duration or continuity of a past action

➡ Language reference and extra practice, pages 144–145

6 Match the beginnings of the sentences with the endings. Then write out the sentences in full with the verbs in the correct form (past continuous or past simple).

1 I (meet) my old boss

2 IBM (offer) me a job

3 The company (have) financial problems

4 The sun (shine) brightly

5 She (find) the missing file

6 We (talk) about our future strategy in a meeting

a) when the President suddenly (announce) her resignation.

b) when I (leave) home at 7 o'clock this morning.

c) while I (travel) to Warsaw for a conference.

d) while I (study) at Harvard.

e) when a lucrative new contract (be) agreed.

f) while she (look for) for some other documents.

pronunciation

7a 1.36 **Weak forms** Listen to the following sentences. Circle the weak forms (/wəz/ and /wə/) and underline the strong forms (/wɒz/ and /wɜː/) of *was* and *were*.

1 We were having a meeting when the fire alarm went off.

2 When the phone rang, I was talking to a customer.

3 'Was he working for you then?' 'No, he wasn't.'

4 'Were they planning to buy another shop?' 'Well, they said they were.'

7b Listen again and repeat the sentences.

8 In groups, think about the events below and discuss them. Describe where you were and what you were doing.

• an accident at home or work

• a big event in your school's/company's recent history

• two important world events

Last month I spilled coffee on my boss's dress while we were having a meeting in the boardroom.

WRITING

9 Write a short paragraph describing the most interesting event you discussed in Exercise 8.

READING

1 In groups, discuss the questions.

1 Which famous business people have you heard of?

2 Why are they famous? What do you know about them?

3 Did you mention any women? Is it more difficult for women to succeed in business than men?

2a Work with a partner to read about some business icons. Try to answer as many of the questions below as you can. Share your answers with your partner.

Student A: read texts 1 and 2.

Student B: turn to page 162 and read texts 3 and 4.

1 What area of business was each person in?

2 What was each person most famous for?

3 Whose business failed due to their competitors' pricing strategy?

4 Who started out:
   a) selling hats?
   b) as a lawyer?
   c) as a scientist?
   d) brushing floors clean?

5 Who:
   a) used words from two languages to come up with the name for their company?
   b) thought that you did not need to succeed at university in order to succeed in business?

6 Which two people:
   a) lived in Europe?
   b) lived in the USA?
   c) liked sports?
   d) wrote a book?
   e) came from a poor family background?

7 Which person:
   a) was married the most?
   b) was born first?
   c) lived the longest?
   d) had the most children?

2b Discuss the similarities and differences between the childhoods and the education of the four people.

OBITUARIES

① Freddie Laker

Sir Freddie Laker died on February 9th, aged 83. Sir Freddie was the pioneer of today's low-cost air travel industry. In 1977, he began his transatlantic Skytrain service flying passengers from London to New York. Tickets cost only £118, which was one third of the price of his competitors. The service was extremely popular and by the end of the first year, Skytrain had made profits of £3 million and the number of passengers from the UK to the USA had increased by 30 percent.

Laker grew up in a small house with no bathroom, and his father left home when he was five. He started as a floor-sweeper in an aircraft factory and then studied aero-engineering. During his schooldays in England, Laker always told teachers that he wanted to be a millionaire. After World War II, he went into business as an aircraft

dealer. Then, in the mid 1960s, he founded his own company – Laker Airways.

After the success of the early Skytrain, other airlines agreed to lower their prices to put Laker out of business. As a result, by 1982, Laker Airways had gone bankrupt.

His last business was running a small airline in the Bahamas.

He was married four times and is survived by a daughter, Elaine, and a son.

Freddie Laker, born August 6 1922; died February 9 2006

② Coco Chanel

COCO CHANEL, fashion designer, died on January 10th in her Paris apartment. Gabrielle 'Coco' Chanel revolutionised the fashion industry with her innovative designs and elegant simplicity. Her themes included simple suits and dresses, trousers for women, and costume jewellery, but she is probably most famous for her perfumes.

She was born in the small city of Saumur, France. Her mother worked in a poorhouse and died when Gabrielle was only six. She was then abandoned by her father and brought up by relatives.

In 1910, she set up a shop in Paris selling ladies' hats. By the 1920s, she had expanded her business to include clothing. At that time she introduced a perfume, Chanel No. 5, which became one of the company's most profitable products. Another instant success was the Chanel suit, which was launched in 1923. The

'little black dress', which could be worn during the day and evening, was also made popular by Coco.

Although she spent most of her life in Paris she moved to Switzerland in her later years. She was still working in 1971 when she died at the age of 87.

Coco Chanel, born August 19 1883; died January 10 1971

VOCABULARY: business word combinations

3a Match the verbs in the box with the words and phrases below. Some verbs can be used with more than one word/phrase.

make found go run introduce launch negotiate

1 a contract
2 a profit
3 a company
4 a product
5 bankrupt
6 into business

3b Write a sentence using some of the combinations from Exercise 3a.

GRAMMAR: past perfect

4a Look at these two sentences from the text about Akio Morita and underline the verbs.

Sony launched the Walkman in 1979 after Morita had noticed young people's love of music.

Before he celebrated his 26th birthday, he had started his own company.

4b Answer the following questions and complete the rule.

1 Which verb in each sentence is in the past simple? (The other verb is in the past perfect.)

2 Which action happened first in each sentence? Write *1* above the correct verb.

3 Which action happened second? Write *2* above the correct verb.

4 Do we use the past perfect for the action that happened first or the action that happened second?

We form the past perfect with _____ + (*not*) + the past participle.

5 Find the two sentences in the texts that start as below. Which tense do we often use to talk about events that happened by a certain time?

1 By the 1920s, …
2 By the end of the first year, …
➡ Language reference and extra practice, pages 144–145

6 Complete the text with the past simple or past perfect of the verbs in brackets.

Warren Buffet, the second richest man in the world, has given almost all his $44 billion fortune away. Buffet [1]_____ (buy) shares before he [2]_____ (be) 12 years old, and by the time he [3]_____ (be) 14, he [4]_____ (make) his first purchase of land. After he [5]_____ (complete) his Masters degree at Columbia Business School, he [6]_____ (begin) his own investment partnership in 1956. Buffet's wife was going to supervise his charity work and donations but she [7]_____ (die) in 2004. They [8]_____ (not live) together since 1977.

Buffet has given his fortune to a charity run by the world's richest man, Bill Gates. Once Gates [9]_____ (make) a fortune with Microsoft, he [10]_____ (set up) the Gates Foundation. Before he [11]_____ (be) 50, Gates [12]_____ (give) $26 billion to charity. The Gates Foundation is now the biggest charitable trust in the world.

SPEAKING

7a What had the following people done by the ages/dates mentioned? Match the phrases with the sentences below.

go bankrupt win the World Cup win an Oscar start his/her own company fly to Australia compose his/her first piece of music become the most powerful person in sport climb Mount Everest expand his/her business

1 By his 26th birthday, Akio Morita …
2 By 1982, Freddie Laker …
3 By the 1920s, Coco Chanel …
4 By 1990, Mark McCormack …
5 By the age of 6, Mozart …
6 By the age of 26, Orson Welles …
7 By the age of 35, Edmund Hillary …
8 By the age of 17, Pelé …
9 By the age of 27, Amy Johnson …

7b Check your answers with a partner by making sentences with the past perfect.

What had Akio Morita done by his 26th birthday?

– He had started his own company.

8 A difficult childhood helps you become a good businessman/businesswoman. Discuss.

SITUATION

1 **Work with a partner to discuss the following.**

1 How often do you negotiate in your everyday life?

2 Who do you need to negotiate with? What about? For example, you may negotiate with a friend or partner about what to watch on television or you may need to negotiate with your boss about a salary increase.

2 **Work with a partner. Which of these tips do you think are most important for a successful negotiation? Try to agree on four.**

• Tell the other person exactly what you want.

• Listen carefully.

• Don't change your plan when you negotiate.

• Have a clear aim.

• Ask a lot of questions.

• Be strong and do your best to win.

• Keep calm. Do not show any emotion.

• Give a lot of reasons for what you want.

3 Read about Domino s.p.r.l. Why is the market for sunglasses growing?

Domino s.p.r.l., an Italian wholesaler, wants to import sunglasses from a manufacturer in the United States or Asia. They will supply retailers all over Europe. Although the peak season for sunglasses is in the summer months, market research suggests that more and more people are wearing sunglasses all year round – even in the evening as fashion accessories!

4a **1.37** Listen to Vanessa from Domino s.p.r.l. speaking to a potential manufacturer in San Francisco, USA. Is the negotiation successful?

4b Listen again and answer the questions.

1 How many pairs of sunglasses did Vanessa want?

2 What were the problems concerning the delivery date and the payment?

OTHER USEFUL PHRASES

What sort of quantity are you thinking of?

We can/would like to offer …

I think we can accept that.

KEY LANGUAGE: making offers, stating a position, bargaining

5a Listen again and complete the extracts.

1 BOB: How many would you like to _____?

2 VANESSA: We're thinking of _____ quite a large order.

3 BOB: I'm _____ that would be a bit difficult, Vanessa.

4 VANESSA: What about if we _____ earlier? _____ you be able to deliver in August?

5 BOB: Let me check if I _____ you – do you mean payment on delivery?

6 VANESSA: How do you _____ about that?

7 VANESSA: I'll think it over and maybe get back to you.

BOB: That sounds _____. Well … I hope to hear from you soon.

5b Match the sentences with similar ones from Exercise 5a.

a) Let's see if I've got this right.

b) We're considering buying a large quantity.

c) What sort of quantity do you have in mind?

d) That seems OK.

e) If we pay more quickly, can you get the goods to us earlier?

f) What do you think of the offer?

g) I'm sorry. That could be a problem.

TASK: negotiating a deal

6a After the failure of the earlier negotiation, a meeting is now arranged between Domino s.p.r.l and Sunspex, another manufacturer based in San Diego, USA. Work in small groups to look at the negotiation details then discuss the questions below.

Group A (Domino representatives): turn to page 159 and read the information carefully.

Group B (Sunspex salespeople): turn to page 163 and read the information carefully.

1 What are your most important needs in the negotiation?

2 Are some of your points less important? Can you offer them to the other side to get what you want?

3 What do you think will be important for the other side?

6b Work in pairs of one Domino representative and one Sunspex salesperson. Negotiate and try to get a good deal for your company.

1

Conclusion

Although there are cost benefits of using *Achieve*, it is clear that *Team Spirit* is a much more professional organisation and therefore the best option to help improve staff morale.

Recommendations

It is recommended that *Team Spirit* are contacted as soon as possible and informed of our requirements.
If possible a staff teambuilding weekend should be arranged for March/April.

2

Jane,
Mr Forster called. I'll get back to him tomorrow about the final details of his visit next month, but can you find out what stuff he needs for his presentation? Also he wants some help with booking a hotel. Let me know what you book as soon as possible.
Thanks,
Dan

3

Dear Mr McLennan,

Further to your letter of 15 March, unfortunately I will be unable to attend the meeting on Friday, due to a previous engagement. However, I would be very grateful if you could send me a copy of the minutes.
Yours sincerely,

Elena D'Angelo

4

Hi Carlos,
Great news: got the contract! Let me know if you want to work with us on this one. I'll be in touch in the next couple of days to firm up on our needs.
Best wishes,
Nils

5

Agenda Item	Discussion	Action
Marketing Plan	The budget for this was approved. Martin Schwarz will prepare in detail for next meeting.	MS to prepare detailed budget by Feb 21st.

STUDY SKILLS: recognising formal and informal language

1a Look at the extracts from different pieces of correspondence. Match them with the types below.

report   letter   email   note   minutes

1b Is each piece of correspondence formal or informal? Why?

2a Recognising formality/informality Which of the following are features of formal/informal writing?

1 use of contractions, e.g. *I'm*

2 no contractions, e.g. *I am*

3 passive constructions

4 phrasal verbs

5 longer words instead of shorter, more common ones, e.g. *assistance* (not *help*), *information* (not *facts*), *reserve* (not *book*), *receive* (not *get*)

6 direct questions, e.g. *Can you …?*

7 missing out words, e.g. subject pronouns

8 use of imperatives

2b Find examples of the features in the extracts.

3 Beginning and ending letters and emails Look again at the email and letter and underline the phrases used to begin and end them.

WRITING SKILLS: writing emails

4 Put the procedure into a logical order for writing emails. (Tip: the answer should spell a word.)

Type … (type a draft)

Who … is the email to? (the reader(s) and your relationship with them)

Send … (add any attachments and send)

Edit … (edit and check)

Register … (is the email formal/neutral/informal?)

Information … (brainstorm the content/functions, and think of the information you need to include)

5 Look at the phrases below and add them to the table of useful expressions on page 67.

I can't make it as …
If I can help in any way, please contact me again.
I regret to inform you …
I would be grateful if you could …
I have some good news (about …)
Got your message on …
Please find attached …
Speak to you / See you soon.

	Formal	Neutral	Informal
First contact	I am writing to enquire/ inform you …	I am writing to ask/tell you …	I'd like to find out / let you know about …
Referring to previous contact	With reference to your letter of …	Thank you for your letter of …	1_____
Giving good news	I am delighted to inform you …	2_____	Great news!
Giving bad news	3_____	Unfortunately, …	Sorry, but …
Making an offer	If you wish, I would be happy to …	Would you like me to …	Shall I …
Making a request	4_____	Could you possibly …	Please can you …
Refusing an invitation	I am unable to attend due to …	I will not be able to come because …	5_____
Apologising	I would like to apologise for …	I am sorry for/about …	Sorry, but …
Closing remarks	If you have any further questions please do not hesitate to contact me.	6_____	Call/Mail me if you need any more help.
Attachments	7_____	I am attaching …	Attached is …
Refer to future	I look forward to hearing from you in the near future.	Looking forward to meeting you.	8_____

6a Using the table, change the parts in bold in the first email from formal to neutral register. Make any other changes necessary.

6b Using the table, change the parts in bold in the second email from informal to formal register. Make any other changes necessary.

7 Write an email for the following situations. Use the W.R.I.T.E.S. procedure.

1 Marco, a colleague from an overseas branch of your company wrote to you last week. You promised to send some documents to him, but forgot. He has just written again to remind you.

2 A customer, Mrs Daley, phoned you and asked you to send her your latest catalogue.

3 Jenny, a friend who works in the same department, wants to go for a drink tonight after work. You are unable to go as you are going to the cinema, but you could go on Friday.

1

Dear Customer

I am writing to advise you of a new development at *Shoes 4U*. **I am delighted to inform you that** in future you will be able to order and pay online. We aim to provide our customers with the best possible service. In order to do this, **I would be grateful if you could** take a few minutes to register your details on the website; after, you will be able to start using the new service right away.
If you have any further questions, please do not hesitate to contact me.
I look forward to hearing from you soon.
Yours sincerely,

2

Dear Louise,
Got your email on Friday. Thank you for the invitation. **Sorry, but I can't make it** as we have a teambuilding seminar that weekend. **Please let Mark know** about the new products.
Please feel free to call/mail me again if you need any more help.
Speak to you soon
Denise

GRAMMAR

1 Do you have any favourite brands? Why do you choose one brand instead of another, do you think?

2 Read the article about neuromarketing and complete gaps 1–11 with the words below.

1 a) don't realise   b) 'm never realising
   c) 'd never realised

2 a) will put   b) puts   c) had put

3 a) was watching   b) 's going to watch
   c) is watching

4 a) would show   b) will show   c) showed

5 a) was telling   b) would tell   c) told

6 a) becomes   b) will become   c) is becoming

7 a) effectiver   b) more effective   c) most effective

8 a) aren't always being   b) weren't always being
   c) won't always be

9 a) quicker   b) quickest   c) most quickest

10 a) lot   b) more   c) much

11 a) as   b) so   c) than

3 What do you think about neuromarketing? Would you agree to do Dr Farwell's test? Why / Why not?

VOCABULARY

4 Read the definitions of the words and write them in the word puzzle. What is the word in 10?

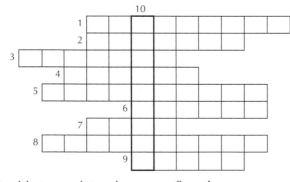

1 able to speak two languages fluently

2 the set of rules for a language

3 sending written messages by phone

4 an easy-to-remember phrase in adverts or commercials

5 able to make people do or believe something

6 the way you say words in a language

7 a sign or symbol on products or adverts

8 an advert on TV or radio

9 informal words or expressions; sometimes used by a particular group of people

Neuromarketing
the advertiser's dream!

I ¹_____ before how much I liked one brand of cream cheese more than any other. But apparently my brain does! That was the conclusion of Dr Larry Farwell. He ²_____ electrodes on my head and, while I was looking at adverts of cheese, he ³_____ the 'response' of my brain. If he ⁴_____ me a special brand of cream cheese, my brain would 'spike'.

This kind of information can be extremely useful for advertisers. For example, if you wanted to know what packaging attracts which type of customer, this test ⁵_____ you.

The good news for companies is that 'neuromarketing' ⁶_____ more and more available in the future. Advertising companies think it will be ⁷_____ than traditional market research. As one advertiser told me, 'If you interview consumers, they ⁸_____ able to say why they buy a brand. So the results can be misleading. On the other hand, if you could get inside their brain, then it would be the ⁹_____ form of market research in the world!'

It would also be a ¹⁰_____ cheaper. The advertising industry currently spends around $10 billion a year on finding out if adverts are effective. Dr Farwell's test could reduce that bill. But not everyone is ¹¹_____ happy as the advertisers. Critics say that reading our brains is unethical and unsafe.

5a Complete the questions with the words in the box.

profit business bankrupt products contracts

1 Can you negotiate _____ and prices successfully?

2 Do you have ideas of _____ to launch that aren't already on the market?

3 Can you focus on making a _____ more than anything else?

4 Would you prefer to run a _____ rather than work for one?

5 If you went _____, would you be happy to carry on and start a new business immediately?

5b Now ask and answer the questions with a partner. If you answered mostly *yes*, you'd make a good entrepreneur. If you answered mostly *no*, you'd better go and work for one.

KEY LANGUAGE

6 **1.38** Listen to a businessman buying mobile phones for his staff and complete his notes below.

Need ¹_____ mobile phones.
They can supply ²_____ for the
weekend. The rest can be delivered
³_____.
Prices:
Pay one fee per ⁴_____.
That includes the cost of the ⁵_____
but not ⁶_____.

7a Complete the dialogue with word pairs from the box. Make any necessary changes.

sound + fine   afraid + idea   check + understand
think + place   afraid + difficult   think + work
what + if   would + order

A: Hello. Can I help?

B: Yes, we're ¹_____ of _____ quite a large order of mobile phones. I run a company and some of my staff need them.

A: Right. How many ²_____ you like to _____?

B: Well, about 20 I think. Five of them are going to a conference this weekend so we'd need them straight away.

A: I'm ³_____ that would be a bit _____ for us. We don't have a lot in stock. But I could probably get you five today and the rest in one week. It depends a bit on the model.

B: That ⁴_____ _____.

A: So when you say you want the phones, are you saying you also want an account with us? We have some good company rates. For example, you can pay a flat monthly fee for all phones.

B: Let me ⁵_____ if I _____ you. We'd pay one fee every month. But how much would the phones be?

A: You don't pay for the phones. Just the calls.

B: So that's even if my salespeople are on the phone all the time, is it?

A: Well, it doesn't include overseas calls of course.

B: Oh. I'm ⁶_____ I don't like that _____. ⁷_____ about _____ we included that as well? What would it cost?

A: You mean include the overseas calls in a flat monthly fee?

B: That's right.

A: Yes, I ⁸_____ that would _____. Look. Let's go through some of the options.

7b Listen again and check your answers.

LANGUAGE CHECK

8 Put the words in the right order to make sentences. Look at the pages to check.

1 I can't … keep with my up friend (page 39)
2 I won't … you let down (page 39)
3 If we … call leave I'll early (page 43)
4 If you … save can a language, then should you (page 43)
5 What … happen if we would late paid? (page 51)
6 The new advert … as as successful the old one isn't (page 52)
7 My computer … powerful than is a little more yours (page 53)
8 This brings … next to my point me (page 55)
9 Thank you … very attention for much your (page 55)
10 By the end of the year … five new products had the company launched (page 63)

LOOK BACK

9 Find the exercises in Units 4–6 where you …

- learn seven new phrasal verbs. (U4)
- read about whether texting can cause problems. (U4)
- read an article about disappearing languages. (U4)
- listen to people's views about adverts. (U5)
- compare which bike to buy. (U5)
- give a marketing presentation. (U5)
- make a business plan. (U6)
- practise using business word combinations. (U6)

7 Design

In this unit

Grammar
- modals
- modals (present deduction)

Vocabulary
- word building, adjectives
- abstract nouns

Scenario
- Martelli design competition

Study skills
- editing and proofreading

Writing skills
- a report

7.1 DESIGN IS EVERYWHERE

If you design something too well, you don't get another job for 30 years.
Raymond Loewy, 1893–1986, US designer

READING AND SPEAKING

1 Think about objects in your home. Which are particularly well-designed? Why?

2a Look at these extracts from an introduction to a design book. In which extract does the writer mention these things?

1 incorrect ideas about design
2 the essential element in good design
3 what design is
4 the restrictions on designers
5 what designers do

2b Read the extracts again and correct the statements below.

1 Designers are the same as scientists and engineers.
2 Magazines don't make mistakes when talking about design.
3 Design is all about appearance.
4 The secret of good design is to be new and different.
5 Designers, like artists, have a lot of freedom.

---

1 ## WHAT IS **DESIGN**?

THE WORD DESIGN means different things to different people. One definition given by designer Richard Seymour is 'making things better for people'.

2 Scientists can invent technologies, manufacturers can make products, engineers can make them work and salespeople can sell them. However, only designers can combine all these things. Designers turn an idea into something that is desirable, commercially successful and adds value to people's lives.

3 Good design begins with the needs of the user. A good design fulfils a user's need. A design doesn't have to be new, different or impressive to be successful in the market place, but it must fulfil a need. However, it is also true that design methods often lead to innovative products and services.

4 Many people have misconceptions about design. Magazines often use the word design when they mean style or fashion. For example, when they show a toaster or bottle opener which is well designed, the result is that people think that design is only about how things look. Design is also about how things work. In reality, the way a product looks is something which happens at the end of a product development process.

5 Designers, unlike artists, can't simply follow their creative feelings. They work in a commercial environment, which means there are many points to consider. Designers have to ask themselves questions such as: 'Is the product really wanted?', 'How is it different from everything else on the market?', 'Does it fulfil a need?', 'Will it cost too much to manufacture?' and 'Is it safe?'

VOCABULARY:
word building, adjectives

3 Work with a partner to complete the word families in the table below. Check your answers in the text.

verb	noun (person)	noun (thing, concept)	adjective
design			
		science	scientific
		manufacturing	
produce	producer		productive
engineer		engineering	
		use	usable
develop	developer		developing
innovate	innovator	innovation	
	inventor	invention	inventive
		art	artistic

pronunciation

4 [1.39] **Word stress** Look up the words in the table in a dictionary. Mark any words that have a different stress pattern from the verb or noun they are related to. Listen and check, then repeat the words.

5a Work with a partner to discuss the following.

1 Can you name an inventor? What did he/she invent?
2 What is the most famous manufacturing company in your country?
3 What are the three products you could not live without?
4 Who do you respect more – artists or scientists? Why?
5 Are artistic people different from other people?
6 What do you think is the best innovation of the 21st century?
7 Is the design of a product important to you? Why / Why not?
8 What products do you think designers will develop in the next ten years?

5b Write some questions of your own to ask other students using words from the table above.

6a The following adjectives are often used to describe designs. Work with a partner to check that you understand them all.

> elegant   functional   futuristic   handmade
> innovative   mass-produced   retro   simple
> streamlined   stylish   traditional   up to date

6b Find words in Exercise 6a that refer to the following.
1 the past (2 words)
2 methods of manufacture (2 words)
3 designs which are new and different (2 words)

6c Find words in Exercise 6a that mean the following.
1 attractive and fashionable
2 modern
3 with a smooth shape
4 attractive and graceful
5 not complicated
6 useful

SPEAKING AND WRITING

7a Think about the following items. In small groups, discuss what qualities you look for in them.

telephones   cars

7b Look at the photos below. Say which design of car and phone you prefer and why.

8 Write a short paragraph describing your favourite design from this page.

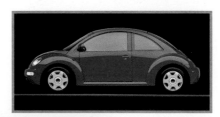

READING

1 You are going to read about design during three different decades of the 20th century: the 1930s, the 1960s and the 1990s. Before you read:

1 Look at the photos of the products and decide which of the three periods each comes from.

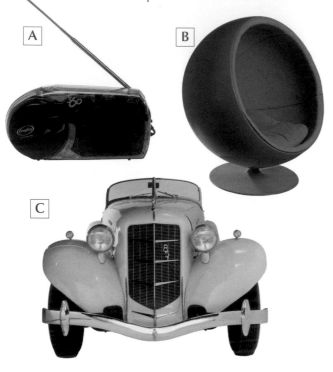

A

B

C

2 Look at the ideas which influenced design at the different times. In small groups, discuss in which period you think they are mentioned and why.

advances in communication   recycling
young consumers   streamlining
short-lived products   ergonomic design (designs adapted to human needs)

2a Read the three texts above quickly to check your answers.

2b Read the texts again and make notes in the table.

	1930s	1960s	1990s
Ideas	*streamlining, ergonomics*		
Designers			
Products			
Materials			

1930-1939

IN THE 1930s designers increased the efficiency of boats and aircraft by giving them smooth and curved shapes. Then, in 1934, Chrysler launched its new streamlined car, the Airflow. This was the start of the use of aerodynamics in car design. Streamlining suggested speed, efficiency and most of all modernity. Designers realised that consumers were attracted to other streamlined products, and they therefore began to use streamlining in a wide range of domestic appliances.

The designer Henry Dreyfuss helped to develop a new theory about design called ergonomics. He believed that machines were more efficient if they were adapted to people's needs. His reputation was based on the Bell 3000 telephone. Because of its ergonomic design, it was easy for people to use.

At this time a number of new materials were used in design, such as Bakelite (an early type of plastic). It was a perfect material for producing smooth, streamlined products.

3 In terms of design, which period was the most interesting, which was the most useful and which was the most exciting, do you think?

VOCABULARY: abstract nouns

4 Match the abstract nouns with their meanings

1 efficiency   3 optimism   5 streamlining
2 modernity   4 consumerism   6 industrialisation

a) using styles that are different from traditional styles
b) the process of becoming an area that has a lot of industry
c) working well without wasting time or energy
d) the belief that good things will happen
e) improving the shape of something so it moves more easily
f) the buying and selling of goods and services

LISTENING

5 **1.40** Listen to two designers talking about ideas for a new product and answer the questions.

1 What product do they discuss?
2 Who will use the product?
3 What materials do they mention?
4 When do they want to launch the product?

1960-1969

THIS WAS a period of optimism and self-belief, when humans travelled faster than sound and walked on the moon. During this period, the power of advertising, particularly on television, created mass consumerism. Manufacturers began to recognise the buying power of teenagers and began to develop products aimed at the youth market. These new young consumers wanted change and variety. It was a time of short-lived products and the idea of a 'throwaway' society. New materials, new shapes, new colours appeared in all areas of design.

There were many radical furniture designs. The Danish designer Verner Panton produced his bright red plastic chair, for example, and Eero Aarnio created his extraordinary Ball Chair.

In fashion, the space age continued to influence design. Designers created clothes in futuristic materials. Courreges' 'silver foil' suits were an example of this.

1990-1999

DURING THE 1990s, many designers worried about the damage to the environment caused by industrialisation. They were especially worried about the destruction of energy sources and raw materials. They wanted to find ways of slowing this down. These concerns influenced design in many areas. For example, solar cars and electric cars were developed. Recycling paper and other materials became popular, as in designer Jane Atfield's plastic shelving unit. The material she used came from old washing-up liquid bottles. Designers created more energy-saving products and products which consumers could repair or recycle. The focus was on product durability. Another big influence on design was advances in communication, in particular the Internet and the mobile telephone.

One product that illustrates the two big concerns of designers in the 1990s was Trevor Baylis' wind-up radio, launched in 1995. This product was particularly useful in Africa because it could generate power without having expensive batteries. People made the radio work simply by turning a small handle.

GRAMMAR: modals

6 Look at these sentences from the conversation in Exercise 5. Underline the modal verbs, and match them with one of the meanings a–h.

1 The chair could be useful for all kinds of people.
2 We can't use steel.
3 We should make it in just three colours.
4 It must be cheap if we want to be competitive.
5 It doesn't have to be very different.
6 It has to be safe because the regulations are very strict now.
7 We could launch it just before the summer.
8 We really mustn't miss this opportunity.
9 … we shouldn't launch until we're really ready.
10 I can do some designs before we meet again.

a) I/We am/are (not) able to …
b) It is possible for me/us to …
c) It is possible/likely that …
d) It is advisable (not) to …
e) It is essential that … (a general rule)
f) It is necessary/important to … (personal opinion)
g) It is not necessary to …
h) It is necessary or important not to …

➡ Language reference and extra practice, pages 146–147

7 Choose the correct modal verb.

1 This material *doesn't have to / mustn't* be used as it harms people's health.
2 This material isn't strong enough. It *must / could* break under pressure.
3 We *must / could* change the design, but I'm not sure that's the answer.
4 We have a problem with the design but it *doesn't have to / shouldn't* be difficult to resolve.
5 We *must / could* be more innovative or we will go out of business.
6 We *could / have to* change the shape of the model so that it meets government regulations.
7 We *can / must* hire that designer. She's the best in the business.

SPEAKING

8 Work in groups. You are designers, and your company has asked you to come up with some ideas for one of the products below. Choose one product, discuss your ideas and sketch a design. Think about shape, colour, materials, size, appearance, rules and regulations. Try to use modal verbs.

a piece of sports equipment   an item of clothing
a household item   a product for a car

READING

1 Look at the logos. Do you recognise any of them? What are the products?

2a Look at the website about Raymond Loewy quickly. Which of the products from Exercise 1 are mentioned?

2b Read the article again and say what the following numbers refer to.

a) 200   b) 1929   c) 40   d) 50
e) $50,000   f) 1940

2c Read the text again and match the sentence halves.

1 Loewy's designs were based on the idea of

2 Loewy's earliest success was

3 Loewy is probably best known for

4 Loewy's logo designs aimed at

5 Loewy's biggest impact was in completely

a) making company symbols very memorable.

b) changing the design industry.

c) re-designing a copying machine.

d) offering original but not revolutionary answers to problems.

e) changing the look and colour of an item of packaging.

HEROES OF DESIGN

HOME

ABOUT US

LINKS

CONTACT US

LOEWY, RAYMOND (1893–1986)

1 Called 'the man who shaped America' and 'the father of modern industrial design', Raymond Loewy must be one of the most influential designers of all time. He revolutionised the industry, working as a consultant for more than 200 companies and creating designs for everything from packaging to refrigerators, from cars to the interiors of spacecraft.

2 Loewy's designs all had one thing in common. They were shaped by the MAYA principle – Most Advanced Yet Acceptable. His idea was that people will not accept solutions to design problems if the solutions are too different from current designs.

3 After a short period as a fashion illustrator, Loewy started his career in industrial design in 1929 by re-designing a copying machine for the British manufacturer, Sigmund Gestetner. The 28-year-old designer completed the task in three days and the design of the machine lasted for the next 40 years.

4 The Gestetner duplicator was the beginning of many designs which used streamlining. He described this as 'beauty through function and simplification'. He spent the next 50 years streamlining everything from postage stamps and company logos to the interiors of stores. The famous Greyhound bus and Studebaker car show his use of streamlining in action.

5 He is perhaps most famous for his re-design of the Lucky Strike packaging. In 1940, the President of the Lucky Strike Manufacturing Company, George Washington Hill, bet Loewy $50,000 that he could not improve the appearance of the green and red Lucky Strike packets. Loewy accepted the challenge. He changed the background of the packet from green to white. Then he put the red lucky strike target on both sides of the packet. This made it more eye-catching and greatly increased sales. It is now recognised as a design classic.

6 Loewy's logo designs aimed at 'visual retention'. He wanted to make sure that anyone who saw the logo, even for a short while, would never forget it. He designed many highly visible logos for famous companies such as Shell Oil, Exxon, Greyhound and Nabisco.

7 By the mid 20th century, his industrial design firm was so famous that he could say 'the average person, leading a normal life … is bound to be in daily contact with some of the things, services or structures' designed by his firm.

Lo   A B C D E F G H I J K L M N
         O P Q R S T U V W X Y Z

LISTENING

3a `1.41` Listen to three pairs of students at a museum of design. In which order do they talk about the things below?

A

B

C

3b Listen again. Are these sentences true, false or not given?

1 The first design is by da Vinci.
2 This design is over 500 years old.
3 Elias and Freddie are looking at a Ferrari.
4 The car was made in the 1950s.
5 The third object is the designer's best-selling design.
6 George would like to buy one of these.

GRAMMAR: modals (present deduction)

4a Look at Track 1.41 on page 175 and underline the modal verbs *must, can't, might* and *could*. Look at the words around them.

4b Match each modal verb with one of these meanings.

1 It can't be true.   a) I think this is possible.
2 It might/could be true.   b) I'm certain that this is true.
3 It must be true.   c) I'm certain that this is not true.

4c Look at the modal verbs in Exercise 4b. What is the opposite of *must be* when we are talking about deduction?

GRAMMAR TIP

We can also use modal verbs with a continuous form:
She might be feeling ill. (= I think she's feeling ill.)
You must be joking! (= I'm certain you're joking.)

➡ Language reference and extra practice, pages 146–147

5 Rewrite the sentences below using *must, can't, could* or *might*.

1 Raymond Loewy is definitely one of the most influential designers of all time.
2 I'm sure this design is by Armani.
3 I'm sure this painting is not by Leonardo.
4 Maybe this painting is by Picasso, but I'm not sure.
5 Not many people are attending the exhibition. I'm sure they aren't promoting it very well.
6 This product looks dangerous to me.
7 People are not sure if it is a Loewy design.
8 I'm sure that designer is working very hard. I've seen a lot of her designs.

6 Work with a partner to discuss what you think the designs below are. Try to use these words and phrases.

must   might   could   can't
I'm sure/certain …   maybe/perhaps
It's possible that …
It's not possible that …

SPEAKING

7 If you had the skills, what would you like to design/re-design?

SITUATION

Look at the advertisement which appeared in the design magazine 'Trendsetter'. You are a member of the jury who will choose the winning designs.

1 Read the advertisement and answer the questions.

1 Who can enter the competition?

2 How can a competitor get an entry form?

3 How much money will the winner receive?

4 How much money is available for special awards?

2a Look at the designs below. Think of three adjectives which describe the qualities of each design, then compare with a partner.

2b Answer the questions.

1 Who do you think might use each product?

2 Where would each one be used?

3 What price do you think each one should be?

3 **2.2** Listen to a judge of the competition and tick (✓) the design qualities below that he mentions.

durable   easy to use   functional   innovative modern   streamlined   stylish   timeless traditional   value for money

FRANCISCO MARTELLI

DESIGN COMPETITION

The competition is open to young designers who are still studying or who have graduated during the last five years. Entry forms will shortly be sent to design schools, university departments and design studios all over the world.

The competition is open to any designer who has produced a prototype of their design. The aim of the competition is to recognise and reward outstanding product designs. Any design which is original and attractive will be considered.

Total prize money is $60,000.
First prize: $30,000   Second prize: $20,000
The remaining prize money will be distributed in the form of special awards, decided by the jury members.

For further information and entry forms, please visit the website below.

Entries deadline: July 30

Additional information: www.martellisprize.com/international

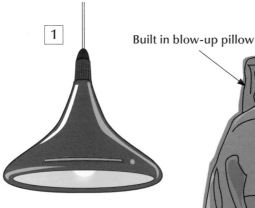

1

Spotlight CD player

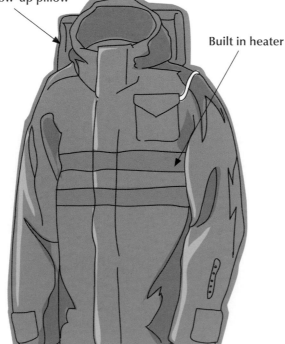

2

Built in blow-up pillow

Built in heater

Commuter jacket

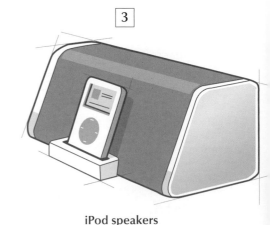

3

iPod speakers

KEY LANGUAGE: describing qualities

4a **2.3** Listen to one of the judges commenting on a design which won first prize last year. The product was a stylish desk. Answer the questions.

1 What special features does the desk have?

2 What kind of person would buy it?

3 What does the judge say about the price of the desk?

4b Listen again and complete the sentences.

1 As you can see, the desk _____ very stylish.

2 It's _____ of solid oak, so it's obviously very durable.

3 There are several _____ I really like.

4 One of the best _____ is that the desk's functional.

5 I'd say it's _____ at home computer use.

6 It would _____ especially to a business person, working from home.

7 It's excellent _____ for money too.

4c Look at the pictures of the designs in Exercise 2a. Choose one of the designs and write five sentences about it, similar to the ones above.

4

Exercise bicycle

TASK: evaluating designs

5a Work in groups of four. You are going to judge this year's competition. Read the description of one of the product designs.

Student A: turn to page 159.
Student B: turn to page 163.
Student C: turn to page 166.
Student D: turn to page 167.

5b Describe your product to the other judges in your group. You may add any other information you wish. Complete the evaluation form for the other three products as you listen to the other judges. Marks are out of ten. Do not evaluate your own product.

5c Add up the marks of the three judges for each product and find the winner.

	Design _____	Design _____	Design _____
stylish			
innovative			
functional			
easy to use			
durable			
value for money			
TOTAL			

OTHER USEFUL PHRASES

Visual appeal

It looks like a (design from the 1960s).

Material

It has a metal/steel/leather/aluminium (top/side/base).

Features

It has several (qualities / special features).

It has a unique feature: it's got a (special thing for …).

One of its weak/strong points is (that it is very difficult/easy to use because …).

Use

It's designed for (opening/keeping …).

It's specially designed to (open/keep …).

It's used for (opening/keeping …) / You (can) use it to (open/keep …).

2a `2.4`

STUDY SKILLS: editing and proofreading

1 It is important to make sure that your writing is accurate and your meaning clear. You are going to listen to a teacher giving some tips on checking written work. Work with a partner. What points do you think she will mention?

2a `2.4` Listen to the conversation. Note down the points she mentions. Are they the same as the points you discussed in Exercise 1?

2b Listen again and answer the questions.

1 What examples does the teacher give of the following mistakes?
   a) spelling
   b) irregular verbs
   c) prepositions

2 Complete the final piece of advice she gives.

Is my meaning _____? Will someone _____ my work _____ what I'm trying to say?

3 What are the main problems you have when you write in English? What mistakes do you often make?

4 Read the report, written as part of a project by two design students, and answer the questions.

1 Which phone:
   a) is cheaper?
   b) is heavier?
   c) has higher sales?
   d) is very well designed?
   e) cannot keep many tunes or photos?
   f) can change its appearance?

2 What feature do both phones have?

3 What is the writer's general opinion of the two phones?

5 **Proof reading** Read the report again and find the following errors.

a) five incorrect spellings
b) two missing capital letters
c) one missing full stop
d) one missing apostrophe
e) one incorrect apostrophe
f) one example of incorrect word order
g) one incorrect verb form
h) one incorrect tense
i) two incorrect prepositions

Report on the...

Nokia 6230i
and the
Samsung SGH-D500

We were asked to compare the above-mentioned mobil phones.

■ The Samsung D500 is a little cheaper than the Nokia 6230i. However, the Samsung model is very stilish and is one of the most popular phones on the market. It's features include a 1.3 Mp camera and music player. It does not have a memory card, so you can store only a limited amont of music tracks and fotos on the phone.

■ The nokia 6230i is small and light. It is weighing only 99g and is very functional It has a 1.3 Mp camera, like the Samsung phone, but it also have a memory card. The panel of the camera can be replaced easily. Covers are in five diferent colours available.

Our opinion
We were a little disappointed for the D500s camera test results. we found that the camera was not very good in capturing movement. However, both the Nokia and Samsung models are very good buys.

WRITING SKILLS: a report

6a **Linkers** Look at the words in *italics* in each sentence below. Which word is used for a contrast, which to add something and which to show a result?

1 The Samsung phone has the best call reception. *Therefore,* there is more chance of staying connected in an area with a weak signal.

2 The Samsung phone has a large colour display. *In addition,* it has a memory card and an excellent camera.

3 The Nokia phone has several good technical features. *However,* it does not have a mobile Internet service.

6b Circle the words and phrases from the list below that are used to introduce results.

also   although   as a result   consequently
moreover   on the other hand

6c Use an appropriate linking word or phrase to make sentences from the prompts.

1 Both models have similar features. The Ericsson model is much cheaper.
Both models have similar features. However, the Ericsson model is much cheaper.

2 The Nokia model has more technical features. It is lighter and cheaper.

3 The Samsung Z320i has a new Internet service. Its battery life is excellent.

4 It is one of the smallest and lightest mobile phones. It is very easy to carry.

5 This phone has the best call reception. It is the cheapest of all the phones.

6 The phone worked perfectly after we poured water on it. We recommend it for people who work outside in all weathers.

7 Pay as you go (PAYG) offers good value if you don't use your phone a lot. A pay-monthly contract is better for heavy users.

8 Our first impressions of the new phone are good. We will have to test it more thoroughly.

7 The editor of a photography magazine has asked you to write a short report on two digital cameras. Your report, together with others, will be used for an article in the magazine on digital cameras. Write the report, using the notes below.

Nikon Coolpix 4600

Price: £125

Overall reliability: average

Shutter delay: well below a second (good for action shots)

Takes 3.5 seconds to be ready for taking pictures after power turned on (slow).

Picture quality: good

Optical viewfinder: good for shots in bad light

Camera can record video, but no sound.

Excellent battery life

Several scene modes but few manual controls

You wait just under 2 seconds before taking shots.

Advantages: picture quality and battery life

Disadvantages: not many manual options, no sound on video

Nikon Coolpix L1

Price: £160

Overall reliability: average

Shutter delay: 0.9 seconds (worse than average)

Takes 5 seconds to be ready for a photo (not good for a quick shot).

Takes 5.3 seconds to be ready for next photo (slow).

Picture quality: below average

Large LCD screen (49mm x 37mm) – good for composing/reviewing shots

No manual focus

Advantages: classic design, quite powerful zoom lens   (38mm–190mm)

Disadvantages: slow – some features (e.g. shutter delay) could be better.

8 Education

Grammar
- defining relative clauses
- non-defining relative clauses

Vocabulary
- education and studying
- word combinations

Scenario
- Trouble at Lakeside

Study skills
- reading strategies

Writing skills
- a formal letter

Education is what remains when you have forgotten everything learned in school.
Albert Einstein, 1879–1955, German-Swiss-US scientist

VOCABULARY: education and studying

1 Work with a partner to discuss the following questions about education in your country. Check that you know all the words in *italics*.

1 What age do children usually start *primary* (or *elementary*) school?

2 What age do children usually leave *secondary* school?

3 What age does *compulsory education* start? At what age does it finish? Do you think these are the correct ages?

4 Do most people go on to *higher education*? Why / Why not? Do they have to pay?

5 Are *exams* or *continuous assessment* more common? Which is the better way of monitoring progress? Why?

2a Look at the phrases below. Which two nouns in each group are correct? Change wrong combinations, adding the correct verb and/or changing the preposition where necessary.

1 **go** to school / ~~to~~ a place at university / to college

2 **revise** for an exam / a subject / a test

3 **graduate** from university / from primary school / from high school

4 **get** a degree / a good grade / an exam

5 **take/retake** homework / an exam / a course

6 **pass/fail** an exam / a course / a good result

7 **hand in** an essay / a seminar / an assignment

8 **do** progress / coursework / your best

9 **make** mistakes / progress / homework

10 **study** an exam / a subject / a language

2b In small groups, ask and answer questions using the combinations above.

How do/did you revise for exams?

READING

3a Read the messages in an Internet chat room. Which messages in the chat room are for mixed-sex schools, which are against, and which are neither for nor against?

3b Read the messages again and find nouns which mean the following.

1 sets of numbers which represent a fact (Hans)

2 the subjects at a school, college, etc. (Martin)

3 the activity of staying away from school without permission (Martin)

4 upsetting and frightening someone smaller and weaker, especially in a school situation (Emily)

3c Which person believes:

1 that mixed schools are less competitive?

2 that there is proof that single-sex schools are better?

3 that school should be the same as real life?

4 that the problem isn't whether a school is single-sex or mixed?

5 that single-sex education caters for girls and boys better?

4 Which of the opinions in the messages do you agree with? Which do you disagree with? Why?

SPEAKING

5 Work in groups and discuss the following. Try to agree on each one.

1 Schools should spend more time teaching the skills people need to get a job.

2 Education is basically a social experience. The atmosphere is the most important thing.

3 There should be no private education. All children should attend state schools/universities.

4 The purpose of secondary education is to prepare you for life.

5 Examination results are the most important aspect of education.

6 Academic achievement depends mainly on your teacher.

7 Teachers should be paid according to the exam results of their students.

8 Sport is the most important subject at school.

WRITING

6 Write a message giving your opinion on one of the statements in Exercise 5 for the *Newsline* chat room.

---

newsline: the online news service   Register / sign in

Discussion: **Single-sex schools are better than mixed schools**

<u>Message 1</u> - posted by *Jane, Amsterdam*
I think mixed-sex schools are the only way for children to learn, because it's natural. In higher education and their working life, they will be mixed so it makes sense for them to be mixed at school. School should reflect the real world.

<u>Message 2</u> - posted by *Hans, Germany*
My reaction to this is very clear. For me, single-sex schools are much better, and the statistics show that they get better exam results, particularly at secondary level. Anything which helps children pass exams must be a good thing.

<u>Message 3</u> - posted by *Bill, USA*
Boys and girls learn in very different ways. I feel that they should be educated separately so teachers can focus on their different needs. The way I see it is that if you have a zoo, you don't put the lions in with the zebras!

<u>Message 4</u> - posted by *Martin, London*
My view on this is that it doesn't really matter. What is important is the curriculum, and keeping students interested. I was a teacher and we had a lot of truancy to deal with, and problems with students missing lessons because they found them boring. Never have a timetable with Maths as the first class on Monday morning!

<u>Message 5</u> - posted by *Emily, Sydney*
I don't think there is any question that mixed schools are better. There is too much competition at single-sex schools, which often means that students don't make enough progress. I also think there is more bullying at single-sex schools, where children are picked on because of the increased competition. Single-sex schools lead to a 'dog eat dog' situation.

Messages 1 - 5 of 5

LISTENING AND SPEAKING

1a **2.5** Listen to a university student talking about a teacher. Does he say the teacher was good or bad?

1b Listen again and tick (✓) which of the following adjectives he uses to describe the teacher.

friendly   informal   easy-going   strict   punctual
late   formal   well prepared   interesting

2 Look at the words from the listening below and use your dictionary to find the meanings of any you do not know.

environment   method   unique   approach
pace   criticise

3 Tell your partner about your favourite/worst teacher at school. Write a short profile (80–100 words) of him or her. Use Track 2.5 on page 176 to help you.

READING

4a Read the article and correct the mistakes in the summary.

Maria Montessori pioneered a new teaching method after she graduated as a nurse in 1896 and taught deprived children. She tried to use everyday objects in the class so the children could develop social skills with each other and learn to be competitive. She taught children to experiment and to depend on the teacher.

4b Read the article again and say what the following dates refer to.

a) 1870   b) 1896   c) 1912   d) 1936   e) 1952

4c Read the article again and answer the questions.

1 What is the main role of the children in the Montessori approach?

2 Why did Montessori want to free children's minds?

3 Why is the furniture light and the cabinets low in a Montessori classroom?

4 What point does the writer make about the children's social life?

5 Do you think children learn best with a formal or informal style of teaching?

Maria Montessori

Maria Montessori (1870–1952) is a famous Italian educationalist whose method of teaching has influenced people all over the world.

Born in the province of Ancona, Italy in 1870, Montessori became the first female doctor in her country after she graduated from medical school in 1896. Later, working with deprived children, she set up a 'Children's House' (Casa dei Bambini) in Rome. This was the place where she developed the Montessori Method, an educational system that encourages an informal style of teaching. Children learn from handling everyday materials and they develop at their own pace. The Montessori philosophy is simple. Children are unique individuals who must be free to learn without being criticised or restricted. It is the child that controls the pace, topic and lessons, not the rest of the class or the teacher. As a result, children enjoy learning and this gives them confidence and makes them happy.

The Montessori Method also teaches children skills to help them become independent. Very young children learn to dress themselves, to cook and to put their toys and clothes away. Children are encouraged to repeat activities as often as they wish, and they develop their observation skills by doing different activities.

A Montessori teacher observes children closely in order to provide them with individual learning programmes. The teacher is a guide, not a leader of the classroom, helping to open students' eyes to the wonders around them.

GRAMMAR: defining relative clauses

Look at the following sentence from the text:

Children are unique individuals **who must be free to learn** …

The words in bold are a defining relative clause.

6a Find and underline the following relative pronouns and adverbs from the text.

who   that   which   whose   where   when

6b Which relative pronouns or adverbs do we use to talk about the things below?

people   things or ideas   places   time
people + possessions/ideas

➡ Language reference and extra practice pages 148–149

| edit this page | history |

Maria Montessori wanted to free children's minds so that they would learn by self-teaching and self-correction. It is an approach to teaching which encourages children to learn by doing and experimenting.

A typical room in a Montessori school has many things children can use, for example, books, objects and games. The furniture is light so they can arrange it as they wish, and the cabinets are low, so the children can reach them. Because the environment offers a range of activities, children like to work together and they develop a social life based on cooperation rather than competition.

Maria Montessori travelled all over the world, training teachers to use her method, but it was only in her final years when she established the teacher-training centres that would take her work forward. There are now many schools in Europe and North America which use the Montessori curriculum and methods.

She wrote *The Montessori Method* in 1912 and *The Secret of Childhood* in 1936.

7 Match the sentence halves, and join them using *who, that, which, whose, where* or *when*.

1 A professor in a British university is someone
2 A university is an institution
3 A thesis is a long piece of writing
4 A seminar is a class at university/college
5 An academic is someone
6 A vacation is a period of the year

a) universities or colleges are officially closed.
b) has the highest rank of the teachers in a department.
c) you do as part of a university degree.
d) students study for degrees and academic research is done.
e) teaches and does research in a college or university.
f) the teacher and students discuss a particular topic.

8a Look at another example of a relative clause and choose the correct answer in the rule below.

A typical room in a Montessori school has <u>many things</u>. Children can use <u>the things</u>. =

A typical room in a Montessori school has many things children can use …

We can leave out the relative pronoun if it is the *subject / object* of the relative clause.

8b Cross out the relative pronoun in the following sentences where possible.

1 Students who enter university may face a number of problems.
2 Is your degree worth the paper that it is written on?
3 There are university tutors who you can phone if you have a problem.
4 The university which I go to is very good.
5 People who have degrees have a better chance at interview.

9a ▮2.6▮ You are going to play 'Call my bluff'. The objective of the game is to listen to three definitions of an unusual word and choose the correct definition. (Two are false and one is correct.) First, listen to two teams playing the game.

Here are three definitions of the word *ammeter*. Listen and say which one is correct.

1 an instrument which is used to measure electric currents
2 a very small creature that only has one cell
3 a machine which is used to measure the temperature in a stable

9b Now work in groups of six. Divide the group into Team A and Team B.

Team A: look at page 159 and follow the instructions.

Team B: look at page 163 and follow the instructions.

READING

1a With a partner, make a list of reasons for going to university. Then read the article quickly and check the reasons given. Are they the same as yours?

1b Read the article again and fill the gaps with these extracts.

a) As it is, with the current virtually non-existent level of financial support in this country, students already often have to take out loans to pay for general living costs.

b) many graduates have to accept positions which are not challenging or well-paid.

c) and most accept that they should pay something towards the benefits they receive from a university education.

d) but the proposed increase is too much.

e) The intended increase in university fees has come at the wrong time.

2 Find reasons in the article for NOT going to university.

3 Discuss the following in small groups.

1 Is it worth going to university?

2 Should almost everyone go to university?

3 Should you have to pay to go to university?

GRAMMAR: non-defining relative clauses

4 Look at the highlighted examples of non-defining relative clauses in the article and choose the correct answers in the rules for this type of relative clause.

Non-defining relative clauses:

1 *have / do not have* commas before them, and after them if necessary.

2 *do / do not* use *that*.

3 give *extra / essential* information about the person, thing or idea in the main clause.

GRAMMAR TIP

Non-defining relative clauses can come in the middle or at the end of the sentence:

Barbara, who spent three years at university in Cambridge, is going back to live there.

Barbara is going back to live in Cambridge, where she spent three years at university.

➡ Language reference and extra practice, pages 148–149

EDITORIAL —AND— OPINION

The true cost of university fees

THE RECENT government announcement of an increase in university fees for the coming academic year has angered young people planning to go to university. In addition, it has caused some of them quite understandably to question the value of a university education.

In an ideal world, university education would be free and open to all. However, in most western countries, students do contribute to the cost of going to university, ¹_____. These benefits include the opportunity to get good jobs in the future, and this of course leads to higher salaries and a more comfortable lifestyle.

But is it that simple? It is true that university graduates may get better jobs, but this clearly means that they will then pay higher taxes, which contribute to the economy of the whole country. So, isn't adding further increases to university fees in effect asking students to pay twice? ²_____. This can result in them getting heavily into debt. Annie Costello, who became President of the National Union of Students earlier this year, says that the average student debt already runs into thousands of pounds. Furthermore, many students have to depend on their parents to finance their education.

³_____. It will discourage some students from going to university because they simply cannot afford it. This is not good news for the Government, whose stated aim is to encourage 50 percent of young people to go on to higher education. Already, many young people are questioning the value of a university education. Everyone seems to have a degree these days, they say, so when they graduate from university, they cannot be sure they will get a well-paid job. And this seems to be the reality: ⁴_____. Therefore the decision to raise university fees will almost certainly affect the student intake, leading to a drop in numbers.

The proposed increase in fees is unfair to students. Many are already having problems dealing with debt. There's nothing wrong with asking students to contribute to the costs of a university education, ⁵_____. We call on the Government to reconsider their decision or risk losing a generation of educated young people.

5 Read the sentences and put commas where necessary.

1 Oxford University which has been the target of government attacks will not give the Prime Minister an honorary degree.

2 John F Kennedy went to Harvard University which is the oldest institution of higher education in the United States.

3 Jean-Jacques Rousseau who was born in 1712 set out his views on education in his book *Emile*.

4 The Kumon method for teaching Maths was developed by Toru Kumon who graduated from Osaka University.

5 Oxford's Bodleian library which is one of the oldest libraries in Europe was originally founded in 1320.

6 Heidelberg University which was founded in 1386 has its own student prison.

6 Join the following pairs of sentences to make one sentence containing a non-defining relative clause. Use *whose, which, who* and *where*. Use commas appropriately.

1 American universities are now facing a lot of competition. They have attracted the world's best students for over 50 years.
American universities, which have attracted the world's best students for over 50 years, are now facing a lot of competition.

2 Last month I went back to Oxford. I studied history there.

3 Annie Costello became President of the NUS earlier this year. Her opinions have always been highly regarded.

4 There are over 36,000 students at the University of Manchester. It's the biggest university in the UK.

5 Aristotle wrote books on many subjects. He studied under Plato.

6 Hilary studied politics at Harvard. She has just been offered a professorship there.

7a Look at the photos of six universities at the bottom of the page. What do you know about them? Work with a partner to exchange information.

Student A: Look at page 159 and follow the instructions.

Student B: Look at page 163 and follow the instructions.

7b Together, write six sentences about the universities. Use non-defining relative clauses.

Oxford University, which is the oldest university in the English-speaking world, allowed women to graduate in 1920.

LISTENING AND SPEAKING

8 **2.7** Listen to four people talking about university. Which speaker(s):

1 thinks going to university was a waste of time?

2 thinks their degree is a big advantage?

3 did not work hard?

4 doesn't think or is unsure that their degree helped them get a job?

9a Work in groups of four. You are going to read some information about the educational system of a country. Make notes, using the prompts below your text as a guide. Write 'no information available' if you cannot answer a question.

Student A: Turn to page 159.

Student B: Turn to page 163.

Student C: Turn to page 166.

Student D: Turn to page 167.

9b Tell your group about the educational system you have read about. Compare the different systems with the system in your country. Which system is most like yours? Which would you most like to study / have studied in?

Brasenose College,
Oxford University

Yasuda Hall, Tokyo University

King's College,
Cambridge University

Heidelberg
University Library

Branford College,
Yale University

Lomonosov Moscow State
University

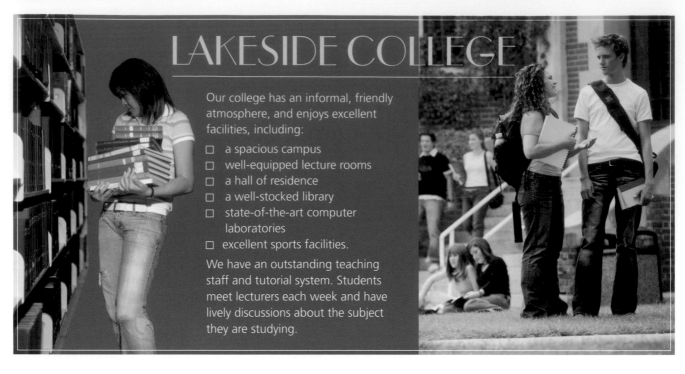

LAKESIDE COLLEGE

Our college has an informal, friendly atmosphere, and enjoys excellent facilities, including:

- ☐ a spacious campus
- ☐ well-equipped lecture rooms
- ☐ a hall of residence
- ☐ a well-stocked library
- ☐ state-of-the-art computer laboratories
- ☐ excellent sports facilities.

We have an outstanding teaching staff and tutorial system. Students meet lecturers each week and have lively discussions about the subject they are studying.

SITUATION

Lakeside College is located in Lausanne, Switzerland. It is a private university with a board of governors, led by the Principal, Marie Laforêt. There are four student representatives on the board, and four staff representatives. During the last three years, serious problems have arisen. The number of students at Lakeside College has fallen from over 1,000 to 560 while complaints from students have greatly increased.

1 Read the situation and the extract from the Lakeside College prospectus. Work with a partner to discuss the following.

1 If you were planning to go to university, which of Lakeside College's facilities would particularly interest you?

2 What sort of things do students at university often complain about?

2 Read part of an email from two student representatives to Marie Laforêt, the Principal of the university. Work with a partner to discuss the following.

1 Which do you think is the most serious problem?

2 Which is the easiest problem to solve? Which is the most difficult problem to solve?

3 What should Marie Laforêt say when she replies to the email?

In the university prospectus, it states that the university offers 'a well-stocked library, state-of-the art computers, a weekly tutorial system and outstanding teaching staff.' This is simply not true.

The library is not well stocked or well run. While there are some copies of the standard course books, there are very few journals, videos and so on and materials are often not in the correct place when you look for them. Because of this, students waste a lot of time and sometimes cannot do their assignments properly, and therefore receive low grades from lecturers. Students have also complained about Internet access. They want more time and facilities to use the Internet.

The computer laboratories are certainly not state-of-the-art. The computers are not modern and frequently break down. Assistants are rarely available to help you when this happens.

Finally, some of the tutorials are a waste of time. There are a few teachers who do not make any effort to motivate students and to develop interesting discussions. We are also very dissatisfied with the standard of lecturing. Some lecturers arrive late and leave early. Many give no handouts to support their lectures, nor do they recommend reading materials to help us prepare for the next tutorial or lecture.

KEY LANGUAGE: discussing possibilities and options

3a 2.8 Listen to a meeting between the student representatives and Marie Laforêt. Complete Marie's notes about some further problems they discuss. Use one or two words in each gap.

- problem 2: late-night 1_____ make
  a lot 2_____.
- Solutions?
(Marie) – ban 3_____.
(Eva) – let each floor of hall have
         one 4_____ semester.
(Koichi) – students can book 5_____
          in the main building
- 6_____'s solution is best. Discuss at next
  7_____ meeting.

3b Listen again. Put the expressions in the order you hear them.

1 … the good thing is that it's fair to everyone, but the bad thing is that it wouldn't be very popular.

2 Yes, good idea. That's the best solution.

3 There are several ways to deal with this.

4 So … the next thing to do is for me to talk to everyone.

5 Supposing we let each floor of the hall have one party each semester.

6 How about letting the students book a room in the main building …

7 Let's see, what other things can we do?

3c Match each expression with one of the headings in the Other Useful Phrases section.

TASK: problem-solving

4a Work in small groups. You are members of the Board of Governors. Turn to page 168 and each read about one problem. Try to think of some solutions.

4b As a group, share your ideas and try to agree how to solve each problem. Choose a chair of the board to lead the discussion.

4c Tell the class about the problems and present your solutions.

5 As a class, decide on the best solutions to each problem.

OTHER USEFUL PHRASES

Thinking about possibilities

We have a number of options.

Talking about options

The advantage is that (it's fair for everyone); the disadvantage is that (it wouldn't be very popular).

Making suggestions

It might be worth [+ -ing]

Changing your approach

Let's look at it another way.

What other options do we have?

Making a decision

The best way is to …

Deciding what to do next

What we've got to do now is … [+ infinitive]

STUDY SKILLS: reading strategies

1 There are two common techniques you can use when getting information from a text: *skimming* and *scanning*. Read the definitions, then answer the questions.

Skimming
You use *skimming* to get a general idea of a text. For example, you look through a text quickly to find out what the topic is about and its main ideas.

Scanning
You use *scanning* to find key words or specific points in a text. In most cases, you know what you are looking for, so you're focusing on finding a particular answer.

Which technique would you use to find:

1 a telephone number in a telephone directory?
2 the name of a village in the index of an atlas?
3 an article in a magazine which was interesting and worth reading?
4 the score of your favourite team in a list of football results?
5 a book you are interested in from a page of book reviews?

2a Skimming Skim the text and answer the questions.

1 Where could the text come from?
2 What is 'lifelong learning'?
3 Do you think that the text will be interesting?

2b Scanning Now scan the text and find the following:

1 three quotes about lifelong learning and teaching.
2 the percentage of adults in Britain following adult education in 2000 and 2004.
3 a reason why lifelong education is increasing in Europe.

3 Work with a partner to discuss the following.

1 What opportunities are there for lifelong education in your country?
2 What are the advantages and disadvantages of distance learning?
3 What do you think the saying 'you can't teach an old dog new tricks' means? Do you agree?

Lifelong Learning

Lifelong learning is the concept that it's never too soon or too late for learning, a way of thinking that many different organisations now believe in. Albert Einstein, the famous scientist, summed up this way of thinking when he said, 'Learning is not a product of schooling, but the lifelong attempt to acquire it.'

Lifelong learning provides adults with learning opportunities at all ages and in various contexts: at work, at home and through leisure activities, not just through formal channels such as school and higher education. In recent years, participation in adult education has increased in most European countries. In Britain, for example, 44 percent of adults participated in adult education programmes in 2004, compared with 40 percent in the year 2000.

Lifelong education is a form of teaching often carried out through distance learning or e-learning, continuing education, home schooling or correspondence courses. It includes postgraduate programmes for those who want to improve their qualifications, bring their skills up to date or retrain for a new line of work. Internal corporate training has similar goals.

One of the reasons why lifelong education has become important is the acceleration in the progress of science and technology. Despite the increased length of primary, secondary and higher education, the knowledge and skills gained there are usually not sufficient for a professional career over three or four decades. As an American educator has said, 'Learning prepares us for change.'

More importantly, lifelong learning is about an attitude – that you can and should be open to new ideas, decisions, skills or behaviours. Lifelong learning does not accept the saying 'You can't teach an old dog new tricks.'

WRITING SKILLS: a formal letter

4a Scan the letter from the Director of the Centre for English Language Studies. Then choose the correct answer to each question.

1 What is the course about?
  a) British culture and education
  b) British politics and government
  c) British life and institutions

2 What visits have been arranged?
  a) the Houses of Parliament and the British Museum
  b) the Scottish Parliament and Edinburgh Castle
  c) the Tower of London and Westminster Abbey

3 When does the course begin?
  a) 1 July   b) 1 June   c) 1 August

4 When does the course end?
  a) 23 August   b) 23 June   c) 23 July

Mr Manfred Lipmann
Maybackstr. 128
50670 Köln
Germany

Centre for English Language Studies
Airdale Castle
University of Helensburgh
Scotland
Telephone: +44 (0) 206 548 3200
Email: info@helens.ac.uk
April 20 2007

Dear Mr Lipmann,

Thank you for your letter enquiring about courses in British life and institutions. I am pleased to tell you that we will be offering such a course in our Summer School programme.

The course will be taught by Professor William Dawson, who has recently published a book entitled *Britain Today*, which has been highly praised by reviewers.

The course is suitable for anyone interested in British culture. It will cover a wide range of topics concerning British life, institutions and attitudes. These include topics such as The Press and Media, Education, the British Sense of Humour and the British Film Industry. There will be a number of guest speakers, and visits have been arranged to institutions such as the Scottish Parliament and Edinburgh Castle.

Finally, as you can see from the enclosed brochure, the course begins on June 1 and ends on June 23, with a farewell dinner.

We look forward to seeing you at the beginning of the course. If you need any further information, please do not hesitate to contact me.

Yours sincerely,

Jane Goodman

Director, English Language Summer School

4b **Letter conventions** Are these statements true or false? Correct the false statements.

1 A formal letter should always have a date.

2 You put the address of the person you are writing to directly under your address.

3 You should begin a formal letter with *Dear* + first name + surname.

4 If you begin your letter with *Dear* + name, you should finish it *Yours faithfully* not *Yours sincerely*.

5 You should end a formal letter by signing it, then printing your name and position.

6 In formal letters, you can use everyday language and short forms such as *I'm* and *we're*.

5 **2.9** Listen to Manfred talking to his English friend, Louise. He needs more information about the course. Note down the SIX points which he needs more information about.

6 Look again at the letter from Jane Goodman and underline the phrases used for beginning and ending the letter, and offering information.

7a You are going to write a reply. Work with a partner to decide in which order you are going to cover the points you noted in Exercise 5, and make a paragraph plan.

7b Work with a partner to draft a reply to Jane Goodman.

7c Work with another pair and exchange your letters. Comment on the other pair's letter, paying attention to its organisation, content, language and style.

7d Make a final draft of your letter.

Engineering

In this unit

Grammar
- the passive
- articles

Vocabulary
- word combinations
- words from the text

Scenario
- The Sky-High project

Study skills
- preparing for a talk

Writing skills
- describing a process

9.1 FROM ENGINES TO ENGINEERS

A scientist can discover a new star but he cannot make one. He would have to ask an engineer to do it for him.
Gordon L Clegg, US engineer

READING

1 What do engineers do? Do you know any? What different types are there?

2a Look at the text. Where do you think it comes from? Who is it aimed at?

A Man's World?

When you hear the word *engineer*, do you think of someone who is a) male?, b) boring? or c) dirty? Or all three? Well, time to think again. Engineers are the people who make our everyday lives easier. How many of the modern world's greatest engineering achievements will you use today? A car, a computer, a telephone?

1_____
Engineers find solutions to problems that are important to society. They control and prevent pollution, develop new medicines, create advanced technologies and help explore new worlds. They make the world a cleaner, safer, healthier place by inventing, building and improving all sorts of things from microchips to household appliances, from skyscrapers to spacecraft.

2_____
Interestingly, the word *engineer* does not come from the word *engine*. In fact it comes from the Latin word *ingeniosus* meaning *skilled*. An engineer is really a clever, practical problem solver. Although the fields of engineering and science are connected, there are also differences.

3_____
While a scientist will ask why a problem occurs or happens, an engineer will want to know how to solve the problem. As one writer once said: scientists build in order to learn, whereas engineers learn in order to build.

4_____
There are all sorts of opportunities in a variety of engineering fields such as aerospace, biomedical, civil, mechanical and computer engineering. Engineers work alone or in teams, and in all sorts of locations such as offices, factories, research labs, outdoors, and even outer space!

5_____
Engineering has often been seen as a male profession. For example, only 9 percent of US engineers are women, while in the UK it is just over 8 percent. However, there is no reason for this: engineers are simply talented people. In fact research shows that women make the best problem solvers. So now is the time for women to engineer the future. Break the stereotype. Build a career. Sign up today!

2b Choose the most suitable heading for each paragraph.

a) Engineers' contribution to society

b) Origin and definition of *engineer*

c) Women in engineering

d) Engineering and science

e) Types of engineers

2c Match these inventions with the type of engineering field mentioned in the text.

1 roads   4 microchips

2 aircraft   5 heart pacemaker

3 a washing machine

roads – civil engineering

LISTENING

3a 2.10 Lindsey Barone is one of the few women engineers in a high position. Listen to the interview. What type of engineering has she worked in?

3b Listen again and correct the statements.

1 She started her career in a car manufacturing company.

2 She worked on military aircraft before her present job.

3 At present she spends most of her time doing tests.

4 She likes engineering because it's well paid.

4 Work with a partner to discuss the following.

1 What did you find most interesting about the interview with Lindsey Barone?

2 Would you like to have her job? Why / Why not?

3 Why do you think there are fewer female engineers than male engineers?

4 Should there be more women in engineering? Why / Why not?

VOCABULARY: word combinations

5a Match the verbs with the most appropriate words and phrases.

1 find   a) safety tests

2 solve   b) a breakthrough

3 do   c) a problem

4 build   d) deadlines

5 do   e) a theory

6 make   f) some research

7 test   g) a model/prototype

8 meet   h) a solution

5b Complete the sentences with an appropriate combination from Exercise 5a. The first letter of the noun is given.

1 Following the accident engineers had to *do* a lot of *safety tests* before the machine could be used again.

2 After a long period of failure, they _____ an important *b_____*.

3 They _____ an imaginative *s_____* to the problem after working with models in the test lab.

4 One part of the engineering process is to _____ a smaller working *m_____* before moving on to a full-size or production version.

5 It can take a long time to fully _____ a complicated *t_____* before putting it into practice.

6 The whole team had to _____ a lot of careful *r_____* into the causes of the problem.

7 In the end we were able to _____ the most serious *p_____*.

8 On many engineering projects there is great pressure to _____ strict *d_____*.

SPEAKING

6 Work with a partner. Look at the list of some great engineering achievements and do the following.

1 Add one more achievement to each category.

2 Decide which is the greatest engineering achievement in each category.

around the house
the refrigerator, the microwave oven, the vacuum cleaner

getting around
the railway engine, the jet airliner, the automobile/car

medicine/health
contact lenses, the thermometer, laser surgery

entertainment
radio, television, compact discs

construction
the pyramids, the Eiffel Tower, the Panama Canal

WRITING

7 Write a short paragraph about what you think is the greatest engineering achievement.

How to avoid asteroids colliding with the Earth

DULIP SINGH ■ SCIENCE CORRESPONDENT

Most scientists agree that the threat of a large asteroid or meteor hitting the Earth is real, although they cannot predict when such an event will occur.

THE EARTH has been struck many times in the past by large objects. A meteorite, estimated to be about 12 kilometres in diameter, collided with the earth in the region of the Yucatan Peninsula (now Mexico) 65 million years ago. Many scientists and historians believe that the extinction of the dinosaurs and other animals was a result of this collision. More recently, an asteroid the size of three football fields (300 metres wide) passed close to the Earth, just twice the distance to the Moon. The rock, 2001 YB5, was first seen in December 2000, leaving little time to change its direction if it had become a real danger.

Scientists agree that we should take action to prevent the collision of an asteroid or comet with the Earth, as the impact of an asteroid larger than one kilometre in diameter hitting the Earth could cause global devastation. It is worrying, too, that only about half of the large Near Earth Objects (NEOs) have been found. It is estimated that about 500 NEOs have not

yet been discovered. A further cause for concern is that 30 percent of the sky hasn't been surveyed.

A research project has just been set up by the EPSRC (Engineering and Physical Sciences Research Council) to track asteroids on a collision course with the Earth. Computer simulations will be used to work out the feasibility of changing the direction of asteroids, using methods proposed by engineers. One such method involves giant mirrors floating in space which could melt the surface of an asteroid and change its course. Another method is to use brute force, such as smashing a rocket into the asteroid to deflect it. The rocket would not physically push the asteroid away but would use the collision to make a hole in the rock, which would push the asteroid in a different direction.

Plans have already been announced by ESA (European Space Agency) to conduct an experiment to see if asteroids can in fact be deflected away from the Earth. Two spacecraft, Hidalgo and Sancho, will be used. Hidalgo will smash into an asteroid named Apophis, which is expected to make its closest pass by the Earth in 2029, when it will be only 32,000 kilometres away. The Sancho spacecraft will watch the collision and record any change in the asteroid's direction.

READING

1 Which of the statements about asteroids is false? Check your answer on page 168.

1 A 1km asteroid hits the Earth every 200,000 years.

2 A 12km asteroid (the size which killed the dinosaurs) hits the Earth every 100m years.

3 Asteroids are mainly rocky bodies that orbit the Earth.

4 Some asteroids have moons.

5 '1-Ceres' is the largest known asteroid.

2a Scan the article. Which of the following do engineers think are possible ways of preventing asteroids hitting the Earth?

1 using mirrors

2 using balloons in space

3 using nuclear power

4 using rockets to smash into the asteroids

5 covering the asteroid with paint to reflect light

6 using electrical currents

2b Read the article again. Match the following information with the correct paragraph.

1 Scientists have not yet identified all the objects that may hit the Earth.

2 There is a project to observe and follow asteroids.

3 One object has been very near the Earth in this century.

4 Only about two thirds of the sky has been surveyed.

5 An investigation will find out if asteroids can be moved away from the Earth using a spaceship.

6 Early animals were possibly wiped out by objects hitting the Earth.

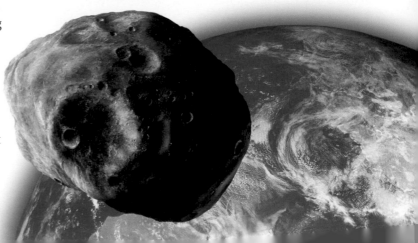

3 Find the following in the article.

1 a verb that means 'to make something move in a different direction'

2 four nouns which refer to things in space which could hit the earth

3 the noun from the verb *collide* which means 'when a moving object hits another violently'

4 nouns in the article that mean:
   a) the risk of something bad happening (paragraph 1)
   b) the force with which one object hits another (para. 3)
   c) severe and widespread damage or destruction (para. 3)

GRAMMAR: the passive

4a Look at the article and find all the examples of the passive you can.

4b Match the sentences you have found with these tenses:

a) the present simple passive

b) the past simple passive

c) the present perfect passive

d) the passive in the future

e) a passive with a modal verb

f) a negative passive

GRAMMAR TIP

We form the present perfect passive with *have* + *been* + past participle:
The Earth has been struck …

4c Which preposition do we use if we introduce the agent?

5a Look at the sentence below. Why is the passive used here? Think about the agent – is it important or known to us?

… about 500 NEOs have not yet been discovered.

5b Find other examples of the passive used for this reason.

6 Look at the sentence below.

The rock, 2001 YB5, was first seen in December 2000.

Another reason for using the passive is to start a sentence with information that is known or has been mentioned before.

Find other examples of this in the text.

➡ Language reference and extra practice, pages 150–151

7a Complete the email with the present perfect active or passive of the verbs in brackets.

7b Find three other examples of the passive in the memo. What tense are they in?

> ✉ ‗□×
>
> ⮰Send 🖫 🖨 ✂ 🖹 📋 🖺 📎 🖼 🔍 ! ↓ ▼ 📇 Options… ❓ ▾
>
> | From… | Assistant Head of Engineering |
> | To… | All engineering staff |
> | Subject: | X3000 engine |
>
> Our company ¹_____ (invest) a lot of money in the X3000 engine. Tests on the new engine ²_____ (finally/complete). Unfortunately, the results ³_____ (show) to be invalid.
> This ⁴_____ (happen) for a number of reasons. Firstly, the correct testing procedure was not followed. Secondly, systems were not checked. Finally, most of the information was deleted from the computer files.
> The Head of Research ⁵_____ (suspend) and funding for research next year ⁶_____ (not/ approve). For these reasons, the research ⁷_____ (not/publish).
> The Head of Engineering ⁸_____ (ask) me to organise a meeting with all staff. He ⁹_____ (arrange) for a new series of tests to start next week. You ¹⁰_____ (all / invest) a lot of effort in this project and we intend to make it a success.

SPEAKING

8a Work with a partner to do a passives quiz. Make passive sentences using the table on page 168. Write as many sentences as you can in ten minutes.

8b Compare your sentences with another pair.
What have you got for number 1?
– The Taj Mahal was built in …

8c Now close all your books. In your groups of four, how many passive sentences can you remember from the quiz? The team with the most correct sentences wins.

SPEAKING

1 Work with a partner to discuss the following.

1 What is the largest man-made structure you have ever been in or on?

2 How did you feel in/on something so big?

3 How would you feel if you were:
a) at the top of a very tall building?
b) in a tunnel deep in the ground?
c) in a building at the bottom of the sea?

GRAMMAR: articles

2 Read the text quickly. Tell a partner what you found most interesting.

TRANSATLANTIC TUNNEL

Engineers have proposed cutting journey times from New York in the United States to London in the United Kingdom to 54 minutes, travelling on a magnetically raised train. The idea is that the train will travel through a tunnel floating in the Atlantic Ocean. The tunnel will be 150 feet below the surface of the sea and it will be nearly 5,000 kilometres long. The train will travel at 8,000 kph (20 times the speed of today's fastest trains).

Giant anchors will be sunk into the bottom of the sea, in some places up to eight kilometres deep. 54,000 tunnel sections will be transported by a special ship and will then be lowered into place. The tunnel sections will then be attached to the anchors. The tunnel will have to stand up to some of the Atlantic's strongest currents including part of the Gulf Stream. The tunnel will probably cost $12 trillion and need one billion tons of steel. It will take decades to build. If it is built, it would be the largest and the most expensive engineering project in the history of the world.

3 Look at the highlighted words in the text and find examples for each of these rules:

We use *a/an* …

1 when we mention something (a singular noun) for the first time. *a train*

We use *the* …

2 when we refer to something that has been mentioned before. ____

3 with the names of some countries. ____

4 with the names of geographical features, e.g. seas, oceans, rivers. ____

5 with superlatives. ____

6 when there is only one of something. ____

7 when we know which thing the speaker/writer refers to. *the sea*

We don't use an article …

8 with general plural countable nouns. ____

9 when we refer to something (a plural noun) for the first time. ____

10 with the names of towns and cities, and most countries. ____

➡ Language reference and extra practice, pages 150–151

4 Complete the text with *the*, *a* or *an*, or leave the space blank if no article is needed.

John, who is an engineer, lives and works in [1]_____ United Arab Emirates. He is currently working in [2]_____ Dubai, the capital city of one of [3]_____ seven emirates that make up the country. There has been a massive number of [4]_____ engineering projects across [5]_____ city recently, and construction in [6]_____ UAE is currently [7]_____ fastest in [8]_____ world. This is mainly because [9]_____ government wants to build in order to spread [10]_____ economy of the country. One of [11]_____ biggest projects is [12]_____ theme park called Dubailand. Others include [13]_____ huge shopping centres and [14]_____ tourist attractions. In fact, everywhere you look at the moment you can see [15]_____ crane. Experts say that 15–20 percent of [16]_____ world's cranes are in Dubai!

READING

5a Look at all three texts and complete as much of the table as you can.

	Tunnel	Sky City	Ski Dubai
height			
width			
cost			
length			
area covered			

5b Read the texts again and answer the questions.

1 What is twenty times the speed of today's fastest train?

2 What is three times the height of the Eiffel Tower?

3 How long will it take from New York to London?

4 What is the depth the anchors would be sunk under the bottom of the sea?

5 What will be the total number of people working and living in Sky City?

6 What will be the maximum number of people in the Sky City lifts?

7 What is the temperature in the snowdome at night?

8 How much snow is there in the snowdome?

5c What problems do the three texts mention?

6a Work in groups of three. If money and time were not a problem, what large structure would you like to design and why? Think about size, location, purpose, materials, transportation and safety.

6b Draw a rough sketch of your design. Show your design to another group and suggest improvements to their design.

SKY CITY 1000

Tokyo has a major problem with overcrowding and a lack of green space. The Takenaka Corporation has proposed Sky City 1000, a vertical city for the 21st century, as a solution.

The Sky City proposal consists of a building 1,000 metres tall (about three times the height of the Eiffel Tower in Paris) and 400 metres wide at the base. It has a total floor area of eight square kilometres. It functions like a medium-sized city with housing, offices, commercial facilities, schools, parks and theatres. It provides for 35,000 full-time residents and 100,000 workers. Sky City 1000 hopes to provide all the services of a city in an attractive natural environment.

The building is made up of 14 dish-shaped levels stacked one upon the other. To get around such a large building high-speed lifts containing up to 70 people will be used in the building and a small train will run around the roof. Engineers have carried out tests using Tokyo's fire helicopter to see what the danger would be if there was a fire.

The main advantage of Sky City 1000 is that people would be able to get to work, the shops, and schools without getting in a car. However, some people would be scared to live in such a tall building, especially with Japan's earthquake problems.

SKI DUBAI

Dubai is an engineer's dream because it has a large number of engineering superprojects. The Gulf Emirate can now boast the largest snowdome in the world, built in the middle of the desert.

Ski Dubai is 85 metres high and 80 metres wide and cost $272m. It has five slopes and 6,000 metric tons of snow, which cover the equivalent of three football pitches. One slope is 400 metres, making the snowdome the Gulf's first indoor ski 'mountain'. It is so steep that engineers had to ensure there were no avalanches.

In the summer, outside temperatures soar over 40°c. During the day the temperature inside is maintained between –1°c and –2°c. The snow-making process is carried out at night when the temperatures inside the building are reduced to –8°c. Liquid water is used to create a cloud. The cloud is then sprinkled with tiny hard ice particles. This allows snow crystals to form. They fall from the cloud as real snow.

The complexity of this unique construction project means that materials from all over the world are used. For many of the locals it offers an exciting experience as it is the first time they have seen snow.

SITUATION

A country in Asia wishes to become better known in the world. It would like to attract more visitors from abroad and to encourage more people to use its conference facilities. However, it has no special advantages to do this.

The Government feels that it needs to have a big project which will capture foreign people's imagination and also be good for its citizens. After some discussion, the Minister of the Environment, Susan Lau, has come up with an interesting idea.

1 Read the situation. In your opinion, what big construction projects might impress foreign visitors?

2a **2.11** Listen to an extract from a television news programme. Discuss the questions.

1 What is Susan Lau's new idea?
2 Why will the project probably appeal to foreigners?

2b Listen again and complete the information.
The Sky-High Project
Type of project: _____
Height: _____
Width: _____
Number of people living in the city: _____
Number of people working in the city: _____
Facilities in the city: _____
Future action by the Minister: _____

3 Read the facts below prepared for the project. Work with a partner to discuss the questions.

1 How might each factor affect the design of the new city?
2 What do you think will be the benefits and the problems of building the vertical city?

- The capital city is overpopulated and polluted. There is a serious housing problem in the city. Many people live in overcrowded apartments and houses.
- Traffic moves slowly, so commuters spend a long time travelling to work.
- In the area chosen for the vertical city, there are many poor and homeless people, and a high crime rate.
- There is a high rate of unemployment in the city, especially in the construction industry.
- Many businesses have closed down in recent years in the area chosen for the vertical city.
- There are strong winds and even hurricanes at times in the country. Also, the area is at risk from earthquakes.
- People in the north of the country wish to create an independent state, against the wishes of the Government.
- There is hot weather throughout the year. Temperatures often reach 45°C.

4 **2.12** Listen to two engineers talking about the benefits of the project. Note down the benefits they mention. Compare them with the ones you discussed in Exercise 3.

KEY LANGUAGE:
discussing options, making decisions

5 `2.13` Listen to four conversations about a name for the vertical city and complete the gaps.

1 A: What ____ ____ ____ ____ the present name, the Sky-High project? It's easy to remember.

   B: I'm not too sure about that. ____ ____ is Tower City. It's short and easy to pronounce.

2 A: I think Hope is a good name for the city. It'll give accommodation for a lot of poor and homeless people.

   B: That's ____ ____ ____.

3 A: Tower City? Yes, I think that's the best name. Why don't we suggest it to the Minister?

   B: Yes, ____ ____ ____. It's the best solution, I think.

4 A: We ____ ____ ____. We'll call it Sky-High City.

   B: OK, let's put the name in our report to the Minister.

TASK: assessing a project

6a You are studying at the capital city's biggest university. Susan Lau has sent the university a list of questions about the new project for discussion. In small groups, look at the questions on page 168 and choose FIVE which interest you. Discuss the questions and make decisions.

6b In your groups, tell another group which questions you chose and what your decisions were, with your reasons.

6c As a class, decide whether the Sky-High project is good for the country. Is it feasible?

OTHER USEFUL PHRASES
What about …
Why don't we …
I suggest …
That sounds good.
I don't think that's a good idea.
OK, that's what we'll do.

STUDY SKILLS: preparing for a talk

1 Have you ever given a talk? How did you find the experience? Was it a success? Why / Why not?

2 You are going to listen to Lisa Martin, an expert on communication, giving a presentation on preparing a talk. Work with a partner to discuss what you think will be her main points.

3a [2.14] Listen to part of the talk. Which point does Lisa make that you find particularly interesting or helpful?

3b Listen again and complete the statements. Use between one and three words.

1 Your talk should match the _____ of your audience.

2 A good way to organise a talk is to divide it _____.

3 You need to think about the _____ you want to make, and have other points that you may use if you have time.

4 Most people use _____ and number them to keep them in order.

5 For a formal talk, many people use software _____.

6 A 'hook' is something you say to _____ of your audience.

7 An example of a hook is _____.

8 You should prepare some memorable sentences which will make _____ on the audience.

4 Are Lisa Martin's points the same as you discussed in Exercise 2? Do you have any other ideas about preparing for a talk?

5 Linkers Look at Track 2.14 on page 178. Underline all the words and phrases that are used to show the order of the different stages of preparing for a talk.

6a You are going to give a five-minute talk to a group of multilingual students in a language class. First choose one of the topics below.

- applying for a driving licence in your country
- getting a place at a university either in your country or abroad
- getting a visa to visit another country
- opening a bank account
- becoming a top professional player in a sport
- any process you are familiar with, at work or where you are studying

Now prepare some ideas for the talk. Think about:

1 how to begin the talk.

2 what your main message will be.

3 what your key points will be.

4 what visual aids you will use.

5 how to end the talk to make an impact on your audience.

6b In small groups, explain how you would give the talk and comment on each other's ideas.

7 Prepare your talk and give it to the rest of the group. Answer their questions.

WRITING SKILLS: describing a process

8a Read the description of how aircraft are made and answer the questions.

1 Why are the following used to produce an aircraft?
a) computers   b) wind tunnels   c) flight tests

2 What document must a construction company get before it can sell its aircraft?

8b Choose the correct meaning for each word.

1 simulation
   a) a test of what someone or something would do in a real situation
   b) features of a product that engineers have to change

2 prototype
   a) the first design of a product before it has been modified by engineers and designers
   b) the first example of a new car, aircraft, etc., used to test the design before it is produced

3 authorises
   a) does tests   b) gives permission

9 Using the passive In English, we prefer to start a sentence with information that is already known, not new. We sometimes use the passive to put known information at the beginning of a sentence. For example:

Aircraft production is a huge and costly business.
↓
Most aircraft are made …

We are unlikely to write:
Aircraft production is a huge and costly business. Companies make most aircraft …

Find two more examples of this in the text.

HOW AIRCRAFT ARE MADE

Aircraft production is a huge and costly business. Most aircraft are made by companies who can produce them in large quantities and who can invest time in planning as well as production. Planning alone can take up to 12 years for a large aircraft and production can also be a very long process. The production stages are as follows.

First, the construction company makes designs of the aircraft. The designs are produced on computers, which are then used for the initial simulations. Then small models of some parts of the aircraft are tested in wind tunnels. Next, a prototype of the aircraft is made, and after that a limited number of aircraft are produced to test on the ground. Representatives from a government aviation agency often make the first flight. Flight tests continue until all the requirements are met. Finally, the government agency authorises the construction company to begin production of the aircraft. A certificate is issued and the aircraft is sold all over the world.

10 There are several stages in the production and launch of a new motorbike. Look at the notes below and put them in the right order. Think about how the passive is sometimes used at the beginning of a sentence.

☐ Show the new motorbike at trade exhibitions all over the world.

☑ 1 Plan the new motorbike and do the first designs. (Design team)

☐ Contact journalists and invite them to test drive the new motorbike.

☐ Changes are made to the prototype and the design is modified. (R&D department)

☑ 2 Build the first prototype, with the help of engineers. (R&D department)

☐ The prototype is tested on special roads. Check if there are any problems and if any changes are necessary.

☐ Do further tests, then make more modifications and changes to the engine.

☐ Results of the test drive are recorded and the journalists prepare articles about the new bike.

☑ 9 Mass-produce the new motorbike. Launch an international marketing campaign.

11 Write an article on the stages in the production and launch of a new motorbike, for inclusion in some school course materials on engineering processes. Use the notes above and the passage about aircraft to help you, and the linking words from Exercise 5.

GRAMMAR

1a Look at the photographs and tell a partner what you think the object is. Use the phrases below.

It might/could be …
It must be …   It can't be …

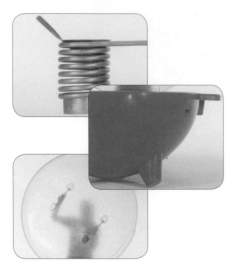

1b Turn to page 168 and look at the whole design. Did you guess correctly in Exercise 1a?

2 Read the article and fill the gaps with the words in the box.

has	a	can	whose	be
can't	might	is	the	
have	was	should		

Designing at a new level!

It ¹_____ look like ²_____ giant tea cup to you or me but the Dutchtub is a lightweight plastic hot tub that ³_____ be used anywhere. Water ⁴_____ heated by a wood fire in the metal coil. The cold water is naturally pulled from the bottom up into ⁵_____ top. It ⁶_____ invented by Floris Schoonderbeek in 2002 and it ⁷_____ recently been selected for a Dutch design award. Floris, ⁸_____ other designs include a mobile library and furniture, believes his invention ⁹_____ take outdoor bathing to 'a new level'! And if you ¹⁰_____ afford the price of €4400, you don't ¹¹_____ to. It can ¹²_____ rented for a day instead.

VOCABULARY

3 Complete the gaps, using the correct form of the word given at the end of each line.

The Three Gorges Dam

It will probably be one of the greatest ¹*engineering* achievements of the 21st century. However, plans were first ²_____ in 1919 by the leader Sun Yat-sen. But it went into ³_____ 70 years later. The dam is admired for its technical ⁴_____, but there are also critics. Electricity which is ⁵_____ from the dam was expected to supply 15 percent of China's energy, including ⁶_____ and industry in the east. Now, some say only three percent of ⁷_____ will benefit from the project.

ENGINEER
DEVELOP
PRODUCE
INNOVATE
PRODUCE
MANUFACTURE
USE

4 Read an email from an e-tutor to a student who is studying on a distance-learning course and choose the correct verbs.

Dear Julia
You have ¹*made / done* good progress this term with your work. ²*Taking / Solving* an online course doesn't seem to have caused you any difficulties. You ³*got / studied* good grades on both your essays even though you ⁴*handed / took* the second in a week late, which affected your overall grade. Please ⁵*make / do* your best to follow the schedule or you may find it difficult to keep up.

With regard to the test that you ⁶*failed / graduated*, remember that you are able to ⁷*retake / remake* it at the beginning of next term. So don't forget to spend part of your winter break ⁸*passing / revising* for it. You also mentioned that you might not be able to ⁹*go / find* to the summer school in July. This is a really important part of the course and will help you ¹⁰*get / make* a good degree, as well as giving you the chance to meet other students and your tutors face to face.

5 Imagine you received a progress report from your English tutor. What do you think it would say? Write the report and show it to your tutor. Does he/she agree with you?

KEY LANGUAGE

6 Look at thee three chairs opposite. Work in pairs and make sentences about them using the phrases below.

It looks very …   It's made of …
One of the best points is …
It's aimed at …
It would appeal to …

7 2.15 Listen to a company discussing ideas for a new type of chair. Are these statements true or false?

1 They are discussing chair B above.

2 They only have one choice of design.

3 When a passenger moves the seat, the TV screen also moves.

4 The seat is the same size as other airline seats.

5 One person would like to improve the visual appeal of the seat.

6 They want the designers to design a completely new chair.

8a Complete the dialogue with the phrases below.

a) you think about   f) would appeal to
b) it looks very   g) Supposing we made
c) let's do that   h) good thing about
d) a possible solution   i) other bad thing
e) several features

A: OK. Thank you all for coming. We have a number of options but I'd like us to look at this one in particular. There are ¹_____ I really like. For example, when the passenger in front moves the seat back the TV screen part stays where it is. The ²_____ this is that the passenger feels they have more space. This is especially interesting because in reality the seat takes up less room than normal seats. What do ³_____ it?

B: I'm sure it's good but ⁴_____ similar to any other airline seat.

A: ⁵_____ it look more stylish or different so passengers feel they are sitting in something completely new – would that help?

B: Yes, that's ⁶_____. And it ⁷_____ low-fare airlines with lots of economy class passengers. But the ⁸_____ is that the head rest doesn't move – sometimes you want to change the position without moving the whole seat. We need to ask the designers what they can do about it.

A: Yes, ⁹_____.

8b Listen again and check your answers.

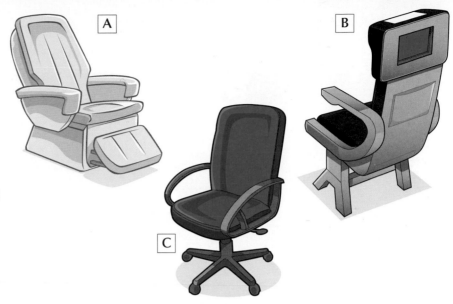

LANGUAGE CHECK

9 Delete the extra word in sentences 1–10. Look at the pages to check.

1 We really don't mustn't miss the flight. (page 73)

2 It might to be true that he designed the first helicopter. (page 75)

3 It's used for to opening tin cans. (page 77)

4 A vacation is a period in the year that when you get a break from school or work. (page 83)

5 This is a room that children can use it at lunchtime. (page 83)

6 Let's us look at this another way. (page 87)

7 We look forward to be seeing you. (page 89)

8 The asteroid was first be seen near our planet in 1891. (page 93)

9 The moving robot will has be used to analyse the surface of Mars. (page 93)

10 I'm going to the London for a weekend break. (page 94)

LOOK BACK

10 Find the exercises in Units 7–9 where you …

• learn to build words into verbs, nouns and adjectives. (U7)

• design some new products. (U7)

• practise the grammar for making deductions. (U7)

• read about the single-sex schools debate. (U8)

• learn which type of relative clause needs commas. (U8)

• write a formal letter. (U8)

• listen to a female engineer. (U9)

• find out about asteroids. (U9)

10 Trends

10.1 IT'S THE NEW THING

Don't follow trends, start trends.
Frank Capra, 1897–1991, US film-maker

SPEAKING

1a Look at the list of trends below and work with a partner to discuss the questions.

1 Which are current trends in your country?

2 Which are trends in other countries?

3 Which could become trends in your country in the future?

4 Which are old-fashioned trends which you think could return?

- recycling and looking after the environment
- being concerned about diet and health
- having cosmetic surgery
- retiring at 70 years old
- reality TV shows
- sunbathing
- getting married later in life
- American-style coffee shops, e.g. Starbucks
- wearing sportswear / training shoes (when not playing sport)
- beauty competitions

1b Think of another trend for each of the four categories in Exercise 1a.

READING

2a Skim the text opposite and answer the questions.

1 What sort of text is it?
   a) a review   b) an article   c) an advertisement

2 Which parts of the text helped you decide?

2b Read the text again. Are these sentences true, false or not given?

1 Gladwell is North American.

2 Gladwell thinks that trends develop in the same way as illnesses.

3 Gladwell has written a number of books on the subject of trends.

4 *Connectors* know many people with the same job.

5 *Connectors* are very common.

6 *Mavens* quickly become aware of changes in fashions.

7 *Salesmen* try to influence people by imitating them.

3 Work with a partner to discuss the following.

1 Think of a recent trend. Where and how do you think it started?

2 What makes trends start?

3 What sort of people are trendsetters? Do you know any?

Books

Tipping points

In his book *The Tipping Point* Canadian author Malcolm Gladwell explains how a trend can take many forms. It can be a general change in social behaviour, an idea or a fashion. However, why do some trends catch on and others not? What makes one particular brand of training shoe suddenly become the must-have product? How do people find out about trends and what makes people want to buy into them? Is it simply a question of keeping up with other people?

In his new work, Gladwell explores the moment when something becomes common and how products, ideas, messages and forms of behaviour spread. He looks at the reasons why trends are similar in the way they develop to outbreaks of disease, or medical epidemics.

Epidemics, like trends, start in a very small way, maybe from a single person with a virus, then spread very quickly until they take over the population and appear to be everywhere. Eventually, they will slow down gradually or die out suddenly. Gladwell shows how these changes happen not gradually but at one dramatic moment.

Gladwell identifies three types of people who are influential in the development of these kinds of social epidemics:

Connectors are people in a community who have wide social circles. They know a lot of people and like to introduce people to each other. The people they know also tend to come from a variety of social, cultural, professional and economic circles.

Mavens are people with a lot of knowledge or experts in a particular field. They wish to pass on their knowledge to others. *Mavens* collect and gather information so are the first to pick up on new trends.

Salesmen are people with charisma and powerful negotiation skills. They have a 'soft' influence over people rather than actual power. This means they are influential because people want to imitate them.

Overall, Gladwell's book is a thought-provoking read for anyone interested in the origins of trends. What's more, he writes in a clear style so even the most difficult ideas are easy to understand.

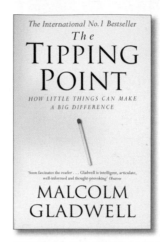

The Tipping Point

Malcolm Gladwell

VOCABULARY: phrasal verbs (3)

4a Look at the phrasal verbs highlighted in the text and match them with their meanings below.

1 become fashionable or popular
2 gain control of something/someone
3 maintain the same level as
4 become less fast/rapid
5 disappear completely
6 discover
7 notice something which is not easy to notice
8 believe in and be influenced by

4b Replace the words in *italics* in the questions below with a phrasal verb from Exercise 4a.

1 What trend do you think will be the next to *become popular*?

2 Do you try to *have the same lifestyle and possessions as* your friends and neighbours?

3 Why do you think trends *become less rapid*?

4 Which trends that have *disappeared* will have a revival, do you think?

5 How do you personally *discover* which trends are becoming popular?

6 Which trends have *become dominant* in your country recently?

7 Which newspapers and magazines are the first to *notice* new trends in your country?

8 Which recent trend are you not going to *be influenced by*? Why / Why not?

pronunciation

5a 2.16 **Stress** Listen to the correct answers and underline the stress in the phrasal verbs.

5b Listen again and practise the questions with the correct intonation and stress.

6 Ask and answer the questions from Exercise 4b in small groups.

WRITING

7 Write a paragraph about a recent trend in your country.

READING

1 In groups, look at the photos and discuss the questions.

1 Who are these people? Do you recognise any of them?

2 Which films were they in?

3 What trends did they start, do you think?

2a Read the article and say which paragraph/ paragraphs contain the following information.

a) a look that is not complicated (2 paragraphs)

b) A relative of the writer saw one of the films.

c) the importance of when a movie comes out in terms of fashion trends

d) accessories (3 paragraphs)

e) The film won an award.

2b Read the article again and complete the table.

Paragraph	1	2	3	4
Name of film				
Main star				
Year of film				
Fashion trend started				

Films and Fashion

by fashion correspondent
Helen Barclay

1 **M**y daughter went to see *The Wild One* for the first time recently and she commented on the fact that Marlon Brando was wearing jeans so long ago. Of course he helped set the trend, so that got me thinking about the link between films and trends in fashion. Fashion and films have gone hand in hand for a long time. *The Wild One* is a good example: it appeared in 1954 and starred Brando. Dressed in a black leather motorcycle jacket, leather cap and cuffed jeans, he created a look which is still considered to be 'cool' today. Everyone from Madonna to middle-aged men have been seen wearing the classic leather motorcycle jacket.

2 Another strong influence on fashion trends was *Breakfast at Tiffany's* (1961), starring Audrey Hepburn. She made famous the simple black dress that looks perfect at either a cocktail party or just standing around outside an exclusive department store like Tiffany's with a pastry and coffee in your hand, as Audrey Hepburn does in the film. She looks so elegant, wearing simple but beautiful dresses, big dark glasses and a string of pearls around her neck. Audrey Hepburn, more than any other film star, still influences women's fashion with her 'Tiffany's' look. As the fashion designer Mary Quant said, 'Audrey was the most stylish woman who ever lived.'

3 In more modern times, the film star Uma Thurman created a major fashion trend when she appeared in the film *Pulp Fiction*, made in 1994. Her style was very simple. Her black trousers, crisp white shirt and unusual hair style – a wig in a sharp black bob – was copied by women all over the world. You can still open up any fashion magazine these days and there will often be pages on the 'crisp white shirt'.

4 Influencing fashion trends can often be about timing. The movie *Memoirs of a Geisha* (2005) came just at the right time to start a trend in Japanese fashion. It starred the Chinese actress Zhang Ziyi, who wore beautiful silk kimonos, and it won an Oscar for Costume Design. A lot of travel companies picked up on the trend and ran 'geisha trips' to Japan. The film has also led to a revived interest in kimonos. It is now quite common to see young Japanese women wearing kimonos not just on traditional occasions, but at a variety of social events. The fashion is also beginning to spread to western countries. For example, kimono accessories are beginning to appear in stores and Max Factor has produced a Geisha mascara.

5 What fashions from films have influenced you? Email your answers to: hbarclay@moddesign.com

VOCABULARY: adjective order

3 Look at the example and put the phrases below in the right order.

	colour	material	function/class	noun
a	black	leather	motorcycle	jacket

1 a   dining   white   pine   table
2 a   garden   chair   green   plastic
3 a   silk   evening   red   dress
4 a   frame   picture   wooden   black

LISTENING

4 Would you like to work in the fashion industry? Why / Why not?

5 [2.17] Listen to a conversation between the manager of the fashion department of a major upmarket store and a new salesperson, Chloe. Tick (✓) the pieces of advice which the manager gives Chloe.

1 Don't talk to the other trainees.
2 Find out about other departments in the store.
3 Always wear the store uniform.
4 Give customers a lot of attention.
5 Pressurise them to buy something.

GRAMMAR: expressions of quantity

6a Listen to the conversation again and complete the sentences with expressions of quantity.

1 We've got _____ _____ time before my next meeting.
2 I've talked to _____ _____ _____ the trainees and served _____ _____ customers.
3 Not really, ... just _____ _____ _____ customers who were a bit difficult.
4 First of all, _____ trainees think they don't need to know …
5 We have _____ rules about uniforms.
6 I used to do all the trips on my own with _____ help but last year I took _____ of the assistants …
7 … we've got _____ _____ ideas and we'll get _____ information from the organisers soon.
8 … give customers _____ time to make up their minds …
9 Give them _____ _____ _____ attention and _____ _____ advice …
10 We have _____ sales assistants to do the job properly.

6b Complete the table using the phrases from Exercise 6a, according to which kind of noun they are used with. Some can be used with both.

used with countable nouns	*a couple of*
used with uncountable nouns	*a little*

➡ Language reference and extra practice, pages 152–153

7 Underline the correct quantifiers in the sentences below. In some sentences both are correct.

1 We met *a little / a few* Italian designers when we were in Milan.
2 They gave us *some / a couple of* advice on how to improve our service.
3 There will be *plenty of / a lot of* journalists at the fashion show.
4 We'll have to do *a lot of / many* work when we get back from the show.
5 We are looking at *a couple of / a few* new designs for the spring collection.

8 Make sentences using the table and as many of the expressions of quantity as possible.

people in your family   people in your town
people in your country   your friends
your colleagues   students in your class

A few	people in my country/town/		
Some	family		
Enough			
Many		the students in	
Plenty	of	my class	are …
A couple		my friends and	
A lot		colleagues	
None			

A lot of my friends are interested in fashion.

SPEAKING

9 In small groups, discuss the following.

1 Do you like getting advice when buying clothes?
2 What trends in fashion do you know about?
3 What factors affect what we wear?
4 What sort of clothes do you like to wear, or not like to wear?

READING

1 **Work with a partner to discuss the following.**

1 What is the retirement age in your country?

2 Do you know anyone who has retired?

3 Who is the oldest working person in your family?

4 Does your country have a state pension scheme? If not, do you have a private pension?

5 Would you like to live to 100? Why / Why not?

2a **Read the article quickly and answer the questions.**

1 Why are people living longer?

2 What is happening to families in Europe?

2b **Complete the sentences below with information from the article.**

1 Many people will live to 100 in _____.

2 Life expectancy has increased a lot since _____.

3 In 1998 the world life expectancy was _____.

4 50 percent of North American and Japanese babies born since 2000 will live to _____.

5 10 percent of North American and Japanese babies born since 2000 will live to _____.

6 Drugs to slow down the ageing process will be available in _____.

7 The world's population could reach _____.

Living to 100

- Scientists expect a sharp rise in life expectancy
- Living to 100 could be common in 2030

Since the mid 1950s, life expectancy around the world has increased dramatically, and many scientists believe that this trend is likely to continue in the future.

The United Nations estimated that in the early 1950s the world life expectancy rate was 46.4 years. By 1998, world life expectancy had increased to 63.0 years. In more developed regions, life expectancy was an average of 75 and in less developed areas it was 62 years. That represents an average increase in life expectancy of about 35 percent for the world.

The main reason for the increase during this period was the decline in infant mortality. Fewer children died at an early age, and this was mainly because of improved healthcare and better food production.

Most experts believe that people will continue to live longer in the future because of medical advances. Researchers predict that at least half of the North American and Japanese babies born since the year 2000 will live to an age of 90, and ten percent to 100 years old.

Furthermore, new drugs are being developed which will slow down the ageing process. These will be available in around 2010, and they will enable people to live 20 years longer.

If the current older populations in many countries become healthier, wealthier and live longer, the trend will have important consequences for people and governments. The cost of medical care for older people will rise, and governments will have to start thinking hard about how to fund state pensions for older citizens. Some people will want to keep on working later in their life, which could lead to changes in the age of retirement in many countries. Others would prefer to retire early to enjoy having more time for themselves. This will create business opportunities for companies in the leisure and entertainment industries and open up new segments of the market.

Finally, the effect on the world population will be great. Europe's population has been in decline for several years now as people prefer to have fewer children and families tend to be smaller. However, the population will not decline as fast once these anti-ageing drugs start to become widely available. It is believed that the populations in China and India could soar by 500 million. An expert on population, Professor Shripad Tuljapurkar, says that 'We could expect to see the world's population top out at about 11 to 12 billion.'

pronunciation

3a `2.18` **Numbers** Say the following figures and phrases. Then listen and repeat.

100   the early 1950s   46.4   40%   the year 2000
the year 2010   500 million

3b Work with a partner. Ask each other what the figures represent.

What does 100 refer to?

– The age we could live to by 2030.

4 Find information in the article to answer these questions.

Why:

1 did life expectancy rise during the 20th century?

2 will life expectancy continue to rise?

3 will the ageing process slow down in 2010?

4 has Europe's population been in decline for several years?

5 will Europe's population not continue to decline so quickly?

GRAMMAR:
infinitives and *-ing* forms

5a Look at the highlighted phrases in the text and choose the correct answer in the rules below. In one case both alternatives are possible.

a) *enable* is followed by an object + the *-ing form* / *infinitive with to*.

b) *want* is followed by the *-ing form* / *infinitive with to*.

c) *start* is followed by the *-ing form* / *infinitive with to*.

d) *enjoy* is followed by the *-ing form* / *infinitive with to*.

5b Complete the table with the verbs in the box. You may want to look at a dictionary.

> like   promise   advise   continue
> manage   expect   love   allow   begin
> suggest   decide   teach   hate   hope

Verbs followed by (object +) infinitive with *to*	Verbs followed by *-ing*	Verbs followed by both forms
want	*enjoy*	*start*

GRAMMAR TIP

When we use a verb after a preposition, the verb is always in the *-ing* form.

… keep on working.

➡ **Language reference and extra practice, pages 152–153**

6 Which two verbs in each sentence below are correct?

1 She _____ following a healthy diet.
   a) enjoyed   b) started   c) hoped

2 He _____ seeing his grandchildren.
   a) expected   b) continued   c) enjoyed

3 We _____ to go to the concert.
   a) promise   b) enjoy   c) want

4 They _____ getting a new job.
   a) talked about   b) succeeded in   c) wanted

5 She _____ going to the cinema.
   a) suggested   b) decided   c) hated

6 He _____ learning Spanish.
   a) gave up   b) started   c) taught

SPEAKING

7a Look at the following statements. Indicate how strongly you agree or disagree with each statement (5 = agree strongly, 1 = disagree strongly).

1 People should stop work at 65.

2 It should be compulsory for people to have children if the birth rate is low.

3 Families should always look after their older members.

4 A sign of a civilised society is that it always treats its old people well.

5 Medicine is for treating illness, not for enabling people to live longer.

6 People who are very overweight (or do extreme sports) should pay for their healthcare.

7b Work with a partner to discuss the statements.

SITUATION

Belleview, UK; 30 years ago

Welcome to Belleview, situated on the south-east coast of England.

BELLEVIEW is one of England's most beautiful towns, with its white villas, historic main street, public gardens and long promenade by the beach. Many retired people come to live in Belleview, attracted by its healthy climate and peaceful, quiet atmosphere. There are ten four-star restaurants in the town, as well as many cafés and tea rooms, several of which are in the picturesque harbour area. The town has a famous spa, a well-stocked aquarium and an interesting museum. Most people spend their Saturday evening taking a leisurely walk along the promenade.

Belleview, UK; today

BELLEVIEW is certainly worth visiting if you are young and looking for an exciting, international atmosphere. Two new universities, numerous English language schools and the building of an airport nearby have totally changed the town. There are now over 200 restaurants and 50 night clubs in Belleview. The town's population has increased greatly in recent years, and now over 60 percent of the population is under 40 years old. Belleview is a lively, noisy seaside town, but it is not the safest of towns and it has its share of social problems – be aware in clubs and on the beaches. On Saturday evenings, the town centre is taken over by young people enjoying themselves and the restaurants and clubs are really lively.

1 Read the extracts from a brochure and travel section of a newspaper about Belleview, a seaside town in the UK. Work with a partner to discuss the following.

1 What differences are there between Belleview today and Belleview 30 years ago?

2 The writer of the extract about Belleview today says, 'Belleview has its share of social problems'. What kind of problems do you think there might be because of the increase in the town's young population?

2a 2.19 Listen to the conversation between the Mayor of Belleview and two members of the town council. What do they say about the following?

cars   beaches   young people

2b Which problem or trend is most serious, do you think?

3a The local newspaper in Belleview recently published an article which raised many criticisms of the town. Work with a partner to read two responses – one of you reads the email below, the other reads the letter.

3b Tell your partner about the main points of your text.

I cannot agree with the opinions expressed in your recent article about Belleview. I am a 21-year-old university student and have been studying here for the last three years. I think Belleview is a great town to live in. There's so much to do here for people like me, and the night life is fantastic. My friends and I go to a new club every weekend. We really enjoy the sports facilities in Belleview, especially the opportunities to go surfboarding and water skiing.
I very much hope the town will sell the aquarium and use the money to build a new sports and swimming pool complex.
Yours sincerely,
Jim Barnes

Sir,
I wish to respond to your recent criticism of our town. I have lived in Belleview for over forty years, so my opinion might be of interest to your readers. Firstly, in recent years, the town seems to be focusing more on young people than on older, more mature people. Many top class restaurants have closed down and been replaced by fast food outlets that attract younger people. There are simply not enough places for older people to go to and enjoy themselves.

The beachfront used to be a lovely place for people to stroll around. Now it has become commercialised and is full of trendy boutiques and amusement arcades, all aimed at younger people. The town centre is not a place to go to at night. It's full of noisy young people, and you don't feel safe there any more.

Finally, there's a rumour that our world-famous aquarium will be sold. I sincerely hope that will not happen.
Yours faithfully,
Sandra Johnson

KEY LANGUAGE: the language of meetings

4a **2.20** Listen to a councillor talking to residents about a parking problem and answer the questions.

1 What three complaints do the residents make about parking?

2 What actions does the councillor agree to take?

4b Listen again. Complete the phrases.

1 We're here _____ _____ the parking problem.

2 I'm very _____ _____ the present situation.

3 It's not _____ – I'm sure you understand that.

4 I'll _____ _____ the matter.

5 Sorry, _____ _____ _____ say something, please?

6 Yes …, please make your _____.

7 Thank you for your _____.

8 To _____ up, …

5 Find expresssions in the Other Useful Phrases that are similar to the phrases in 4b.

TASK: participating in a meeting

6a The Mayor of Belleview has set up a meeting between councillors and residents to discuss the town's main problems and to try to come up with ideas for solving them. Work in groups of two or three and read some information about the problems.

Group A (Mayor and councillors): turn to page 160.

Group B (younger residents): turn to page 163.

Group C (older residents): turn to page 166.

6b Now form larger groups and hold the meeting. One Group A, one Group B and one Group C works together. The mayor leads the discussion. Discuss each of the problems below and decide on the best solution for each problem.

- parking
- fees for beaches
- behaviour of young people
- lack of facilities for older people
- the proposal to sell the aquarium

OTHER USEFUL PHRASES

Stating the purpose of the meeting
The purpose of the meeting is to …

Showing understanding of people's feelings
I see how you feel.

Encouraging people to speak
Go ahead.

Thanking people for their ideas
That was very interesting.

Saying you will take action
I'll see what I can do.

Making a point
Can I make a point?

I'm very concerned about … (the present situation)

I'm afraid I can't agree.

I'm very unhappy about …

Stating the key points that have been agreed
Let me summarise.

STUDY SKILLS: recording and learning vocabulary

1 Do you find it easier to learn vocabulary or grammar? Which is more important, do you think?

2 Complete the extract from a website with the words in the box.

> communicate   active   grammar   read   vocabulary   words

Question: How many words are there in English?

Answer: A lot, perhaps as many as one million, and growing all the time! English certainly has a huge ^{1}_____, and while it is sometimes quite easy to ^{2}_____ in English, it can be very difficult to say exactly what you mean. This is a problem of vocabulary, not ^{3}_____. Students of English often overvalue the importance of learning grammar and undervalue the importance of vocabulary. So, how many ^{4}_____ do you need to learn? According to the American author Stuart Berg Flexner, an average well-read person has a passive vocabulary of 20,000 words, but an ^{5}_____ vocabulary which is a lot less. However, don't worry too much – only about 2,500 words make up about 80 percent of everything we ^{6}_____ or hear.

[edit]

3 Which of the following do you note when you record new vocabulary? Write 1 for *always*, 2 for *sometimes*, and 3 for *never* in the gaps. Compare your answers with a partner.

1 write a translation of the word/phrase into your own language ☐

2 write an explanation of the word/phrase in English ☐

3 record the pronunciation, including stress ☐

4 write the part of speech (verb, noun, etc.) ☐

5 write synonyms/antonyms (words with the same/ opposite meaning) ☐

6 write other words in the same family (e.g. *trend* – noun, *trendy* – adj, *a trendsetter* – noun, person) ☐

7 record collocations (words often used together, e.g. *upward trend, fashion conscious*) ☐

8 record grammatical patterns (e.g. verb patterns, prepositions etc.) ☐

4 It is a good idea to organise your vocabulary in a variety of ways. This will help you to see patterns and make connections. Do the exercises to see the different methods. Which methods do you find useful?

a Topic headings Match the verbs and nouns in the two boxes below and then put them under the most appropriate heading.

Education	Engineering	Trends
get a degree		

> build   do   follow   get   go out
> hand in   revise   solve   start

> for exams   of fashion   an essay
> a prototype   a degree   a problem
> fashion   a craze   safety tests

b Diagrams Add some words to the branch diagram.

CLOTHES — skirt, blouse, dress, shoes (trainers, boots), kimono
accessories — scarf, hats, belt, bag

c Pictures/symbols Match the chart types with the pictures below.

(line) graph   table   bar chart   flow chart   pie chart

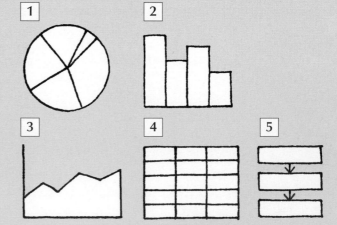

5a 🔊 2.21 **Learning vocabulary** Listen to six students talking about how they learn vocabulary. Write the number of the speaker by the method he/she describes.

a) putting vocabulary into categories

b) displaying new words on a wall

c) filling gaps in sentences

d) hearing and saying words several times

e) learning groups of words with the same origin

f) remembering a key word, i.e. something that reminds you of the word

5b Will you use or try any of these techniques in the future, do you think?

WRITING SKILLS: describing a trend

6a Complete the table with the words and phrases in the box. Use a dictionary to check whether each word and phrase is a noun or a verb, or both.

| increase | drop | decline | level off | rise | fall |
| grow | go up | decrease | stabilise | remain stable |

↑	↓	↘	→

6b Describe each of the graphs below, using an adjective from the box and a noun from Exercise 6a. Use a dictionary to help you decide which words collocate. There may be more than one possibility.

| dramatic | significant | steady | sharp |
| slow | gradual | slight | sudden |

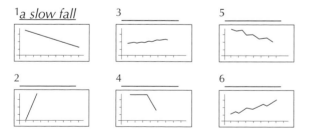

¹*a slow fall*

7a Read the extract from a report on spending on entertainment in different parts of the world, and match each paragraph with its purpose.

a) gives the main trend

b) gives the conclusion

c) gives more detail and any surprising or opposite trends

d) gives where the information comes from and what it shows

7b **Avoiding repetition** Read the extract again and replace the words in **bold** with one of the expressions in the box.

commissioned by	findings	finds	largest rise
marked fall	relatively stable	small
sudden increase	survey	twice as much as

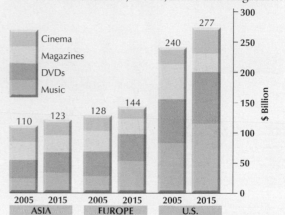

This bar chart shows the **results** of a study **carried out** for World Statistics Inc into spending on entertainment in Asia, Europe and the United States. The **study** compares spending in 2005 with a forecast for 2015 across different sources of entertainment: cinema, DVDs, music and magazines.

Overall, the survey **shows** that total spending on entertainment in the US is **double** that of Europe and Asia combined, in both 2005 and 2015. Also, the US will show the **greatest increase** in spending between 2005 and 2015. The level of spending for Europe and Asia between the two years shows a **slight** increase.

For all three markets the biggest change in spending will be on music and DVDs, which both show **a sharp rise**. Interestingly, the only **significant decrease** in spending between 2005 and 2015 is on magazines. For all markets the spending on cinema will remain **fairly constant**.

We conclude that there is no point at present in entering the magazine or cinema market, but there are real possibilities in the music market. More research into this market is recommended.

8 Look at the chart showing trends in household types in the UK from 2003 to 2026. Write a description of the changes the chart shows. Use the description above as a model and the words and phrases from Exercise 6.

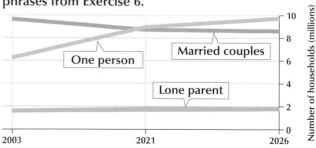

Arts and media

11.1 TYPES OF MEDIA

In the future everyone will be famous for 15 minutes.
Andy Warhol, 1928–1987, U.S. artist and filmmaker

READING AND LISTENING

1a Look at the different types of media. How often do you use each of them?

radio   newspapers   magazines   cinema
TV   books   CDs   DVDs   Internet websites
computer games

1b Which of the types of media from Exercise 1a do you prefer for:

1 finding out about news?   3 education?

2 entertainment?   4 research?

2a Read the three reviews. Match each one with one of the types of media in Exercise 1a. Which words or phrases helped you to decide?

2b Which of the following star ratings do you think the critic gave at the end of each review? Which words or expressions helped you make your choice?

0 TERRIBLE   * POOR   ** AVERAGE   *** GOOD
****   VERY GOOD   ***** EXCELLENT

3a 2.22 Listen to three more reviews and match each with one of the types of media in Exercise 1a.

3b Listen again and give each review a star rating.

1

NEW SERIES...

This ambitious new series is a breathtaking exploration of the Earth. The fantastic attention to sound, the groundbreaking new filming techniques used, and David Attenborough's superb narration have created a documentary which is surely a masterpiece. Over eight million people in the UK have watched each of the episodes.

2

This is a two-disc set, one with relaxing music for bedtime, the other for playtime. Exposing your child to classical music is an interesting idea. The high cost of the package might make some people think twice, but because we all love Mozart, it might still be worth buying.

3

REVIEW   'I was disappointed with Roller Coaster World'

I have to say I was disappointed with *Roller Coaster World*. The graphics are just about adequate but the instruction menus were impossible to follow. Nothing exciting happens after you have created the roller coaster. I would think long and hard before buying this one.

VOCABULARY: media genres

Harry Potter and the Order of the Phoenix is the gripping and electrifying new ¹_____ from the incomparable J.K. Rowling. The ²_____ is excellent and the book is full of suspense. It does contain some violent and frightening scenes, but I enjoyed reading every ³_____.

✚ HOSPITAL DRAMA

So far I have found nearly every ⁴_____ of the hospital drama *ER* to be very moving, with powerful storylines and groundbreaking use of the camera.

4a Complete the reviews above with the words in the box.

| atmosphere | plot | series |
| episode | chapter | novel |

4b Find adjectives in the texts that mean the following.

1 keeps your attention and interest
2 so good that no one else can be compared to them
3 has a strong effect on your emotions
4 using new ideas and methods
5 excellent, very good
6 very funny
7 important and typical of its type
8 incredible and exciting

5a Look at the mind map with some of the types of media mentioned in the reviews. Find examples of genres (e.g. *documentary*) from Exercises 2 and 4 and fit them in the mind map.

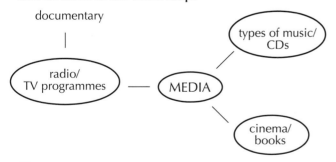

5b Add the words below to the mind map.

| sitcom page-turner soap jazz crime |
| current affairs programme reggae reality |
| folk country hip hop animation soul |
| autobiography science fiction opera |

Radioweek

It's a laugh is an outstanding new radio ⁵_____, on every Monday evening. Listen out for **Shop Trek**, a hilarious sketch based on shopping in the future.

FILM REVIEW

Another classic horror is released on DVD this week. Hitchcock's *Psycho*, with its brooding dark ⁶_____ in the house on the hill, and the breathtaking shower scene in the motel, is the perfect example of 'edge-of-your-seat suspense'.

5c Can you think of any other examples to add to the mind map?

6 In groups, discuss the following.

1 What type of TV and radio programmes, books, music and films do you like? Can you describe one of your favourites from each field?

2 Have any documentaries recently particularly impressed you? Which one(s)?

3 Tell your group about your favourite TV series. Talk about the main characters and the plot and describe your favourite episode.

WRITING

7 Write a review for a newspaper, website, magazine or radio programme. Use the reviews to help you write your own review.

SPEAKING

8 Work in three groups to have a debate about the media. Read the situation and your roles.

Your organisation has just been awarded a grant from the Arts Council to set up a museum collection for either films, books or recorded music for entertainment. There is not enough money and resources to have a collection for all three.

Group A: you represent film.
Group B: you represent books.
Group C: you represent recorded music.

Prepare a case for why your media:

1 is important.
2 is better than the other two.
3 should be chosen.

READING

1 You are going to read about a famous recluse. What is a recluse? Guess, then read the introduction below to check your answer.

A recluse is someone who:

a) likes media attention.

b) avoids media attention.

c) comes back after a period away from media attention.

Out of **sight**, out of **mind**?

In today's multi-media age, it seems no artist with something to sell can afford not to do interviews and chat shows to publicise their latest product. People's interest in celebrity means we often know more about the artists than their work. Below, our reporter Wendy Finch profiles three recluses from the world of the arts who decided not to play the media game. Why are we fascinated by the artists themselves when really their work should speak for them?

2a In groups of three, each read more about one recluse and answer the questions.

Student A: read the article below.

Student B: read the article on page 164.

Student C: read the article on page 165.

1 How is the person's character described in the article?

2 What is their most famous piece of work?

3 How was their relationship with the media?

4 What did they do later in life?

5 Is there anything surprising in the article?

2b Tell your group about your article. Use the questions in Exercise 2a to help you.

2c In your group, discuss which person/people:

1 was/were worried about personal safety?

2 moved to the countryside?

3 pretended to be someone else?

4 won an award?

5 had their work associated with a famous crime?

6 returned to his place of birth?

7 moved to another country?

8 was/were offered a lot of money for any new work?

9 didn't like travelling by air?

10 had a book written about them by one of their children.

1

SYD BARRETT
(1946–2006)

At the Pink Floyd reunion in London's Hyde Park for Live8, there was one member missing.

Often called an eccentric genius, Syd Barrett formed the supergroup Pink Floyd in 1965 and wrote, sang and played guitar on all their early hit records, including the 1967 masterpiece *Piper at the Gates of Dawn*. He left the band in 1968 after experiencing some kind of breakdown due to the pressures of stardom and touring. He made two solo albums, *The Madcap Laughs* and *Barrett*, both released in 1970, which continue to sell well.

Barrett then left the music business completely, deciding a musician's life was not for him. He did not make any music at all after 1974. Once a household name, he is now more or less forgotten except by his fans. He moved

back to his home town of Cambridge and started to use his original name of Roger Barrett. He lived alone, quietly spending his time painting and gardening. He received a six-figure income from his Pink Floyd royalties, but his contact with the outside world was minimal. Although he hadn't appeared or spoken in public since the mid-1970s, fans and journalists still attempted to contact him.

In 1971 a journalist tracked him down. Syd told the reporter that he walked a lot, painted, wasted time and feared getting old. He also said that he felt full of dust and guitars. Another journalist reported that a bald, fat man answered the door and said that Syd couldn't talk. In 1992, Atlantic Records offered half a million dollars for any new Syd Barrett recordings.

His family reported that he was content and reasonably healthy. More recently, when fans or journalists called on him he was polite and coherent, but unwilling to discuss his past as a famous rock star. Talking to one journalist on his doorstep in 2001, Syd asked him to leave as he didn't do interviews any more.

VOCABULARY: words connected with the arts

3 Find words or phrases in the texts that mean the following.

1 a very successful record or CD (text 1, paragraph 1)
2 a very successful book (2.3)
3 a very successful film (3.3)
4 a great work of art (1.1, 2.4, 3.1)
5 a very well-known person (1.2)
6 a person whose job it is to give their opinions of books, films, etc. (3.3)
7 payments made to a writer of a book, song, etc. (1.2)
8 a very long book or film (3.2)
9 a piece of information which may or may not be true (2.1)

SPEAKING

4 In groups, discuss the following.

1 Which of the three profiles did you think was the most interesting? Why?
2 Do you think celebrities have the right to a private life?
3 Which books, songs and films do you think are masterpieces?
4 What rumours about media celebrities have you heard recently?

GRAMMAR: reported speech

5a Look at this example of how Stanley Kubrick's words are reported. What two changes are there between the two sentences?

'I travel to London four or five times a year.' =

He once told a friend that *he travelled to London four or five times a year*.

5b Now find examples of reported speech from the profiles of Syd Barrett and J.D. Salinger that match these direct quotes. Write them down.

1 Syd: 'I walk a lot.'
Syd told the reporter that he walked a lot.
2 A bald, fat man: 'Syd can't talk.'
3 Syd: 'Please leave.'
4 A professor: 'You are the worst English student in the history of the college.'
5 JD Salinger: 'I like to write but I write for myself.'
6 Salinger's daughter: 'He also enjoys being with people.'

6a Look at the examples of reported speech that you have written and answer the questions.

1 What do you notice about verbs in reported speech?
2 Which verbs are used to report the statements in Exercise 5b (e.g. *told*)? Write them.
3 Look at the structures following the reporting verbs. When do we use the infinitive with *to* instead of a *that*-clause?
4 Look at the verbs *say* and *tell*. Which one needs a personal object (*him, her, them,* etc.)?

In reported speech we usually change the tense of the speech we are reporting (e.g. present perfect → past perfect, present continious → past continuous).

6b How do we change the present simple and *can* when we report them? Look again at the examples in Exercise 5b.

GRAMMAR TIP

In reported speech, we often also make changes to pronouns, e.g. *I* = *he/she*, *our* = *their*, and to adverbs, e.g. *today* = *then/that day, yesterday = the day before*.

➡ Language reference and extra practice, pages 154–155

7 Change the sentences below to reported speech. Use the phrases in brackets to help you.

1 We expect our new CD to be a big hit. (*The band said …*)
The band said that they expected their new CD to be a big hit.
2 I am writing a new article today. (*He said he …*)
3 I have just finished writing a new book for my publisher. (*She said …*)
4 Val refused to speak to the reporters yesterday. (*He said Val …*)
5 We'll finish the recording tomorrow. (*They said …*)

8 Think of or make up a rumour about a celebrity. Tells as many people as you can, and then write down as many rumours as you can remember in reported speech.

Did you know that Brad Pitt is going to get married again?

Mehmet said that Brad Pitt was going to get married again.

LISTENING

1 You are going to listen to a journalist, Richard, talking about an interview he attended for a job as a foreign correspondent. Discuss the questions.

1 What does a foreign correspondent do?

2 What questions do you think the interviewer will ask the journalist?

2a ▨2.23 Listen to the conversation and answer the questions.

1 Why does Richard want to become a foreign correspondent?

2 Does he think he will get the job?

2b Listen to the conversation again. Tick (✓) the questions that Richard was asked in his interview.

1 Why do you want to be a foreign correspondent?

2 What parts of the world are you interested in?

3 Have you travelled a lot?

4 Do you speak any foreign languages?

5 Where did you go to university?

6 Have you taken any further qualifications?

7 What articles have you written?

8 What qualities does a journalist need to be a foreign correspondent?

9 When can you start work?

10 Are you physically fit?

3 Would you like to be a foreign correspondent? Why / Why not?

GRAMMAR: reported questions

4a In the conversation, Richard told Nura about the interview. Look at the questions you ticked in Exercise 2b. Find the reported versions of these questions in Track 2.23 on page 180.

Why do you want to be a foreign correspondent?
She asked me why I wanted to be a foreign correspondent.

4b Choose the correct answer in each rule.

1 We use *if* or *whether* to report *yes/no questions* / *wh- questions*.

2 When questions are reported, the word order *changes* / *doesn't change* from the order of the original direct question.

3 The reported question has the same word order as a *statement* / *question*.

4 The verb in the reported question *often changes tense* / *never changes tense* from the tense in the direct question.

➡ Language reference and extra practice, pages 154-155

5 You are a reporter. You were interviewed about your job by some university students. Write their questions below in reported speech. Start with 'They asked me ...'.

1 Are you good at reporting?

2 Are you able to write notes quickly?

3 What time do you usually start work?

4 Do you enjoy working as a reporter?

5 What do you do when people don't answer your questions?

6 How much time do you spend travelling abroad?

7 Do you ever feel afraid in a crisis?

8 What problems do you have when you are reporting?

READING

6 Why do you think people choose to be foreign correspondents? What qualities do you think you need to be a foreign correspondent?

7a Read the extracts from an interview with Rageh Omar, a foreign correspondent. Fill the gaps with these questions.

a) What was your best experience?

b) What advice do you have for those starting out?

c) What was your first salary?

d) What was your first job?

e) How did you become interested in journalism?

MEUTYA HAFID DARI BAGHDAD

Me and my career:

Rageh Omar

Foreign correspondent

1 _____
I first became interested in my teens. I'm originally from Somalia and lots of my family have travelled far and wide, throughout Africa, the Middle East and Europe.
I saw journalism as a really good way of getting out into the world and, as someone who was born in Somalia, educated in the west and is a Muslim, I feel at home in several different cultures.

2 _____
I wangled my way into a month's traineeship at the _Voice_ newspaper in Brixton but my first real job in journalism was as a stringer for the BBC in Ethiopia. I really didn't want to go back into education, so I went out to Ethiopia in May 1991 with £800 in my pocket in the hope of getting some work. BBC Africa said they'd take occasional pieces from me. I came back a year later and was offered a job with the World Service.

3 _____
It's hard to single out one in particular but one moment that was really touching was when we were covering Kosovo along with thousands of other journalists. We were in a village on the border with the Former Yugoslav Republic of Macedonia, doing a story about a hospital. All the soldiers had left and we were interviewing one of the main surgeons.
After we had switched off the camera, he said that it felt as though we had been with him every night. He had been hiding in a basement there because there was no way of getting into Kosovo and every night he would translate our reports to all the others present. It brought home to me how much responsibility we had.

4 _____
As a stringer I was paid by the piece. I got £45 for each dispatch and £60 for a live radio interview. Each month the BBC would send me out my little cheque with details of how many dispatches I'd done. Obviously it depended on how much news there was around at the time but it was quite tough to survive for that first year, even in Ethiopia.

5 _____
Don't be daunted and don't be shy in any sense. If there's a programme or an organisation you really like, call them, ask to come in and see them. You'd be amazed how often you get a positive response.
You need that chutzpah but also remember it's about integrity and storytelling. You must be able to listen as well as talk and convey the story as accurately as possible.

Note: a stringer is a person who regularly sends new stories to a newspaper but who is not employed by that newspaper.

7b In which paragraph can you find this information?
1 what qualities a foreign correspondent needs to have
2 where Rageh Omar was trained
3 why he decided to be a journalist
4 where he was born
5 when he first went to Ethiopia
6 how he was paid
7 an experience that showed him that journalism was an important job

8 Find words and phrases in the interview that mean the following.
1 got something by clever, and maybe dishonest, methods (paragraph 2)
2 a short period when someone learns about a job (para. 2)
3 to choose one thing from many others (para. 3)
4 made me realise (para. 3)
5 discouraged, worried (para. 5)
6 confidence and courage to do something, especially against authority (para. 5)
7 the quality of being honest and having high moral standards (para. 5)

SPEAKING AND WRITING

9 Work with a partner. One of you witnessed an important news event. Decide together what the event was (e.g., the effect of an earthquake or hurricane on a city).

Student A: you are a reporter. Write five questions about what Student B saw. Then interview him/her.

Student B: you are an eyewitness. Make a few notes about what you saw. Then answer A's questions.

After the interview, write an account of it. Use reported speech.

I asked (Juan) what exactly he had seen. He said …

The reporter asked me what exactly I had seen. I said …

SITUATION

Gemini Television is a large independent broadcaster. They have had success in television with mini-series and situation comedies. Recently the company has decided to move into film-making in order to both raise its profile and to increase profits. They have received some film proposals or 'pitches' from directors working in different countries. They are considering investing in one of the projects, which they will sell around the world.

1 Read the situation. What sort of film do you think would be good to invest in?

2a `2.24` Listen to two executives from Gemini Television talking about the move into film-making. Do they agree on the direction they want to follow?

2b Listen again. Tick (✓) the things the executives mention.

1 originality of the idea
2 actors
3 experience of the director
4 locations used
5 how easy it will be to sell around the world
6 the genre of the film
7 the surprise element
8 the cost

KEY LANGUAGE: comparing and contrasting

3 Listen again and complete the sentences and phrases.

1 It's very _____ _____ the kind of things we've done in the past.
2 It's the _____ _____ TV really, just everything's bigger.
3 … which is _____ _____ _____ the sort of stuff we usually make.
4 … something _____ _____ _____ what we've been doing recently.
5 I think the director is _____ _____ _____ the location, though.
6 … and find we have something _____ _____ _____ than our usual TV series.

---

1 Title: <u>Hands up for Happiness</u>

Genre: Romantic comedy

Plot: Two pairs of identical twins, one Italian and one Russian, meet and start relationships. They have problems telling the difference between each twin. Will they end up with the right person?

Cast: unknown actors as need to be real twins

Special features: very romantic locations, e.g. Venice, St Petersburg. Also will travel well and promotes international relations.

Budget: $40–50 million max.

Audience: 20–35 year olds

---

2 Title: <u>Alien Attack</u>

Genre: science fiction

Plot: Story takes place 500 years in the future. The Earth is attacked by aliens. A small group survive the attack and try to save the planet. Will they succeed before the aliens breed?

Cast: to be decided (by the director)

Special features: stunning special effects, exciting visually

Budget: $60–80 million max.

Audience: 15 upwards

TASK: choosing a film to produce

4 Work in small groups. You are executives at Gemini Television. It is your job to decide which film Gemini should make. Read the pitches for the films and add any information to the chart that you can.

	Hands up	Alien Attack	Exit Strategy	Midnight Sun
Genre				
Locations				
Actors/cast				
Special features				
Ending				
Budget				

5a 2.25 Listen to the director of each film talking about their pitch. Match each director with one of the pitches from Exercise 4.

5b Listen again and complete the other sections of the table.

6 Look back at the list of criteria the executives discussed in Exercise 2b. Add any others you think are important. Discuss the advantages and disadvantages of each film, and decide in your groups which film you want to produce.

7 Make a final decision as a class.

OTHER USEFUL PHRASES

We could do a lot worse than … (a good crime film).

The best thing about this film is …

What's great about this is …

What I really like about this is … (the story).

I think … is really good because …

The worst thing about this is …

The biggest drawback is that …

What I don't like is …

3

Title: **Exit Strategy**

Genre: thriller

Plot: A woman picks up the wrong bag at an airport and is mistaken for a foreign agent who has secret documents. She is chased around the world by criminals, government agents and the real owner of the bag.

Cast: major Hollywood star as lead actress

Special features: many locations around the world, lots of twists and turns in the story, strong possibility for a sequel, and for turning the lead character into a female James Bond

Budget: at least $100-120 million

Audience: 15 upwards

4

Title: **Midnight Sun**

Genre: action/adventure

Plot: A story of family honour, revenge, great love and of good versus evil. A young Japanese man brought up in the USA returns to the country of his birth. He discovers the dark secret of the family, and the reason he was brought up in the USA. His search for the truth leads him to the Philippines and to the beautiful princess Satsuki.

Cast: young, unknown actors

Special features: superbly choreographed fight scenes

Budget: $50-70 million max.

Audience: worldwide, but probably over 18 due to violence

1a Work with a partner to discuss the statements below about delivering a talk. Say whether you agree or disagree, and give your reasons.

1 You should keep eye contact with the audience for at least 80 percent of the time.

2 At the beginning, explain clearly what you are going to talk about.

3 Try to start the talk with a joke or a funny story.

4 Speak in a loud voice during your talk.

5 Speak slowly at first, then speed up.

6 Give a maximum of two examples during the talk.

7 Make sure you have numbered notes.

8 Do not interact with the audience until the end of the talk.

9 Your talk will be much better if you use visual aids (tables, graphs, etc.).

10 Do not encourage too many questions because you may not be able to answer them.

1b Compare your answers with another pair.

2 `2.26` Read the descriptions below of four common mistakes that people make when giving a talk. Listen to the beginning of four talks by an organiser of a festival and match each with one of the mistakes.

The gabbler

This person talks so quickly that the audience cannot understand what they are saying.

The 'no plan' presenter

This person does not have any plan or outline of the talk to give to the audience.

The mumbler

This person talks too quietly, or not clearly enough for someone to understand them.

The rambler

This person talks in a very confused way, not keeping to the point.

3 `2.27` Listen to the beginning of another talk, which is well organised and is delivered well. Work with a partner to practise delivering it, using the transcript below.

Good morning, everyone. Thank you for coming to my talk. I'm going to tell you about our plans for the music and dance festival in September. I've divided my talk into three parts. I'll start by telling you about the kind of performers we're trying to attract and I'll mention some well-known people who'll attend the festival. Next, I'll discuss how we're advertising the event – what plans we have for that. I know that's of interest to you. Finally, I'll explain why this will be the ideal festival for you to sponsor. I'll be pleased to answer any questions at the end of my talk. Is that OK, everyone? Good. Right, let me tell you about the performers we hope to …

4 Work with a partner to practise giving a talk.

Student A: follow the instructions below to give your talk. Then listen to Student B's talk and ask questions.

Student B: listen to Student A's talk. Then follow the instructions on page 165.

Student A: You are an organiser of a street festival (a festival with people who perform their acts in the street to passers-by) in the area where you live. Read the notes below, and give a short talk about the festival to your partner. He/she should ask questions at the end of your talk and you should answer them.

Location: in the city centre – main square

History of the festival: has been held for the last ten years. Always very successful. People of all ages attend. Children love the festival.

Dates: April 15–20.

Times: 11 a.m.–6 p.m.

Performers: singers, dancers, jugglers, puppeteers, comedians, etc., local acts and from abroad. Interest from all over the world.

Special event: performance by a famous US singer.

Advertising: newspaper ads, radio spots, leaflets, posters.

Advantages to sponsors: low charges for all types of advertising, e.g. posters, banners, etc. Thousands of people will see the advertisements.

Other information? Other special events? Food? Security?

5 Prepare a short talk (five minutes) about a festival or event you have been to / regularly go to. Work in small groups and deliver your talk to the rest of your group. Answer any questions they may have.

WRITING SKILLS: a report

6a Read the report by an organiser of a street festival. Choose the most suitable heading for each paragraph.

1 Conclusion
2 Audiences
3 Performers
4 Recommendations
5 Refreshments
6 ~~Introduction~~

6b Work with a partner to discuss the following.

1 What were the good points about the festival?
2 How can the organisers improve next year's festival?

7 **Making generalisations** There are several examples of making generalisations in this report. When you generalise, you say that something is true about most people or things. Look at two examples of words/phrases used to generalise from the report.

Overall, the festival was highly successful …

Most of the performers were excellent …

Work with a partner to find other examples of generalising in sections B–E of the report.

8 Imagine that the festival you talked about in Exercise 4 has now taken place. Write a report on the festival, with recommendations for improving it next year. Use 'generalising language' where appropriate.

Report on our Street Festival (April 15–21)

A *Introduction*

Overall, the festival was highly successful, attracting over 50,000 people. The weather was good, although it rained heavily on the first day. Most of the performers were excellent and well received by the public.

B _____

People attending were mainly families. However, there were people of all ages, and a large number from the various ethnic groups in our community. The acts appealing to children were particularly popular.

C _____

The majority were singers and dancers, but there was a wide variety of acts from over 20 countries. Almost all of the performers started and finished their acts on time. Perhaps the highlight of the festival was the music and dance routines of a group from Ethiopia.

D _____

There were many outlets offering hot and cold food. On the whole, people were satisfied with the quality of the food and service. However, some people complained that the queues were too long at the more popular outlets and said that there needed to be a greater variety of ethnic foods.

E _____

The festival gave great pleasure to a large number of people and it brought together the different cultural communities within our city. In general, the sponsors were very pleased with the organisation of the festival. Most of them wanted to participate in next year's festival.

F _____

1 Ways of reducing crowds at the most popular events should be considered.
2 More signs need to be provided and a wider variety of food offered.
3 Programmes showing daily events should be sold to spectators.
4 Accommodation for mothers with young children could be arranged.
5 It is vital to hire more security staff.
6 We must start to advertise the event much earlier.

12.1 REAL CRIMES?

I think crime pays. The hours are good, you travel a lot.
Woody Allen, 1935–, US film-maker and actor

SPEAKING

1a Work in groups. Look at the following activities. In your opinion, is each one:

a) quite a serious crime?

b) a crime, but not a serious one?

c) not a crime at all?

• writing graffiti

• making personal phone calls from work

• taking small items from hotel bedrooms when you are a guest

• saying nothing when you get too much change in a supermarket

• parking in a space for disabled drivers

• driving at 20kmh more than the speed limit on a motorway

• finding a wallet/purse containing money and not taking it to the police

• buying an essay on the Internet

• making your CV/resume better by not including information or putting incorrect information

• not giving all the facts when making an insurance claim

1b Think of one more activity for a), b) and c) in Exercise 1a. Then discuss your ideas in groups.

READING

2 You are going to read a text about a teenager who did something wrong. What kind of things do teenagers do that are against the law? Discuss your ideas with a partner.

3a Read the newspaper report and answer the questions.

1 What did the boy buy?

2 Where did he live?

3 How did he buy it?

4 Who supplied what he ordered?

5 Who paid?

6 How long did it take for the product to arrive?

7 What happened to the boy and the chocolate?

Dublin's first cyber criminal

A teenage boy with a sweet tooth has become Ireland's first Internet criminal after ordering £1,600 of chocolate on the credit card of an Argentinian.

The case began in Dublin, where a 15-year-old boy was surfing the Net on his parents' computer. He found an American company offering home deliveries of chocolate. The boy called up the order form, filled in his name and address and placed an order for $2,000 of chocolate. When asked for his credit card number, he made one up. He typed in 16 digits at random. Four days later, while his parents were out, a courier delivered the chocolate. The boy, who cannot be named for legal reasons, hid the goods in his room.

Meanwhile, the credit card holder in Argentina was distressed to discover that he had paid $2,000 to an American company supplying chocolates. He denied any knowledge of the order. The American suppliers checked the order form, realised the order had gone to Dublin rather than to Argentina and contacted the Irish police. The Irish fraud squad began investigating its first case of Internet fraud.

Police called at the boy's home and witnessed him eating the evidence. According to one Irish weekend newspaper, his parents were 'dumbfounded' at the discovery. All three cooperated fully with the police and recovered the remains of the chocolate.

As a juvenile, the boy will not be charged with obtaining goods by false pretences and the American company donated the chocolate to a children's charity in Dublin. The offender is said to be 'remorseful and sick of the sight of chocolate'.

3b Read the text again and choose the correct answer.

1 The Argentinean felt:
a) unhappy and upset.
b) angry and worried.
c) surprised and annoyed.

2 The boy's parents felt:
a) angry.   b) surprised.   c) amused.

3 At the end of the story the boy felt:
a) sorry.   b) worried.   c) angry.

4 Tell a partner about a time when you experienced these feelings.

distressed   dumbfounded   remorseful

VOCABULARY: crime, technology and money

5a Underline all the words and phrases in the report connected with the topics in the table. Write them in the correct column and decide if they are verbs, nouns or adjectives.

Crime/law	Technology	Money/business
criminal (noun)	surf (verb)	credit card (noun)

5b Find words in the crime column of the table that mean the following.

1 an event that the police look into
2 relating to the law
3 the crime of tricking people to get money
4 to try to discover the truth
5 to see something happen
6 facts or things which prove the truth
7 a young person, not yet an adult
8 to say officially that someone is accused of a crime
9 a person who has committed a crime

6 In groups, discuss the following.

1 In your opinion, did the boy commit a real crime?
2 Imagine that you are involved in this case. What would you do if you were:
a) the American company?
b) the boy's parents?
c) the police?
d) the Argentinean?
3 At what age do you think people are responsible for their actions?
4 Is there such a thing as a perfect crime?

WRITING

7 Write a short letter to the newspaper giving your views on the case. Use the beginning and ending below to help you.

Sir,

I read with interest your story yesterday about the young Internet criminal. My view of this case is …

… and I think you will find that the majority of sensible people feel the same way.

Name, Place of writing

LISTENING

1 What are the main reasons why people commit crime? Think of some recent famous crimes in your country. Why did the offenders commit them, do you think?

2a [2.28] Listen to three extracts from interviews with criminals. Which of the reasons you thought of in Exercise 1 are mentioned?

2b Listen to the extracts again. Complete the table with information from the interviews.

	1 Carlos	2 Frank	3 Gina
1 Crime?			
2 Age of criminal?			
3 Reason for crime?			
4 Plans for future?			

READING

3a Read the text and match one of the three causes of crime mentioned in the text (genetic, environment, choice) with each speaker from Exercise 2.

3b Read the text again. Look at the summary statements below and match them with one of the causes in the text (genetic, environment, choice).

1 Anti-social adults often produce anti-social children.

2 Criminals think carefully before they decide on a life of crime.

3 Young people who behave badly tend to become criminals.

4 People used to think that someone's physical features were a cause of crime.

5 Some experts now believe that people commit crimes because of their genes.

6 Criminals consider what they can lose and gain by committing a crime.

4 Which reason in the text do you think is the most common cause of crime?

WHY DO WE COMMIT CRIMES?

All adults at some time or another commit a crime, sometimes by accident, but why do some people intentionally commit crimes? Here are three theories that try to explain the causes of criminal behaviour.

GENETIC CAUSES

The idea that some people commit crimes because of biological factors has a long tradition. This theory suggests that criminals are born, not made. In the 19th century some people even thought brain sizes and skull shapes could explain criminal behaviour. Although experts today no longer believe this, they do argue that human behaviour can be linked to an individual's genes. Studies of adopted children who show criminal behaviour suggest that their behaviour is more similar to their biological parents' behaviour than their adoptive parents', showing a genetic link.

ENVIRONMENT

This theory states that a person's surroundings influence their behaviour. Just as children learn good behaviour from their parents and siblings, so children can learn bad behaviour from their families and other close relationships. Researchers in this area argue that early anti-social behaviour in childhood often leads to a future of criminal behaviour. It is a vicious circle, as one expert states: 'Problem children tend to grow up into problem adults, and problem adults tend to produce more problem children.'

CHOICE

The central idea of this theory is that crime is a career decision, an alternative way of making a living. The theory argues that most criminals are rational people, who know what they want and the different ways of getting it, i.e. work or crime. They are able to balance the risks of committing a crime, such as going to prison, against its benefits, i.e. what they gain if they aren't caught. The conclusion is: if there are more benefits than risks, do it, but if there are more risks than benefits, don't do it.

Research is continuing into people's motivation for committing crimes as understanding this may help us apply the correct punishments for crime. It is important to understand the causes of crime. With more knowledge, it will be easier to prevent crime and to help criminals to lead a more useful life.

VOCABULARY: word combinations

5a Find words in the text that can be used with the nouns below.

1 _____ behaviour (x5)   4 _____ relationships
2 _____ tradition   5 _____ decision
3 _____ link   6 _____ circle

5b Complete the sentences with phrases from Exercise 5a.

1 He spent many years in prison because of his _____.

2 Her parents were away from the house so often that she was unable to form _____ with either of them.

3 The United States has a _____ of allowing its citizens to own guns.

4 There are some teenagers in our town whose _____ is beginning to annoy us – they write on walls and shout at people all the time.

5 Some people make a _____ at an early age, but others need time to decide what to do in their lives.

GRAMMAR: third conditional

6a Look at these examples and answer the questions.

1 If they *had done* the job more quickly, they *would have left* in time.
   a) Did they do the job quickly?
   b) Did they leave in time?

2 If I *had wanted* to, I *could have become* a top businessman.
   a) Did he want to become a top businessman?
   b) Did he become a top businessman?

3 I *would have studied* at night school if I *had found* a good job.
   a) Did she study at night school?
   b) Did she get a good job?

4 I *might have tried* harder if I *hadn't been* unemployed.
   a) Was she unemployed?
   b) Did she try harder?

We use the third conditional to talk about unreal situations in the past, i.e. situations that are contrary to the facts.

6b Look at the examples of the third conditional in Exercise 6a and complete the rule.

The third conditional is *if* + past _____, + *would(n't)* _____ + _____ participle. We can also use _____ or *might* in the main clause.

➡ Language reference and extra practice, pages 156–157

7 Complete the sentences using the correct form of the verbs in brackets. Use *could or might* if possible.

1 If they _____ (plan) the robbery better, they _____ (succeed).

2 If the police _____ (act) more quickly, they _____ (prevent) the robbery.

3 If he _____ (not drive) so fast, he _____ (not have) an accident.

4 The crime rate _____ (not increase) if the last government's policy _____ (be) more efficient.

5 The police _____ (not catch) him if he _____ (not leave) his fingerprints on the door.

8 Think about how your life could have been different. Complete the sentences below using the third conditional.

1 If I had gone to a different school/university …
   If I had gone to a different school, I wouldn't have met any of my friends.

2 If I hadn't learned how to …

3 If I hadn't met …

4 If I hadn't visited …

SPEAKING

9 In groups, discuss the following.

1 Criminals are born, not made.
2 Most criminals are either greedy or lazy.
3 Crime doesn't pay.
4 Petty crimes lead to serious crimes.
5 Once a criminal, always a criminal.
6 Television programmes are a major cause of crime.

VOCABULARY: people in crime

1a Look at the words and find the following. There are three extra words.

1 four words for people who are or may be criminals
2 one word for people who are victims
3 three words for people who work for the law
4 two crimes

robbery	lawyer	attorney	captor
fingerprints	prosecutor	thief	
bank robber	getaway	kidnapping	
suspect	ransom	hostage	

1b Are the three extra words connected with crimes or the law?

READING

2a Work with a partner to read two crime reports. Then answer the questions for your crime.

Student A: read the report below.

Student B: read the report on page 164.

1 Where was the crime?
2 Describe the tunnel.
3 What was the total value of money and items stolen?
4 What exactly was stolen?
5 How much money has been retrieved?
6 What progress has been made by police?

2b Tell your partner about your text.

3 Without looking back at the texts, put the events in the correct order.

Student A: order the list below, then check with your text.

Student B: order the list on page 165, then check with your text.

a) One of the suspected robbers was kidnapped. ☐
b) The police arrested some suspects. ☐
c) A sign appeared in front of a house. ☐
d) The robbers dug a tunnel. ☐
e) The robbers entered the bank. ☐
f) The robbers fitted the tunnel with lights and air conditioning. ☐
g) The robbery was discovered. ☐

4 Have there been any spectacular robberies in your country?

LISTENING

5 [2.29] You are going to listen to eight speakers giving their opinion of a robbery of about £50 million in the town of Tonbridge in the UK in February 2006. Which speaker:

a) talks about people in this country and abroad knowing about the crime?
b) says how much money was stolen?
c) talks about someone who found some money?
d) says that some members of staff weren't careful enough?
e) says how big the reward was?
f) says too many people were involved?
g) talks about someone who worked there being involved?
h) talks about tracing bank notes?

Bank Robbers Tunnel Their Way to Millions

■ **By Monte Reel**

Tunnelling bank robbers in South America have broken world records of crime, snatching millions of dollars from banks and making their getaways through narrow passages beneath busy city streets. One of the biggest robberies was a $68 million job in Fortaleza, Brazil.

About 100 yards from Fortaleza's Central Bank, a sign appeared in front of a building that described it as a landscaping store, selling natural and artificial grass as well as plants. This was a trick, apparently, to avoid suspicion when the robbers removed large quantities of earth from the premises. The thieves dug a 260-foot tunnel from the house to the bank, putting in electric lights, air conditioning and wooden walls. The robbers entered the bank when it was closed for the weekend and got away with about $68 million.

The robbers managed to avoid or disable the bank's alarm systems. The robbery remained undiscovered until the bank opened for business the following Monday.

'They worked for several months', police said. 'They had sophisticated equipment and experts in math, engineering and excavation.' Police found a pick-up truck at the rented house. They also discovered that the house was covered in white powder, which made it difficult to take fingerprints.

In the months since the Fortaleza robbery, police have recovered about $8 million and arrested eight people they

GRAMMAR: modals (past deduction)

6a Look at these opinions from Exercise 5. From the speaker's point of view, answer *yes*, *no* or *not sure* to the question that follows each opinion.

1 They might have wanted to use the money in Europe. *Did they want to use the money in Europe?*

2 They shouldn't have stolen such a large amount of money. *Did they steal a large amount of money?*

3 Basically, they can't have planned it properly. *Did they plan it properly?*

4 They should have involved fewer people. *Did they involve fewer people?*

5 The £2 million reward might have got some informers and other criminals very interested. *Did the reward get some informers and other criminals interested?*

6 Someone with inside knowledge could have been involved. *Was someone with inside knowledge involved?*

7 They must have been very careless. *Were they careless?*

8 It couldn't have been more successful. *Was it successful?*

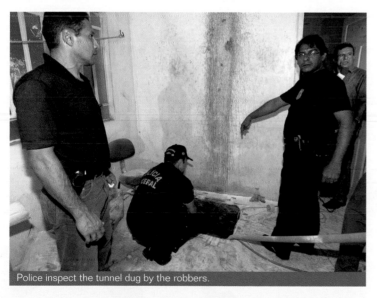
Police inspect the tunnel dug by the robbers.

suspect were part of the gang of thieves responsible for the crime. Five men were arrested with about $5.4 million of the money and told the police they had helped to dig the tunnel. Eighteen suspects remain free. Prosecutors have said that the robbers tried unsuccessfully to hire a small plane days before the robbery to move the money out of the country.

The massive amount of money still missing has led to kidnappings of alleged suspects for ransom. In October, one of the suspected robbers was kidnapped, then found dead after his family reportedly paid $890,000 in ransom. The police also suspect that some members of the gang might be connected to other tunnelling bank robberies in Uruguay and the Argentine city of Cordoba.

According to Brazilian press reports, one potential suspect sought by authorities is Moises Teixeira da Silva, who was sentenced to 25 years in prison for organizing bank robberies using tunnels.

He escaped from a Sao Paulo prison in 2001 – through a tunnel.

© 2006 The Washington Post Company

6b Look at the examples in Exercise 6a. Match them with the meanings a–e. There may be more than one example for each meaning.

a) This wasn't a good idea, but it happened.

b) This was a good idea but it didn't happen.

c) It is possible, but not certain, that this happened.

d) It is logically certain that this happened.

e) It was not possible for this to have happened.

6c Complete the rule.

The modal perfect is formed with a modal verb (*must, can, should*) + _____ + past participle.

➡ **Language reference and extra practice, pages 156–157**

7 What are your opinions of the robberies described in this lesson? Write five sentences using modal perfects, then discuss them with a partner.

The robbers in Argentina shouldn't have taken hostages.

SPEAKING

8 **The perfect murder** You are going to try and solve a crime. Work in groups of six. You are police detectives and each of you knows only the information on your card. Read the newspaper report below, and the information on your card, and discuss who committed the crime and how it was committed.

Student A: turn to page 160.

Student B: turn to page 164.

Student C: turn to page 166.

Student D: turn to page 167.

Student E: turn to page 167.

Student F: turn to page 168.

This morning the body of beautiful millionairess Susan Shapiro was found on the banks of Lake Minoria. The police know from the autopsy report that the victim died last night between 8 p.m. and 10 p.m. The small lake and surroundings have been searched extensively by police and divers and no murder weapon has been found. It appears that she was stabbed in the chest.

SITUATION

In England criminal cases usually go to a Crown Court. In this court there is a judge and a jury. The jury is made up of 12 people. The jury listens to the arguments and evidence presented by the prosecution and defence lawyers. The jury then delivers a verdict: guilty or not guilty. The jury have to reach their verdict by discussing the case together. During the trial the judge is like a referee, making sure that both sides act fairly. The judge also decides on a punishment if the defendant is found guilty by the jury.

1 Read the situation. Is this system similar to the one in your country?

2 **2.30** Listen to three extracts from a court case. A homeless man was accused of stealing some books from a store in a railway station. Which extract is:

a) the prosecution presenting a case?

b) the defence presenting a case?

c) members of the jury discussing the case?

KEY LANGUAGE: presenting a case and discussing a verdict

3a Read the sentences and try to guess what goes in each gap. Listen again and check your answers.

1 The _____ clearly shows that the manager of the bookshop …

2 I will bring _____ to confirm that he is an honest man.

3 I am sure that you will find my _____ innocent.

4 The facts of the _____ are clear. Let me summarise the _____ for you.

5 There should be no _____ in your minds that this man is guilty of theft.

6 I am confident that you will find the _____ guilty.

7 You can look at it in two _____.

8 I _____ he's innocent because …

9 I'm not _____ he's guilty because …

10 It's _____ to me that …

3b Match the sentences in Exercise 3a with:

a) the prosecution

b) the defence

c) the prosecution or the defence

d) the jury

TASK: discussing court cases

4 Read the information about three court cases. Which crime:

1 involved people eating something?

2 involved someone taking pictures?

3 took place in the countryside?

4 went on for a number of months?

5 took place at night?

6 involved a vehicle?

Case 1

A burglar broke into the home of a woman who lives in a remote rural area. The burglary took place at 2 a.m. The woman, who is a martial arts expert, woke up and realised someone had broken into her house. She went downstairs quietly and, without warning, attacked the burglar. She knocked him unconscious and then, losing control, she kicked him repeatedly. The burglar was badly injured and spent a long time in hospital recovering. The burglar is now permanently disabled. The woman was arrested and charged with using excessive force.

You, the jury

Case 2

A woman in her late 30s became obsessed with a younger man of 25 who lives in the same town. He moved to the area a year ago and she first noticed him at the railway station as they both take the same train to work. They talked briefly on the platform on several occasions. More recently, she started following him, appearing outside his work and visiting places where he meets his friends. She found his address and started taking photographs of him. She also started phoning him at work, and at home, and when he answered she hung up. The man found out that she is planning to move into a flat opposite him. After several complaints the woman was arrested and charged with stalking the man.

Case 3

A 35-year-old man was driving his two children (aged five and six) to a theme park. The son and daughter were in the back of the car. The man gave them a packet of sweets to eat during the journey. They started fighting and one of the children began to choke on the sweets. The child could not breathe and was in difficulties. The driver turned round to help and lost control of the car. It crashed into a group of people sitting at tables outside a café. Five people were injured, two seriously. The man was arrested and charged with dangerous driving.

5 **Work in groups of five to discuss each of the cases. Follow the steps below.**

For case 1:
Student A (prosecution): turn to page 160.
Student B (defence): turn to page 165.
Students C, D, E (the jury): see jury instructions below.

For case 2 change roles:
Student B (prosecution): turn to page 165.
Student C (defence): turn to page 166.
Students D, E, A (the jury): see jury instructions below.

For case 3 change roles again:
Student C (prosecution): turn to page 166.
Student D (defence): turn to page 167.
Students E, A, B (the jury): see jury instructions below.

Jury instructions:
Listen to the prosecution and defence lawyers. You may have some questions to ask. When they have finished you should think about the following:
1 **Judgement:** you should give a verdict of guilty or not guilty.
2 **Sentence:** if you reach a not guilty verdict, you should explain your reasons. If you reach a guilty verdict, you should also take the role of the judge and decide the most appropriate sentence, e.g. prison, a fine, community service (unpaid work in the community).

OTHER USEFUL PHRASES
Presenting a case
Let me summarise the facts/events for you.
There is no evidence that a crime was committed.
There can be no doubt that …
Members of the jury, the facts of this case are simple.
Discussing a verdict
On the one hand … On the other hand …
Don't you think that … ?
I don't think the facts of the case are very clear.
I've made up my mind.

STUDY SKILLS: summarising

1 Read the extract from a writing guide about summarising. What are the most important things to remember when you summarise?

> You often need to summarise something you have read, heard or seen. In each case you should pick out the main points. If you need to summarise something written, for example an article or an extract from a book, it is important to use your own words to express the ideas. After writing a summary it is a good idea to read the original again to make sure you have not missed any key points. A summary is not notes. It is a shorter version of the original text.

2a [2.31] Listen to part of a lecture on home security. What does the speaker say about the following?

a) windows   d) safety chains

b) notes   e) burglar alarms

c) ID cards

2b Read two sample summaries of the lecture. Work with a partner to decide which summary is the best.

2c Listen to the lecture again. Work with your partner and read either summary A or summary B while you are listening. Check that the points in the lecture are covered in the summary. Compare with your partner and decide if your original decision about the better summary is still true.

3 Which pieces of information are in the lecture and which does each writer use in making the summary? Tick (✓) the appropriate gaps in the table. Look at Track 2.31 on page 182 to check your answers.

	Lecture	Summary A	Summary B
1 Gives the name of the speaker.			
2 Gives the main topic (home security).			
3 Gives the order in which the information will be / is presented.			
4 Points out that people don't always use safety chains.			
5 Lists the methods for creating security.			
6 Finishes with a conclusion.			

4a [2.32] Listen to a lecture on car security and make notes. Use these headings.

- Topic
- Main points
- Conclusions

4b Use your notes to write a summary. Remember to use only the main points and note if there is a conclusion.

A

On the topic of home security, the expert mentioned a number of methods to protect you and your home, ranging from methods that cost nothing to some that are quite expensive. The methods, from the cheapest to the most expensive, were: keeping front doors and windows closed; not leaving signs that you are not at home; asking for identification; fitting window locks; installing and using a safety chain on the front door; fitting more secure locks to all doors; and installing a burglar alarm. Using these methods will prevent most burglaries. [91 words]

B

There are a number of methods you can use to prevent security problems in your house. You can do simple things like closing your windows and leaving a security chain on the front and back door or you can put plenty of locks on the windows and install a burglar alarm that makes a lot of noise if someone is trying to break into the house. Never let anyone into the house unless you know them well. [76 words]

WRITING SKILL: a narrative using cause and effect

5a Linkers Match the sentence halves below to make sentences showing cause and effect. What linking words do we use to introduce an effect?

1 There was an accident on the motorway in the rush hour.

2 The tutor was ill that morning

3 The lecturer said that we were all in danger of failing the exam.

4 The police caught him speeding.

a) As a result, we all worked very hard and passed.

b) … so he made an appointment with the doctor.

c) The result was a substantial fine.

d) Consequently, everyone was late for work.

5b Write sentences describing the results of these situations. Use the linking words from Exercise 5a.

1 The radio news did not report the accident.
The radio news did not report the accident. As a result huge queues formed on the motorway.

2 The child was bitten by a dog.

3 Police presence in the city centre has decreased.

4 Her managers were really pleased with her work.

5 The train was very overcrowded …

6 The plane had a tailwind of 100 kilometres per hour.

6 Read the witness statement and make a list of five causes and effects in the statement.

7 Narrative using cause and effect Read the points below and write a witness statement (the story of what happened).

Situation: Witness on foot near the traffic lights at Westward Hill

Date: Today's date

Time: 8.30 a.m.

Location: Crossroads of Westward Hill and Consort Road

Weather: Raining; poor visibility

Incident: Driver of blue van talking on mobile; van goes through red light

Result 1: Van crashes into a taxi.

Result 2: Taxi crashes into a bus stop.

Result 3: Taxi driver and four people at the bus stop injured.

Result 4: All injured taken to hospital.

Result 5: Van driver arrested by police.

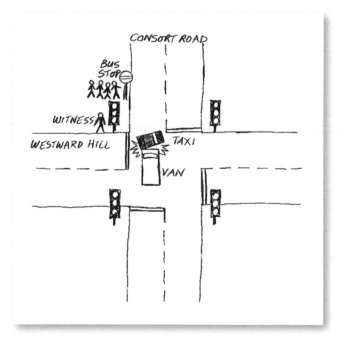

WITNESS STATEMENT

On Monday 17 December 2007, at approximately 9.30 a.m. I was riding my bicycle along George Street in the direction of the town centre. I was late for work due to the heavy traffic. A new, silver Mercedes, registration number KD57PRL, was coming towards me and passed very close to me at speed. This caused me to lose my balance, which then resulted in me falling off the bicycle. As a result, I injured my ankle quite badly. I do not know the speed at which the vehicle was travelling but it appeared to me that he passed by me very closely and very quickly.

As I was falling onto the road, I looked up and saw the Mercedes crash into a white van opposite the newsagent's. However, the driver did not stop and check what he had done. I think he was scared so he reversed and then drove away. The driver was a male in his thirties with blond hair wearing a dark leather coat.

1

A 15-year-old schoolgirl has been sent to prison in Germany for missing school. Maggie Haineder, from Goerlitz in Saxony, was given two weeks in prison after she missed more than three weeks of school. One critic said, 'The judge's decision is crazy,' but Judge Andreas Pech replied, 'She received a fine which she did not pay. She has to go to jail.'

2

A prisoner who had escaped from a prison in Ghent tried to return but they wouldn't let him in. The robber Hakim Ghazouani, 24, had escaped from the prison after a visit to the doctor last month. After talking to his solicitor the robber returned to the prison and asked, 'Can I come back in?' However, he didn't have his identity card. The Prison Director Pierre Detilloux said, 'We didn't know who he was. It would have been a scandal if we had locked up the wrong person.'

3

A prisoner posted himself from a high-security prison in Germany in a large cardboard box. The box was picked up by the postman and taken to the local post office. It is the second time a convict has tried this in the last month. An Austrian prisoner also escaped from Graz prison by posting himself. A German police spokesperson said, 'We are still looking for the man.'

GRAMMAR

1a Read the three articles quickly and match each with one of the headlines a–c below.

a) ADDRESSED TO FREEDOM   b) LET ME IN!

c) TEENAGER LEARNS HER LESSON

1b Read the opinions below and match them with the correct article from Exercise 1a. Then choose the correct answer in each.

1 He *can get / could have got* the idea from reading about the other prisoner. _____

2 If she*'d paid / paid* the fine, she could have gone home. _____

3 They *can't / can* have checked the box before it was sent out. _____

4 They should *have / had* seen him get inside. _____

5 It might not have happened if prison security would *have / had* been better. _____

6 If he'd had his identity card, they *would / wouldn't* have let him in. _____

7 He *must / might* have lost the card somewhere. That's the only explanation. _____

8 If she*'d gone / went* to her lessons, she wouldn't have been sent to prison. _____

2 Read the articles again and complete the sentences below using reported speech.

1 One critic said that the judge's decision _____ crazy.

2 The judge replied that she _____ paid her fine.

3 The prisoner asked _____ back in.

4 The prison director said that they _____ the man was.

5 A German police spokesperson said that they _____ the man.

VOCABULARY

3 Read the TV guide and complete gaps 1–10 with the words below.

	Channel 1	The News Channel	Movie Plus
8.00	**Mr Bean** The hilarious 1_____ show returns with all the usual characters.	**Technology Now** Keep up to date with the latest 4_____ in the world of cyberspace.	**Behind the scenes** Looking at how film-makers produce breathtaking special 6_____.
9.00	**The Chase** A new detective 2_____ begins starring Ralph Roland. In this first episode he begins by 3_____ a kidnapping.	**Financial News** All the city news, with a special report on the continued 5_____ in IT shares.	**Star Wars III** The classic science 7_____ adventure continues. This time our 8_____ must choose between good and evil.

1 a) comedy   b) documentary   c) page turner
   d) genre

2 a) series   b) crime   c) chapter   d) novel

3 a) placing   b) investigating   c) increasing
   d) looking

4 a) modern   b) trends   c) recent   d) steady

5 a) stable   b) growth   c) level off   d) chart

6 a) affairs   b) effects   c) fiction   d) drama

7 a) episode   b) atmosphere   c) moving
   d) fiction

8 a) hero   b) sequel   c) set   d) pitch

KEY LANGUAGE

4 **2.33** Listen to three university students discussing their new recreation area and answer the questions.

1 What was wrong with the previous coffee bar?

2 What are the benefits of the new area?

5a Complete the words in the dialogue.

A: OK. Thank you all for coming. We're here to ¹d_____ the new space the University has given us for a coffee bar. Firstly, I'd like to say that it's ²c_____ to me that the new area is much better than what we had before so I'd like us to be positive about it.

B: I agree. I was very ³u_____ with the appearance of the old coffee bar. It had lots of bad paintings on the wall and really uncomfortable seats. I think this new area could be a much nicer place to relax.

A: Thank you for your ⁴c_____ – I think we'd all agree with you. This is very ⁵d_____ from the old recreation area. For a start, the room is in a completely new building and nearer the lecture rooms.

C: Sorry, could I just ⁶s_____ something please? I think the university could give us ⁷s_____ much better than this area. After all, we pay fees …

A: I understand that but you can look at it in two ⁸w_____. Yes, it's not perfect, but it's better than what we had.

5b Listen again and check your answers.

LANGUAGE CHECK

6 Write in the missing words in sentences 1–10. Look at the pages to check your answers.

1 I've met plenty designers who come from Italy. (page 105)

2 A lot fashion models don't eat enough. (page 105)

3 The government wants to continue discuss it until they make a decision. (page 107)

4 My father is really good listening. (page 107)

5 I'm very concerned the current situation. (page 109)

6 Sales tend to level after the Christmas period. (page 111)

7 He told me call back later. (page 115)

8 When we spoke earlier he told that he wasn't coming in today. (page 115)

9 The customer asked she could return the dress. (page 116)

10 If they'd learnt this the first time, we wouldn't had to do it again. (page 125)

LOOK BACK

7 Find the exercises in Units 10–12 where you …

• learn the order of adjectives. (U10)

• take part in a meeting. (U10)

• write a review. (U11)

• read about a recluse. (U11)

• listen to a journalist talking about an interview. (U11)

• learn words for different types of criminals. (U12)

• solve a crime. (U12)

• summarise a lecture. (U12)

Language reference

GRAMMAR

G1 Question forms

Present simple questions

Use present simple questions to ask about regular or habitual actions and general truths or states. In questions with the verb *to be* and with modal verbs, put the verb before the subject.

Am I a suitable person for the job?
Can they take the test today?

With other questions in the present simple, use the auxiliary verb *do/does*.

Do you feel happier about college now?
How often **do** they travel to work together?

Past simple questions

Use past simple questions to ask about a past action. Form this question in the same way as the present simple but put the auxiliary verbs in their past form.

Was she very intelligent when you knew her?
Did you feel embarrassed when it happened?

Present continuous questions

Use present continuous questions to ask about an action happening at the moment or around the time of speaking or about a changing situation. Form this question by putting the verb *to be* before the subject.

Is he **interviewing** students at the moment?
Are they **considering** what to study at university?

Present perfect questions

Use this question to ask about the recent past or an event at an unknown time. Form this question by putting the verb *has/have* before the subject.

Has Martin found out his score?
Have they ever measured their intelligence?

! Don't use the auxiliary *do/does* with questions in the present continuous and present perfect.
~~Do you working~~ at the moment? ✗
~~Do you have finished~~ your work? ✗

G2 Subject and object questions

Subject questions ask about the **subject** of a sentence.

subject
↓
Who designed the IQ tests?
Philip Carter designed the IQ tests.

Object questions ask about the **object** of a sentence.

object
↓
What did Philip Carter design?
He designed **the IQ tests**.

For subject questions, don't add an auxiliary verb:
Who gave you that present? ✓
Who did give you that present? ✗

We usually only use *who*, *what* and *which* to ask subject questions.
Who wrote the test?
What happened last night?

G3 Present simple and present continuous

Use the present simple to describe:

• a regular or habitual action.
She usually **takes** the train to work.

We often use adverbs or time expressions of frequency with this use of the present simple: *often, usually, sometimes, once a week, twice a month*.

• a fact or general truth.
Many people **don't believe** in horoscopes.
Bill Clinton **spends** most of his time in his home country of the USA.

Use the present continuous to describe:

• an action happening around now (often temporary).
Sorry, she**'s speaking** to someone at the moment.
We**'re** currently **looking** for new people.

• a trend or changing situation.
Prices **are rising** steadily at present.
More and more people **are learning** English.

• a photograph or a scene.
In the photograph, the two people **are talking**.

G4 State verbs

State verbs describe something passive or a state, for example the verbs *be*, *like*, *believe*, *understand*, *know*, *prefer*, *depend*. We rarely use state verbs in the continuous.

I know lots of ambitious people. ✓
~~I'm knowing~~ lots of ambitious people. ✗

KEY LANGUAGE

KL Giving opinions, agreeing and disagreeing

I don't know.	Come on …	I don't agree.
I think …	Well, it's true.	Great idea.

VOCABULARY

V1 Personality adjectives

adventurous, ambitious, assertive, bossy, cautious, creative, easy-going, energetic, even-tempered, generous, hard-working, moody, open-minded, organised, quiet, reliable, self-confident, sensible, sensitive, serious, sociable, strong-willed, talkative, thoughtful

V2 Prefixes

antisocial, bicycle, bilingual, discomfort, dislike, ex-baseball player, ex-boss, ex-president, misbehave, misunderstand, monorail, outperform, outrun, overconfident, overshadowed, redefine, redo, semicircle, underrated, underuse

G1 **1** Write the missing words in sentences 1–10.

1 A: _____ he the right person for the job?
   B: Yes, I'd say so.

2 A: _____ you feel better about taking the test?
   B: Yes, I'm less nervous now I know what it is.

3 A: _____ he work well in a team?
   B: Yes, he's good with other people.

4 A: What exactly _____ your horoscope say?
   B: The same as usual. That I'll be lucky this week.

5 A: _____ they _____ all their homework?
   B: Yes, they have.

6 A: What _____ you working on at the moment?
   B: I'm working on a proposal for a film.

7 A: _____ we ask you a few questions?
   B: Yes, of course.

8 A: When _____ Carl Jung born?
   B: In 1875.

9 A: What _____ he study at university?
   B: Medicine, from 1894 to 1900.

10 A: _____ he _____ his final exam?
   B: Yes, he took it last week.

G2 **2** Read the sentences and complete the questions. The underlined word(s) should be the answer.

1 Bill Clinton is an ex-President.
   Who is *Bill Clinton*?

2 Myers Briggs designed the test.
   Who _____?

3 Oprah Winfrey owns several houses.
   What _____?

4 Marilyn Monroe married Joe DiMaggio.
   Who _____?

5 He's able to speak three languages.
   How many _____?

6 Spring is my favourite time of the year.
   What _____?

7 My boss is the reason I'm leaving.
   What _____?

G3,4 **3** A university lecturer is interviewing a new student. Write the verbs in the present simple or present continuous.

A: How ¹_____ you _____ (study)? What's your approach?

B: Well I ²_____ (work) really well early in the mornings. Most of my friends stay up late but I ³_____ (prefer) the early hours.

A: So do you find it difficult to work with others?

B: Not necessarily. It ⁴_____ (depend) what the task is. For example, at the moment I ⁵_____ (work) with a group of people. We ⁶_____ (set up) a club for young kids in the town centre.

A: Really? That's good. Now, ⁷_____ you _____ (know) about the exam at the end of every term?

B: Yes, I read about that.

A: How do you find exams?

B: Well! I ⁸_____ (get) worried before exams but I think I ⁹_____ (get) better at staying calm.

KL **4** Complete the dialogue with the phrases below. There is one extra phrase.

a) I don't agree   c) Great idea!   e) it's true
b) I think   d) I don't know f) come on

A: ¹_____ we should employ Sandra. She's the most cheerful.

B: Well, ²_____ that she was the happiest of everyone but ³_____ – she has absolutely no previous experience.

A: But you don't need experience to answer the phone.

B: ⁴_____. How you answer the phone can make the difference in business.

A: Do you think we could train her?

B: ⁵_____. That might take too much time and money …

V1 **5** Write the missing vowels in the adjectives.

1 You need to be an _dv_nt_r__s sort of person to go climbing in the mountains.

2 Don't be too c__t___s about saying what you think in meetings.

3 Running at 6 a.m. looks a bit too _n_rg_t_c for me. I prefer sleeping.

4 Don't talk to him. He's always m__dy on a Monday morning.

5 Gill is one of our most r_l__bl_ employees. She's always on time.

6 You look rather th__ghtf_l. What's are you considering?

7 People who are _p_n-m_nd_d are often good listeners.

8 This job needs someone who is s_lf-c_nf_d_nt.

V2 **6** Complete the words with a prefix from the box.

| out | bi | anti | over | re | under |
| dis | mis | mono | ex- | | |

1 _____social   6 _____shadowed
2 _____cycle   7 _____define
3 _____comfort   8 _____perform
4 _____understand   9 _____president
5 _____rail   10 _____rated

7 Complete the sentences with words from Exercise 6.

1 Can I borrow your _____? It's too far to walk.

2 Every time I ask you to do something, you seem to _____ what I say.

3 This new film is _____. The critics said it was boring but I thought it was great.

4 My brother was always better than me at school and completely _____ me.

5 At the airport, take the _____ from one terminal to the other. It's faster than the bus.

8 Make five more sentences with the other words.

Language reference

GRAMMAR

G1 Past simple

Form the past simple of most regular verbs by adding -*ed* to the end of the verb.

jump – jump**ed**
last – last**ed**

With verbs ending in -*e*, add -*d* only.

dance – danc**ed**
die – di**ed**

With verbs ending in -*y*, remove -*y* and add -*ied*.

carry – carr**ied**
hurry – hurr**ied**

Where a verb ends with the letter *t* or *d*, the -*ed* is an extra syllable and is pronounced /ɪd/.

lasted /'laːstɪd/
landed /'lændɪd/

For other verbs the -*ed* is pronounced either /t/ or /d/, depending on the sound at the end of the verb.

jumped /dʒʌmpt/
received /rɪ'siːvd/

Many commonly used verbs have an irregular past simple form, for example:

become – became   lead – lead
begin – began   take – took
write – wrote   go – went

Use the past simple to refer to finished actions that are in the past.

I began school in 1989.
He set out across Europe in 1271.

We often use the past simple when we know or say the exact time of the action and with time expressions such as *yesterday*, *last week*, *in 1271*.

G2 Present perfect

Form the present perfect with *has/have* (*'s/'ve*) + past participle of the verb.

She**'s sailed** round the world.
They**'ve climbed** Mount Everest.

Use the present perfect to talk about:

• finished actions in a time period that continues up to now. We often use time expressions such as *today*, *this week*, *this year*.
  We've been really busy **all week**.
  You've worked hard **all year**.

• experiences in our lives when we don't say when they happened. We often use adverbs such as *never*, *ever*, *already*, *yet*, *just*.
  Have you **ever** visited their house?
  They've **never** climbed Mont Blanc.

already, yet and ever

These three adverbs are often used in conjunction with the present perfect:

• *ever* is used in questions to refer to any time up to the present:
  Have you **ever** been to Germany?

• *already* is used in affirmative sentences and questions to refer to an event close to the present that has happened:
  We've **already** done that. What's next?

• *yet* is used in questions and negative sentences to refer to an event that is planned or expected but not completed:
  I haven't had time to do it **yet**.

! We use *already* and *ever* before the main verb but *yet* comes at the end of the sentence.
  I have **already** finished it.
  Sorry, I haven't finished it **yet**.

G3 Present perfect and past simple

The present perfect and past simple both refer to the past but the present perfect doesn't necessarily say or imply when something happened.

We've already found someone suitable.

The present perfect and past simple can both refer to finished actions but the past simple refers to a specific past time and the present perfect to a time continuing up to now.

We looked for someone suitable last year.
We've looked for someone suitable this year.

! We rarely use adverbs such as *ever*, *already*, *yet* with the past simple.

KEY LANGUAGE

KL Discussing advantages and disadvantages, making suggestions

There are arguments for and against.
On the one hand … On the other hand …
Another disadvantage of … is that …
I think we should …
It'd be a good idea to …
I suggest we …
How about …

VOCABULARY

V1 Travel

abroad, destination, home, journey, package holiday, travel (n), trip

V2 Travel expressions

become more independent, broaden your horizons, experience different cultures, explore new places, find yourself, get away from it all, learn a new language, learn new skills, meet new people, see new sights

V3 Phrasal verbs

get back, look around, carry on, set out, get to, stop off

Extra practice

G1 **1** Complete the text with the past simple form of the verbs in the box.

lead	start	have	cross	run
stop	be	fly	complete	

Sir Ranulph Fiennes ^{1}_____ born in 1944. In the army he ^{2}_____ several expeditions, including a hovercraft expedition on the White Nile and crossing from the North to the South Pole. He ^{3}_____ the Antarctic on foot, but seven years later illness ^{4}_____ his solo trek to the North Pole and in 2003, he ^{5}_____ heart surgery to save his life. Only four months after the operation, he ^{6}_____ seven marathons in seven continents in seven days. He ^{7}_____ in Santiago, Chile and then ^{8}_____ to the Falkland Islands, Sydney, Singapore, London and Cairo. He ^{9}_____ the marathons in New York.

2 Speaking practice Work with a partner to talk about:
- one thing you did last weekend.
- how you celebrated your last birthday.
- what you learnt in your last English lesson.

G2 **3** Put the word in brackets in the correct place in each sentence.

1 Have you been to France? (ever)
2 I've told you that – don't ask me again. (already)
3 Bill and Martin have seen it so let's watch it now. (never)
4 Haven't you finished it? (yet)
5 Have you finished your lunch? (already)
6 Why haven't you told me? (ever)
7 I haven't had time to speak to her. (yet)
8 Has he been late for class? (ever)

G3 **4** Write the words in brackets in the past simple or the present perfect.

1 They _____ (climb) Mount Everest twice before and are going for a third time this year.
2 _____ you ever _____ (ride) on a camel?
3 When _____ he _____ (die)?
4 _____ he _____ (have) time to see Martin last week?
5 He _____ (just announce) another attempt to reach the South Pole.
6 She _____ (raise) money for charity last year by crossing the desert.
7 I _____ (never live) abroad. What's it like?
8 We _____ (meet) loads of wonderful people when we went to Ethiopia last year.
9 How many exams _____ you _____ (have) so far this month?
10 I _____ (visit) so many countries in my life that I can't remember them all.

KL **5** Put the words in the correct order to make expressions.

1 On the … cold   one   hand   it's
2 On the … beautiful   it's   other   hand
3 There are … for   arguments   against   and
4 Another … is that   expensive   disadvantage   it's
5 It'd be … to   a   idea   ask   people   other   good
6 I think … see   should   what   we   say   they

V1 **6** Match the words in the box with the meanings below.

abroad	travel	destination
journey	trip	package holiday

1 going to different places _____
2 in a different country _____
3 the time spent travelling from one place to another, often over a long distance _____
4 a short journey, often for work _____
5 where you're trying to get to _____
6 a holiday that has a fixed price and includes travel, accommodation, etc. _____

V2 **7** Match the sentence halves.

1 They say travel helps you to find
2 You should broaden
3 I prefer to explore
4 Most people just go abroad to
5 Travel makes you become
6 I like places where you experience different
7 We saw some incredible

a) more independent.
b) yourself but I think it's just running away.
c) new sights.
d) your horizons with a journey.
e) get away from it all.
f) cultures.
g) new places and meet new people.

V3 **8** Underline the correct word.

1 Did you have time to look *out / around*?
2 We set *out / in* on our adventure as the sun was rising.
3 Ask the taxi driver to carry *on / along* to the end of the road.
4 Let's stop *out / off* at the temple on the way.
5 How do you get *out / to* the market?
6 What time does he get *return / back* from work?

GRAMMAR

G1 Present perfect continuous

Form the present perfect continuous with *have/has* (*'ve/'s*) + *been* + *-ing*.

> He**'s been working** from home.
> Employers **have been investing** in video conference technology.

We use the present perfect continuous to talk about actions and situations that continue into the present.

> I've been studying at Oxford University for two years (and I am still studying there).
> They've been talking on the phone for two hours (and they are still talking).

We often use the present perfect continuous with the time expressions *since* and *for*. Use *since* to refer to a point in time and *for* to indicate a period of time.

> I've been studying at Oxford University **since 2006.**
> I've been studying at Oxford University **for two years.**

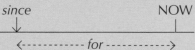

We don't usually use state verbs with the continuous form.

> I've ~~been knowing~~ John for years. ✗
> I've known John for years. ✓

G2 Present perfect simple and present perfect continuous

We use the present perfect simple to emphasise:

- that an action started in the past and is completed.
  I've prepared the leaflets you asked for.
  They've interviewed everyone.

- the result of the activity, for example by telling us how much or how many.
  We've asked over five hundred people.
  He's done all his homework.
  How many people have you interviewed?
  How much of your work have you done?

We use the present perfect continuous to emphasise:

- that an action started in the past and is still continuing.
  She's been working here for over three years.
  We've been writing letters to all the candidates.

- the activity and its duration, for example by telling us how long.
  Roger has been playing tennis for years.
  Roger has been playing tennis since he was a boy.
  How long have you been working here?

KEY LANGUAGE

KL Asking questions, giving answers

Framing questions

I'd also like to know …
I'm (also) interested in knowing …
A question we like to ask all our …
I was wondering what/if/when …
A question now about …
Let me follow that up with another question.
Moving on, can/could you tell me …
Just one last/final question …

Framing answers

I'm glad you asked me that.
That's a very good question.
Without going into too much detail, …
Let me just think about that for a moment.
I thought you might ask me that.
I haven't really thought about that.
I'm not an expert, but …
I'm afraid I don't know the answer to that.

VOCABULARY

V1 Adjectives connected with work

boring, challenging, exciting, flexible, glamorous, repetitive, rewarding, satisfying, stressful

V2 Dependent prepositions

depend on, experience of, fluency in, knowledge of, look for, prospects for, report to, responsible for

V3 Expressions connected with time and work

spend time, time-consuming, time management, work-life balance, workstation

Extra practice

G1 **1 Complete the sentences with *for* or *since*.**

1 I've been trying to call you _____ hours – where have you been?
2 _____ the last six years he's been living in France.
3 She's been studying English _____ she left school.
4 _____ 1990, the council have been spending much more on public transport.
5 I've been looking for that _____ weeks – where did you find it?

2 Complete the sentences with the words in the box.

you	since	watching	been	long	haven't
has	for	hasn't	teaching	having	

1 Rose _____ been building this house _____ 1995.
2 I've _____ reading all day.
3 How _____ have _____ been working here?
4 They _____ been studying hard enough. They must work harder.
5 We've been _____ at this school _____ two years. The kids are great.
6 He _____ been getting enough sleep. He's really tired.
7 She's been _____ guitar lessons for ages but she still can't play a tune.
8 I don't know what happened in the series. I haven't been _____ the TV recently.

G2 **3 Underline the correct verb form.**

1 We've *prepared / been preparing* three boxes and they're all ready to be sent.
2 Can you take over? I've *packed / been packing* these all morning. I need a rest.
3 Have you *waited / been waiting* long?
4 How long have we *driven / been driving* now?
5 I've *written / been writing* fifty letters so far today.
6 We've only *seen / been seeing* the first five minutes of the film, so sit down.
7 How long have they *been / been being* here?
8 I've *worked / been working* all morning so I'm really tired.

KL **4 Write the missing prepositions in sentences 1–6.**

1 I'm also interested _____ knowing about your last job.
2 A question now _____ your long-term ambitions.
3 Moving _____, can you tell me why you want the job?
4 Let me follow that _____ with another question.
5 Without going _____ too much detail, can you tell us why?
6 I'm afraid I don't know the answer _____ that.

5 Put the words in the correct order to make expressions.

1 one last question just
2 I'm you asked that me glad
3 question good that's a very
4 just think for a let about that moment me
5 you might me thought ask I that

V1 **6 Match the descriptions of people's jobs with the adjectives in the box.**

flexible glamorous stressful
challenging rewarding

1 'I'm a Hollywood actress. I'll be at the Oscars next month.' _____
2 'We work long hours and take complaints from members of the public. I need to see a doctor!' _____
3 'As long as I work 35 hours a week my boss doesn't mind when I work. So some days I start at 9 a.m. and some days at midday.' _____
4 'I work with a children's charity. It's hard work but I really feel I'm helping people.' _____
5 'The next expedition is through the Amazon rainforest by boat.' _____

V2 **7 Match the sentence halves.**

1 We're looking
2 I wouldn't depend
3 We need someone with fluency
4 Knowledge
5 My experience
6 You'll report
7 There's good prospects

a) in Polish.
b) to me.
c) on her to remember.
d) of management is limited.
e) for promotion.
f) of Java programming would be helpful.
g) for a candidate with a degree.

V3 **8 Complete the sentences with either *work* or *time*.**

1 Don't spend too much _____ on this.
2 We don't have our own offices where I work but I have my own _____ station.
3 You can improve your _____ management with proper planning.
4 Nowadays more and more people are trying to get a good _____-life balance.
5 Meetings are really _____-consuming and not always useful.

Language reference

GRAMMAR

G1 Future forms

Will

Use *will* (*'ll*) to:

* make decisions and promises at the time of speaking.
  He hasn't arrived yet, so we**'ll** just have to go without him.
  Sorry, I'm a bit busy. I**'ll** call you back in five minutes.
* make predictions about the future.
  Don't worry, I'm sure you**'ll** pass your exam.

We often introduce the *will* future with words and expressions like *think*, *probably*, *it's (un)likely*, *I'm certain*.

  I (don't) think you'll be able to learn Spanish.
  They'll **probably** call us before they leave.
  It's (un)likely that we'll stop for a meal somewhere.
  I'm certain Rachel will be there.

Going to

Use *going to* to talk about plans or intentions (something which you have already decided).

  We're **going to** visit my friends next week.
  They're **going to** watch a film tonight.

The present continuous

Use the present continuous to talk about fixed future arrangements, usually involving other people.

  I'm meeting Peter at the cinema at seven.
  Nobody else **is coming** to the party.

G2 First conditional

Form the first conditional in the following way:

if-clause	+	main clause
if + present simple		*will/may/might/should,* etc.

  If people only **learn** English at school, other languages **will die** out.
  If you **come** to my house first, we **can go** together.
  If he **asks** you for help, you **should say** yes.

We don't use *will* in the if-clause.

  If people ~~will only learn~~ English at school, other language ~~die out~~. ✗

Use the first conditional to talk about real possibilities.

  If they don't hurry, they'll miss the plane!
  I'll revise more if it helps me pass the exam.

We can put the main clause first. If we do this, we don't use a comma.

  We might buy a car if I save enough money.

Unless

Unless means the same as *if not*.

  Unless we protect languages, they'll become extinct.
  = **If** we **don't** protect languages, they'll become extinct.

! We don't use a negative structure in the *unless*-clause.

  ~~Unless we don't~~ protect languages, they'll become extinct. ✗

When and *as soon as*

When and *as soon as* can replace *if* in the first conditional. We use them when we are very certain that something will happen.

  When they arrive, call me and I**'ll** meet them.
  As soon as they arrive, we**'ll** start the meeting.

! We never use a future tense with these time expressions.

  ~~When the train will arrive,~~ I'll give you a call. ✗

KEY LANGUAGE

KL Accepting and rejecting ideas, considering consequences

I don't know about that.
I think you're right.
Yes, I think that would work.
I'm afraid I don't like that idea.
Good idea.
It's definitely worth considering.
I'm not sure about that.
If we do that, it will … (cause some problems).

VOCABULARY

V1 Language learning

accent, bilingual, dialect, foreign, grammar, native (adj), slang

V2 Phrasal verbs

catch on, fall behind, get by, keep up with, let down, pick up, take up

V3 Permission

allow, let, permit

V4 Extinction

devastate, die out, disappear, disappearance, disastrous, extinct, extinction

G1 **1** Write the words in brackets in the correct tense: *will*, *going to* or present continuous.

1 A: I bought this phone from you but it doesn't work.
   B: OK. Leave it here and I _____ (look) at it as soon as I have time.
2 It's all arranged. We _____ (meet) at 2 p.m. by the market square.
3 We've discussed it and we _____ (get) married!
4 I don't think I _____ (do) anything on Monday. Can we meet then?
5 A: What do you intend to do about Lillian?
   B: We _____ (offer) her an extension on the essay.
6 I haven't made up my mind yet but I _____ (probably go) to the lesson tonight.
7 You should go to the party. I'm certain that Frank _____ (be) there.
8 Thanks for the offer, but I think I _____ (stay) at home tonight.

G2 **2** Complete the second sentence so that it has a similar meaning to the first, using the words given.

1 If you don't revise, you won't pass your exams.
   If you revise, _____.
2 If we see your teacher, we should ask him for the correct answer.
   We should ask your teacher for the correct answer when _____.
3 The world might only have one or two languages in the future if we don't protect them.
   The world might only have one or two languages in the future unless _____.
4 I won't go if you don't go.
   I won't go unless _____.
5 I'll be there at about 5 p.m. unless there's lots of traffic.
   If _____, I'll be there at about 5 p.m.
6 We'll go for coffee as soon as the class ends.
   When _____.
7 I'll give you a call if I'm not busy this afternoon.
   Unless _____ I'll give you a call.
8 You shouldn't go out so much if you don't have much money.
   If you don't have _____ stay in.

KL **3** Complete the words in the dialogue.

A: So we all agree our staff need English lessons. But the problem is when? What about at lunchtime?
B: No, I'm not ¹s_____ about that. Staff won't like it. They'll complain.
C: I ²t_____ you're right. When are they supposed to eat? I think after work is better.
A: If we do that, it will ³c_____ some problems because people finish at different times.
B: Let's look at the consequences. If we have them during working hours, it'll cost us money.

C: Yes, but they would work harder. It's definitely ⁴w_____ considering.
A: I'm afraid I don't ⁵l_____ that idea. Money isn't the only problem. How can we have everyone joining the class in the middle of the day?

V1 **4** Match the words in the box to their definitions.

> foreign   dialect   grammar   accent   bilingual   native

1 the way you say words in a language _____
2 from another country _____
3 able to speak two languages fluently _____
4 a way of speaking in a particular region of a country _____
5 from or belonging to a particular country _____
6 the rules of language _____

V2 **5** Choose the correct word.

1 When I'm nervous, my English lets me *off / down*.
2 Don't fall *behind / ahead* with your homework.
3 I have a friend who just seems to pick languages *off / up*. I think she knows six!
4 I can get *by / on* in Spanish – in restaurants, for example.
5 Children tend to catch *on / along* more quickly.
6 Have you ever thought of taking *off / up* Chinese?
7 Slow down! I can't keep up *at / with* you.

V3,4 **6** Read the opinion and complete the gaps with the words in the box.

> allow   die   disastrous   extinction   let   disappearance

'In my opinion we can't ¹_____ so many languages to ²_____ out. It would be ³_____ if eventually the only language anyone spoke in the world was, for example, English. The ⁴_____ of languages is rather like what has happened to so many of our species of animals in the past. Their ⁵_____ has made the world a less interesting and varied place today. In some countries everyone has to speak the official language and governments don't ⁶_____ children use their native tongue in schools. We must do more to protect the world's languages.'

5 Language reference

GRAMMAR

G1 Second conditional
Form the second conditional in the following way:

   if-clause   +   **main clause**
   if + past simple   *would/could/might,* etc.

If she **knew** the answer, she **could help** you.
If they **gave** a discount, **would** you **buy** it?

We use the second conditional to talk about an unreal situation in the present or future.

As with the first conditional, we can put the main clause first.

I'd help you if I had time.

were and *was*

Both are possible in the second conditional, with no change in meaning.

If I **was** a politician, I'd make some big changes.
If I **were** a politician, I'd make some big changes.

When we give advice, we often use *were*.

If I **were** you, I'd take the job.

G2 Comparison
Form the comparative of one-syllable adjectives by adding -er, and the superlative of one-syllable adjectives by adding -est.

  great – greater – greatest
  big – bigger – biggest

With two-syllable adjectives ending in -ow and -er, add -er or -est. With adjectives ending in y, add -ier or -iest.

  narrow – narrower – narrowest
  clever – cleverer – cleverest
  happy – happier – happiest

Form the comparative of other two-syllable adjectives and longer adjectives by adding *more* before the adjective, and the superlative by adding *most* before the adjective.

  hopeful – more hopeful – most hopeful
  interesting – more interesting – most interesting

! There are exceptions. Put *more/most* (not -er/-est) before one syllable adjectives which are past participles, for example:
  tired – more tired – most tired
  lost – more lost – most lost

less and *least*

Use *less* or *least* before any adjective. The number of syllables is not important.

It's **less** expensive.
It's **the least** expensive.

Irregular adjectives

The adjectives *good* and *bad* are irregular and do not follow the rules above.

  good – better – best
  bad – worse – worst

Modifiers

Modifiers help us to comment on the size of the difference in the comparison. To talk about a large difference, use *a lot* or *much*. To talk about a small difference, use *a little* or *not much*.

China is **a lot** more populated than Norway.
Italy isn't **much** bigger than England.

as … as

Use *as* + adjective + *as* to say there is no difference.

This Coca-Cola advert is **as good as** this Pepsi advert.
The twins are **as tall as** each other.

Use *not as* + adjective + *as* to make the adjective weaker.

I'm **not as sure as** you that this is a good idea.
The film wasn't **as good as** I expected it would be.

KEY LANGUAGE

KL The language of presentations
Beginning a presentation
I'd like to introduce my colleagues …

Stating the main purpose of the presentation
Our purpose today is to …

Giving the plan/structure
My presentation is divided into three/four parts.
If you have any questions, we'd be pleased to answer them at the end of the presentation.

Talking about a new point
Moving on now, …

Referring to a visual aid
This brings me to my next point.
Please look at the screen.

Ending a presentation
Now, let me summarise our main points.
Thank you very much for your attention.
Are there any questions?

VOCABULARY

V1 Advertising
attention-grabbing, catchy, commercial (n), dull, effective, endorse, exotic, eye-catching, logo, misleading, original, persuasive, promote, shocking, slogan, sponsorship, witty

V2 Advertising methods
classified ad, endorsement, handbill, mail order, poster, product placement, TV commercial, wall/rock painting, word-of-mouth

V3 Word combinations
advertising manager, attractive target, fast food, interactive website, junk food, persuasive message, television advertisement, vast sums

G1 **1** Write the verb in brackets in the correct form to make second conditional sentences. Use *could* and *might* when possible.

1 If we _____ (advertise) more, we'd sell more.
2 What _____ (happen) if we put a poster up?
3 If I knew the number, I _____ (give) them a call.
4 If _____ (be) you, I'd find a new USP.
5 Could you do it if I _____ (ask) you?
6 You _____ (not know) what this advert is for if you looked at it.
7 _____ you _____ (give) us a bigger budget if we needed it?
8 If we used the Internet more, the company _____ (reach) more people.

2 Speaking practice Tell a partner what you would do in different situations. Use the phrases below.
If I had …
• more money, I'd …
• a new career, it …
• time, I'd …
If I was …
• President / Prime Minister, I'd …
• ten years younger, I'd …

G2 **3** Choose the correct form.
When I first started working in the business, advertising was much ¹*less important / the most important* than it is nowadays and our budgets weren't anything like as ²*big / bigger* as they are now. Companies now realise that marketing is ³*more complex / complexer* because there are so many different kinds of media. For example, the Internet is one of the ⁴*fastest / most fast* ways of launching a new product, especially to young people. At the click of a button you can send out adverts. It's also ⁵*cheaper / cheapest* than television advertising, which takes months of planning and costs a fortune. It's true that television reaches the ⁶*higher / highest* number of people at once but in many cases Internet advertising can be just as effective ⁷*than / as* TV. For example, by choosing the right websites you are ⁸*more / most* likely to reach your target market.

4 Complete the sentences with the words and phrases in the box.

| as interesting   a little   much better |
| much more   the least |

1 My exam results weren't _____ than yours, so don't worry.
2 We can make the product _____ cheaper than it is now, but not much.
3 His new book isn't _____ as his first one.
4 This is a _____ attractive design than the last one – well done.
5 This is _____ important problem – let's discuss the other points first.

KL **5** Match the sentence halves.
1 Our presentation is divided into
2 Please look
3 I'd like to introduce
4 Let me summarise our
5 Are there
6 Thank you very much for
7 If you have any questions, we'd be pleased to answer them

a) your attention.
b) my colleagues.
c) any questions?
d) main points.
e) four parts.
f) at the screen
g) at the end.

V1 **6** Complete the words.
1 We've got a famous singer to e_____ our new soft drink.
2 That's a really e_____-c_____ image. Where was it photographed?
3 We've just agreed a s_____ deal with a Formula 1 racing team.
4 If we make a radio advert, we'll need to have a c_____ song that everyone knows.
5 Coca-Cola must have the most famous l_____ in the world.
6 It's a rather dull s_____. Can we make it wittier?
7 How about having the actors drinking the product in a really e_____ location with a beach, islands and palm trees?

V2,3 **7** Match the words to make word combinations.

1 advertising
2 TV
3 vast
4 mail
5 product
6 interactive
7 fast
8 junk
9 persuasive
10 word-of-

a) food
b) message
c) mouth
d) order
e) manager
f) website
g) food
h) placement
i) commercial
j) sums

8 Speaking practice Work with a partner. Take turns to define the word combinations in Exercise 7. Can your partner guess your definition?
The person in charge of things like TV commercials and slogans.
– *Is it the advertising manager?*

GRAMMAR

G1 Past continuous

Form the past continuous with *was/were + verb + -ing*:

I **was working** on a project for six months.
The children **weren't working** very hard.

Use the past continuous:

- to talk about background actions

  It was a beautiful day – the sun was shining and the birds were singing.

  <---- *sun was shining, birds were singing* ----> NOW

- to talk about a longer background action in the past when a shorter action interrupts it or happens during it:

  We were talking about you when you rang.

  you rang
  ↓
  <------------------- *talking* --------------------> NOW

  (the background action is interrupted and stops)

  I was having a staff meeting when Julia arrived five minutes late.

  Julia arrived
  ↓
  <------- *having a meeting* --------------> NOW

  (the action happens during the background action)

- to talk about repeated actions in the past that take place over a temporary period of time:

  People were coming in all day to buy this item.

  people coming in
  ↓ ↓ ↓ ↓ ↓   NOW
  <------- *all day* ------>

- to emphasise the duration or continuity of a past action:

  For the whole of last month we were trying to solve this same problem.

  <------- *trying to solve problem* -------> NOW

  <------------- *last month* -------------> NOW

! We rarely use state verbs such as *be, like, know, believe, understand* in the continuous form.
  I ~~was liking~~ the fish soup ✗
  I liked the fish soup. ✓

G2 Past perfect

Form the past perfect with *had + past participle*:

I called but he**'d** already **left**.
When I checked, it was obvious they **hadn't understood** the instructions.

Use the past perfect to emphasise that one action happened before another in the past:

The film had already started when we arrived at the cinema.

film started   arrived at the cinema   NOW
↓   ↓

The past perfect is often used with the conjunctions *when, before, after* and *by*:

I had left **when** he called.
She had been to Australia twice **before** we went together.
We went out **after** we had eaten breakfast.
By the age of 80 he had written over a hundred books.

If the sequence of events is clear, we can also use the past simple.

I called my friend after I finished work.

KEY LANGUAGE

KL Making offers, stating a position, bargaining

How many would you like to order?
We are thinking of placing a large order.
I'm afraid that would be a bit/very difficult.
What about if we paid earlier? Would you be able to …?
Let me check if I understand you.
How do you feel about that?
That sounds fine.

VOCABULARY

V1 Business terms and roles

charge (v), community, competitor, customer, entrepreneur, invest, law, loss, manufacturer, partner, prices, profit, retailer, staff, supplier, taxes, wages, wholesaler

V2 Business word combinations

found a company, go bankrupt, go into business, introduce a product, launch a company, launch a product, make a profit, negotiate a contract, run a company

G1 **1** Write the verbs in brackets in the past continuous or the past simple.

'When I ¹_____ (study) at university, I took a part-time job as a security guard at a factory to earn some extra money. I often ²_____ (work) at night, and one evening I ³_____ (check) the warehouse when I heard a noise. I was really scared so I ⁴_____ (call) the police. They arrived and while they ⁵_____ (search) the area they found someone asleep in a small cupboard next to the warehouse. The person ⁶_____ (be) the daytime security guard, who ⁷_____ (live) in the factory because he couldn't afford to rent a flat. He ⁸_____ (wear) pyjamas produced in the factory. The factory owners were furious at first and ⁹_____ (plan) to sack the young man but in the end they found him a cheap flat and he ¹⁰_____ (keep) his job.'

G2 **2** Match the sentence halves.

1 By the time they got to the cinema
2 He stayed out late
3 By the end of his first year at university
4 I'd just gone to sleep
5 After I'd booked the tickets

a) after I'd told him not to.
b) when the phone rang and woke me up.
c) the film had already started.
d) she changed her mind and said she wanted to eat out instead.
e) he'd already decided he didn't want to be a doctor.

G1,2 **3** Choose the correct tense.

1 We launched the second version once we *had seen / were seeing* how successful the first one was.
2 By the time he *was applying / 'd applied*, the job had already gone.
3 He called while I *tried / was trying* to finish this essay.
4 After he *had invested / was investing* more money, the business took off.
5 The entrepreneur *gave / had given* another billion dollars to charity after he had already given three billion.
6 We didn't need to clean the house, because he *had already done / already did* it.
7 I studied business in the evening while I *was working / had worked* in a kitchen.
8 She left before anyone *had had / was having* a chance to explain the situation.
9 The business *went / was going* bankrupt last month and they couldn't save it.
10 All last year, the company *had looked / was looking* for ways to survive the crisis.

G2 **4** Speaking practice Tell a partner about yourself, using the phrases below.

By the age of five, I had …
By the age of ten, I had …
By the age of 15, I had …

KL **5** Complete the sentences with the words in the box.

| placing would sounds |
| afraid feel paid check |

1 How many _____ you like to order?
2 We are thinking of _____ a large order.
3 I'm _____ that would be very difficult.
4 What if we _____ earlier?
5 Let me _____ if I understand you.
6 How do you _____ about that?
7 That _____ fine.

V1 **6** Complete the words.

1 How many s_____ do you have working here?
2 The first rule of business is that the c_____ is always right.
3 How much money did you i_____ in the company?
4 We made a huge p_____ last year.
5 Malcolm is my p_____ in the business.
6 The p_____ of computers keeps going down.
7 This government keeps putting up t_____.
8 It's much cheaper to buy products from a w_____ than from a shop.

V2 **7** Choose the correct verb(s) in each group. There may be more than one correct in each.

1 *go / make / found* … bankrupt
2 *do / launch / go into* … a company
3 *launch / introduce / found* … a product
4 *make / go into / launch* … a profit
5 *negotiate / found / run* … a contract

GRAMMAR

G1 Modals

can/can't

Use *can/can't* to talk about present ability and possibility.

> We **can** ask him if he'd like to join us.
> I **can't** ski. I don't know how to.

could

Use *could* to say something is possible or likely in the future.

> Your work on this **could** be useful later on.
> That table **could** be good for my office.

should/shouldn't

Use *should/shouldn't* to say if something is advisable or not.

> I think we **should** ask customers what they want.
> We probably **shouldn't** wait any longer to start work on this.

have to / must

We use both *have to* and *must* to talk about something that is necessary and important, but there are some differences in meaning.

- Use *have to* to say something is essential or that it is a general rule.
  > When you develop a new design you **have to** try it out a number of times.
  > It **has to** be strong enough to carry eight people.

- Use *must* to say something is necessary or important in your personal opinion.
  > I feel that we **must** make the design more modern.
  > It **must** be on my desk by the end of the day.

> ❗ We do not normally use *you must* or *you mustn't* in face-to-face conversation. Use *should* instead.
> You ~~must~~ be more careful. ✗
> You **should** be more careful. ✓

don't have to / mustn't

Use *don't have to* to say something is not necessary.

> It **doesn't have to** be made of metal. Plastic is fine.
> They **don't have to** be here. We can decide ourselves.

Use *mustn't* to say it is necessary or important **not** to do something.

> We **mustn't** forget to tell them about the party.
> They **mustn't** find out about our plans. They wouldn't like them.

G2 Modals for present deduction

Use modal verbs to make guesses (deductions) about the present, based on evidence. The different modal verbs express different levels of certainty.

must

Use *must* to say that you are certain something is true.

> The door is open so Michael **must** be home.
> Jane was ill but she's running around so she **must** be a lot better!

can't

Use *can't* to say that you are certain something is **not** true.

> This painting **can't** be by Rembrandt. It's much too modern.
> The police say he attacked someone at 7 p.m. but it **can't** be true because he was with me at that time.

could/might

Use *could* or *might* to say something is possible.

> It **could** be true that it was all his own work. It's definitely possible.
> The package **might** be from David. Open it and find out!

We can also use modal verbs with a continuous form.

> He **must be feeling** better!
> They **might be coming** later.

KEY LANGUAGE

KL Describing qualities

It looks very …

It's made of (wood/metal/leather).

There are several features I really like.

One of the best points is …

It's aimed at …

It would appeal to …

It's excellent value for money.

VOCABULARY

V1 Word building, adjectives

art, artist, artistic, design (n/v), designer, develop, developer, developing, development, engineer (n/v), engineering, innovate, innovator, innovation, innovative, invent, inventor, invention, inventive, manufacture, manufacturer, manufacturing, produce, producer, product, productive, science, scientific, scientist, use (n/v), usable, user, well-designed

V2 Design

elegant, functional, futuristic, handmade, mass-produced, retro, simple, streamlined, stylish, traditional, up to date

V3 Abstract nouns

consumerism, efficiency, industrialisation, modernity, optimism, streamlining

Extra practice

G1 **1 Complete the second sentence so that it has a similar meaning to the first, using a modal verb and any other words necessary.**

1 Sorry but I'm unable to help you with this.
  Sorry but _____ you with this.
2 I think it's important that we make it stronger.
  We _____ it stronger.
3 Is it possible for you to come with us tonight?
  _____ with us tonight?
4 It isn't necessary to ask for his permission.
  You don't _____ for his permission.
5 I'm able to use steel in this design.
  I _____ in this design.
6 I'd advise you not to bother him until after lunch.
  You _____ him until after lunch.
7 Keep that wood. It's likely to be useful later.
  Keep that wood. It _____ later.
8 The new law says that it's essential that you use recyclable products.
  You _____ recyclable products because of the new law.

G2 **2 Match replies a–f with sentences 1–6.**

1 I heard that it never rains in England.
2 My son is eating again now.
3 The front door is open.
4 He said if he was free, he'd be here by nine at the latest. It's midnight now.
5 There was a rumour about them getting married and then I saw them buying an engagement ring together.
6 Just because it's specially designed, this tiny pen cost over €200.

a) My flatmate must be home.
b) You must be joking! It never stopped when I was there.
c) He must be feeling better.
d) So what they say about them must be true.
e) That can't be true. It's only plastic.
f) He can't be coming.

G1,2 **3 Complete the sentences with the modal verbs in the box.**

> have to   must (x2)   don't have to
> shouldn't   can't   could   can

1 You _____ that now – we'll have time tomorrow.
2 You _____ speak to her like that – she's very sensitive.
3 Don't forget that you _____ buy a ticket before you get on the train.
4 I _____ start working harder or I'll fail the exams.
5 This _____ be the right way. Let's stop and ask someone.
6 Our new secretary _____ speak two foreign languages – she's really clever.

7 He's not answering the phone – he _____ be out somewhere.
8 Take something to read – there _____ be delays at the airport.

KL **4 Complete the sentences with the words in the box.**

> appeal   points   value   looks
> made   aimed   several

1 There are _____ features I really like.
2 It's _____ of metal.
3 It would _____ to business people.
4 It's excellent _____ for money.
5 It _____ very stylish.
6 It's _____ at the younger market.
7 One of the best _____ is its flexibility.

V1,2 **5 Complete the words with -ic, -er, -ive or -al.**

1 I don't think he'll like the idea – he has very tradition_____ views.
2 My nephew is a software design_____.
3 This new keyboard layout is very us_____ friendly.
4 This plan of yours is very innovat_____. Will it work?
5 He's a very artist_____ person with great skill in painting.
6 One scientif_____ theory says there's no such thing as global warming but no one takes it seriously.
7 For that spare part we'll have to contact the manufactur_____.
8 That new science fiction film is really futurist_____, with spaceships and lasers.
9 I'd like a kitchen that's function_____ rather than fashionable.
10 I'm an engine_____ specialising in bridges.

V3 **6 Complete the sentences with the words in the box.**

> industrialisation   modernity   optimism
> consumerism   streamlining   efficiency

1 I think our society is completely based on _____ these days. All we do is shop!
2 We need to improve the _____ of these machines. They currently use too much energy.
3 This all used to be countryside but all the _____ in the late eighties destroyed the landscape.
4 The _____ of this car makes it go faster and also looks great.
5 I love the _____ of this painting. The artist has thrown all the traditional ideas away and come up with something really new.
6 There's a lot of _____ in the country. People really believe things are going to get better.

8 Language reference

GRAMMAR

G1 Defining relative clauses

Use defining relative clauses to identify or define things, ideas, places, time and possessions.

> Children like subjects **which interest them.**

! Don't repeat the noun from the main clause or introduce a personal pronoun to replace it:

> Have you ever been to that museum which we just drove past it? ✗
>
> That's the man who he helped me yesterday. ✗

A defining relative clause begins with a relative pronoun or adverb.

Relative pronouns

Use *that* to refer to things, people or ideas.

> That's the book **that** I was looking for.
>
> Are you the person **that** I spoke to yesterday?
>
> You're ignoring the point **that** I was making.

Use *which* to refer to things or ideas.

> Yesterday we went to the restaurant **which** you recommended to us.

Use *who* to refer to people.

> That's the man **who** I bought my car from.

Use *whose* to refer to possession.

> He's the teacher **whose** students get the best grades.

Relative adverbs

Use *where* to refer to places.

> He studies at a university **where** some of our politicians got their degrees.

Use *when* to refer to time.

> I still remember the day **when** we first met.

If we use a relative adverb we don't normally use a preposition in the relative clause.

> That's the house where I was born in. ✗
>
> That's the hotel where we stayed last year. ✓

Subject/object relative clauses

The relative pronoun can be the subject or object of the relative clause.

> What's the name of the film that we saw yesterday? (We saw **the film**.)
>
> That's the shop which has the dress I want to buy. (**The shop** has the dress.)

If the relative pronoun is the object of the relative clause, then it can be omitted.

> What's the name of the film (that) we saw yesterday?
>
> Is she the person (who) I need to speak to?

G2 Non-defining relative clauses

Non-defining relative clauses give information about something in the main clause, but do not help to identify or define it.

> The President, **who is currently on a trip to the USA**, said he disagreed with the decision.
> (We know who the President is without the information in the relative clause.)

Non-defining relative clauses must have a comma before and after the clause.

> Our history course, which was started by Professor Smith, is ending next year.

! Do not use *that* in non-defining relative clauses. Use *who* or *which* instead.

> The course, that was also started by Professor Smith, is ending next year. ✗
>
> The course, which was also started by Professor Smith, is ending next year. ✓

We can also use non-defining relative clauses at the end of a sentence.

> Last year we visited Rome, which we thought was a really beautiful city.

Non-defining relative clauses are not common in spoken English.

KEY LANGUAGE

KL Discussing possibilities and options

Thinking about possibilities
There are several ways to deal with this.

Talking about options
The good thing is … the bad thing is …

Making suggestions
How about [+ -ing]
Supposing we …

Changing your approach
Let's see, what other things can we do?

Making a decision
That's the best solution.

Deciding what to do next
So, the next thing to do is …

VOCABULARY

V1 Education and studying

approach, compulsory education, continuous assessment, criticise, elementary school, environment, exam, fail, graduate, hand in, higher education, method, pace, pass, primary school, secondary school, unique

V2 Learning

continuing education, corporate training, correspondence course, distance learning, e-learning, home schooling, lifelong learning, postgraduate programme

Extra practice

8

G1 1 Complete the sentences with a relative pronoun or adverb. If it is possible to omit the pronoun, do not include it.

1 He's the person _____ I told you about.
2 Is this the place _____ you grew up?
3 She's the one _____ sister goes to the same class as us.
4 Do you remember the day _____ we went there all together?
5 Is this the book _____ we need to buy?
6 Do you still remember the first house _____ you lived in?
7 We need to hire someone _____ can really help the business grow.
8 It's the story of a man _____ life changes forever the day he meets a stranger in a café.

2 Combine the two sentences to make one sentence with a defining relative clause.

1 The school gets good results. I studied there.
   The school _____ gets good results.
2 The people are friendly. They live next door.
   The people _____ are friendly.
3 The girl works at the library. She was at the meeting.
   The girl _____ was at the meeting.
4 This is the station. I met John there.
   This is the station _____ I met John.
5 The idea is a good one. You suggested it yesterday.
   The idea _____ is a good one.
6 I bought the band's CD last week. They're playing here tonight.
   The band _____ CD I bought last week are playing here tonight.

G2 3 There is one mistake in each sentence. Correct it.

1 Maria Montessori who was an Italian educationalist, developed the Montessori method.
2 This course, that is run by Professor Jones, is my favourite.
3 His theory, whose is really nothing new, says we learn best by doing.
4 The university, which was founded in 1803 is the most famous in our country.
5 The Prime Minister, who he was a student at this university, is going to make a visit here next month.
6 The manager of Westtown Bank, who we spoke to her yesterday, gave us the wrong information.
7 I gave the book to my friend John, which always likes to try new authors.
8 They want to knock down King's Hospital, where I was born in.

KL 4 Complete the words in the dialogue.

A: I don't know which university to apply to.
B: Well, there are several [1]_____ to _____ with that problem.
A: Really?
B: Of course. [2]_____ _____ visiting both before deciding?
A: I've done that. London seems more fun but the [3]_____ _____ about Oxford is that everyone has heard of it.
B: OK, well make a list of pros and cons for each.
A: Yes, that's the [4]_____ _____
B: So the [5]_____ thing to _____ is to fill in the application forms.

V1 5 Complete the sentences with the words in the box.

| graduate criticise unique |
| exams approach hand in |

1 Did you _____ your essay on time?
2 Do you _____ this year or next?
3 How many _____ have you got this term?
4 What's your _____ to teaching?
5 People never _____ teachers in my country.
6 He has a _____ method of learning English.

V2 6 Make phrases using one word from each box and match them with the definitions below.

| compulsory higher primary |
| corporate continuous distance |

| assessment education training |
| education school learning |

1 the number of years at school that you have to do:
   _____ _____
2 a system that checks progress over a period of time:
   _____ _____
3 the school where children between four and 11 go to in the UK: _____ _____
4 where you can go to study after you leave school:
   _____ _____
5 education for business people: _____ _____
6 teaching children at home instead of at school:
   _____ _____

GRAMMAR

G1 The passive

We form the passive with the verb *to be* + the past participle of the main verb:

The test **is carried** out.

Form the passive for each tense as follows:

Present simple	The Earth **is struck.**
Past simple	Meteorites **were discovered.**
Present perfect	The theory **hasn't been agreed** on.
Future	Mars **will be explored.**
Modal	The rock **must be destroyed.**

If we include the person who does the action, we introduce them with the preposition *by*.

The test is carried out **by scientists.**

Use the passive when the person doing the action is not important or known.

A strange message about an object in the sky **was left** on a police answering machine.

The space shuttle **will be flown** twice around the moon.

We also use the passive when we want to start a sentence with information that is known or has been mentioned before.

20 scientists are currently on the team. By the end of the year, they **will be joined** by 25 more.

G2 Articles

Use articles in the following ways:

• first and second mention

Use *a/an* when you mention a singular noun for the first time.

Tokyo has **a** major problem with space.

An alternative idea has been suggested.

Use *the* when we refer to something that has been mentioned before.

(Tokyo has **a** major **problem** with space.) At last city planners are trying to solve **the problem**.

Don't use an article with general plural countable nouns, and when we mention a plural noun for the first time.

Scientists still haven't found a way to deter meteorites.

Satellites will be launched into space. (Scientists will then use **the** satellites to look for alien life.)

• known things

Use *the* when there is only one of something.

The Earth's moon is a natural satellite.

Engineers are designing a train which will travel under **the** city.

• set uses

Use *the* with the names of some countries.

the United States, **the** United Kingdom, **the** Netherlands

Use *the* with the names of geographical features:

the Baltic sea, **the** Pacific ocean, **the** Amazon, **the** Alps

Use *the* with superlatives.

It's **the** largest engineering project of its kind.

Use *a/an* when talking about a job someone does:

I'm **a** teacher.

She works as **a** lawyer.

Don't use an article with the names of towns and cities, and most countries.

Venice, Paris, Tokyo, Japan, China

KEY LANGUAGE

KL Discussing options, making decisions

What do you think about …?

Another possibility is …

That's a possible solution.

Yes, let's do that.

We all agree then. We'll …

VOCABULARY

V1 Word combinations

build a model, do (some) research, do safety tests, find a solution, make a breakthrough, meet a deadline, solve a problem, test a theory

V2 Space

asteroid, collision, comet, deflect, devastation, impact, meteor, meteorite, threat

V3 Production

aircraft, aviation, flight test, mass-produce, modification, prototype, simulation, wind tunnel

G1 **1** Complete the second sentence so that it has a similar meaning to the first, using a passive form.

1 Astronauts fly the shuttle into space.
   The shuttle _____ into space.
2 Scientists did the tests yesterday.
   The tests _____ yesterday.
3 The company has launched the new brand.
   The new brand _____.
4 They haven't answered our questions.
   Our questions _____.
5 Engineers built the new plane in Seattle.
   The new plane _____ in Seattle.
6 You can play tennis in the morning.
   Tennis _____ in the morning.
7 The President has announced a new environmental policy.
   A new environmental policy _____.
8 We fire the rockets from mission control.
   The rockets _____ from mission control.

2 Read the sentences and delete the agent if it is unnecessary.

1 She was sacked ~~by her employer~~ yesterday.
2 It was announced by the Prime Minister today that he would resign within the week.
3 It is the third time that the Earth has been hit by an asteroid in recent years.
4 The bridge was first built by people in the 1920s.
5 The emergency meeting was organised by our managing director.
6 The criminal was sent to prison by the judge for three years.

G2 **3** Complete the gaps with *the*, *a* or *an*, or leave a space if no article is necessary.

1 I'm _____ engineer for a large building firm.
2 The flight stops in _____ Tokyo.
3 There's _____ major problem with this idea.
4 We're going skiing in _____ Swiss Alps this winter.
5 We thought we might go to _____ Canada for our next holiday.
6 She wants to become _____ nurse when she finishes school.
7 I think _____ cars are the most serious cause of pollution in the world.
8 This is one of _____ slowest trains I've ever been on.
9 The tunnel passes under _____ sea from England to France.
10 Now, _____ trains run several times a day between London and Paris. Tickets for _____ trains cost from £25 single.

KL **4** A local council is discussing what to call a new bridge across the city's river. Complete the dialogue with phrases a–e.

a) Another possibility is
b) We all agree then
c) That's a possible solution
d) Yes, let's do that
e) What do you think about this idea

A: [1]_____? We could name it Peterson Bridge, after Gerald Peterson, who did so much for the city in his life.
B: [2]_____, but I'm not sure if it's the best idea. The park in the centre is already called Peterson Park, so it might be confusing. [3]_____ to call it Broad Bridge. Then people will know you go down Broad Street to get to it.
A: [4]_____.
C: Yes, I like that idea too.
A: [5]_____. We'll call it Broad Bridge

V1 **5** Choose the correct verb.

1 Finally, they've *solved* / *made* a breakthrough.
2 We've been *doing* / *finding* some research into it.
3 Did you *make* / *do* the safety tests?
4 Have they *built* / *met* the prototype yet?
5 I'd like to *make* / *test* your theory.
6 We still haven't *found* / *done* a good solution.
7 I've *met* / *solved* the problem with the machine.
8 Do you think we'll *meet* / *do* the deadline?

V2,3 **6** Choose the correct word in each sentence.

1 There was a terrible _____ between the two football players.
   a) collision   b) devastation   c) threat
2 Can we make some _____ to the designs?
   a) modifications   b) simulations   c) impact
3 The _____ industry needs to reduce pollution from its engines.
   a) comet   b) wind   c) aviation
4 Can we _____ the asteroid so it doesn't hit us?
   a) modify   b) deflect   c) test
5 Let's run another _____ on the computer to see what will happen in a real situation.
   a) modification   b) devastation   c) simulation
6 We're doing another flight _____ on the prototype plane.
   a) tunnel   b) test   c) mass-produce

GRAMMAR

G1 Expressions of quantity

Use expressions of quantity to comment on the quantity of a noun. They can be used with subjects and objects.

> I only have **a couple of shirts** left.
> **Plenty of people** want to go there.

Countable and uncountable nouns

Some quantifiers can only be used with a countable or uncountable noun.

Use these quantifiers with countable nouns:
a couple of, a few, many

Use these quantifiers with uncountable nouns:
a little, much

Use these quantifiers with both countable and uncountable nouns:
a lot of, no, none, some, plenty of, enough

General and specific nouns

Use *some* and *no* with general nouns without an article.

> **Some people** aren't interested in sport.
> I'd like **some meat**.
> **No bikes** are allowed on the pathway.

Use *some of, none of, plenty of, a couple of, a lot of* with specific plural or uncountable nouns.

> **Some of the people** we were expecting didn't come.
> You can use **some of the meat in the fridge**.
> **None of them** wanted to go.
> **A couple of my friends** live there.
> **A lot of the students** are getting good marks.

G2 Infinitives and *-ing* forms

When one verb follows another, it may appear in the infinitive or *-ing* form. The form depends on the first verb, and the following structures are possible.

- verb + (object +) infinitive with *to*
  > Most people **want to live** for a 100 years.
  > Everyone **wants the champion to win** again.

  Other verbs include: *allow* (object + to), *decide, hope, manage, promise, teach* (object + to).

We also use the infinitive with *to* with *would* + verb.

> I like to play tennis. ✓
> I like playing tennis. ✓
> I'd like to play tennis. ✓
> I'd like playing tennis. ✗

- verb + *-ing*
  > We **prefer watching** comedies.
  > They **enjoy playing** tennis on Saturdays.

  Other verbs include: *practise, recommend, suggest, understand*.

  We also use the *-ing* form after a preposition:
  > I'm going to give **up learning** Spanish.
  > I'm good **at making** friends.

- verb + infinitive with *to* or *-ing*
  > I **like to travel**.
  > I **like travelling**.

  Other verbs include: *advise, begin, continue, like, love, hate*.

KEY LANGUAGE

KL The language of meetings

Stating the purpose of the meeting
We're here to discuss …

Encouraging people to speak
Please make your point.

Thanking people for their ideas
Thank you for your comment.

Saying you will take action
I'll look into the matter.

Making a point
I'm very unhappy with …
It's not acceptable – I'm sure you understand that.
Sorry, could I just say something please?

Stating the key points that have been agreed
Well, to sum up …

VOCABULARY

V1 Phrasal verbs

buy into, catch on, die out, find out, keep up with, pick up on, slow down, take over

V2 Describing trends

decline (v), decrease (v), dramatic, drop (v), fall (v), go up, gradual, grow, increase (n/v), level off, remain stable, rise (v), sharp rise, significant, slight, slow, stabilise, steady, sudden, top out (at)

Extra practice

G1 **1** **Choose the correct answer.**

1 Sorry, I only have *a lot / a couple* of hours to do this and I won't have time tomorrow.
2 We never have *a little / enough* money for holidays.
3 *A few / A little* people couldn't come this evening.
4 We still have *plenty of / many* sugar in the cupboard.
5 *Some / Much* of you need to stay late but most of you can leave.
6 *No / None* of them know about our secret. Shall I tell them?
7 *A lot / A couple* of customers – nearly 80 percent – complained about the price, so I suggest we lower it.

2 **Write in the missing words in sentences 1–8.**

1 A few my old friends work in the fashion industry. They all really like it.
2 Plenty people I know only wear black but I prefer different coloured clothes.
3 Can I talk to you about something for couple of minutes?
4 Give him little more time – I'm sure he'll finish it.
5 There are lot of students in my class that want to study English.
6 None the people in my family went to University. I was the first.

G2 **3** **Match the sentence halves.**

1 I really enjoyed
2 You're not allowed
3 Most people want
4 He's not good at
5 They started
6 We advise you

a) to use a dictionary in the exam. It's against the rules.
b) making friends. That's why he's so lonely.
c) to make a booking before you travel.
d) working here before I did.
e) playing tennis. Let's do it again sometime.
f) to live to 100.

4 **Complete the sentences with the verb in brackets in the correct form.**

1 Most people want _____ (live) in this part of town.
2 She decided _____ (cancel) the appointment.
3 Do you enjoy _____ (watch) nature films?
4 He taught me _____ (play) chess.
5 They're really good at _____ (help) with problems.
6 We should carry on _____ (drive) for another hour.
7 Are you allowed _____ (come) with me?
8 They suggested _____ (take) the train.
9 I'd love _____ (see) that new film about Shakespeare.

KL **5** **Complete the phrases with the words in the box.**

> acceptable   matter   unhappy   point
> here   say   sum   comment

1 Please make your _____.
2 I'll look into the _____.
3 Sorry, could I just _____ something please?
4 Thank you for your _____.
5 We're _____ to discuss transport.
6 Well, to _____ up, we are all agreed about the solution.
7 It's not _____ – I'm sure you understand that.
8 I'm very _____ with these plans.

V1,2 **6** **Complete the gaps with a preposition.**

1 I don't buy _____ this new trend.
2 Enthusiasm for the new sports hall died _____ when they saw the price.
3 The growth in the population has slowed _____ in recent years.
4 I just can't keep _____ with young people's fashions these days.
5 Do you think this fashion for pink will catch _____?
6 Did you pick up _____ the anger in his voice?
7 Life expectancy will top _____ at 100 by the end of the century and stop rising.
8 The new craze for red hair is taking _____ the population!
9 I should buy it before the prices go _____.
10 The company's share price levelled _____ at $50 today.

V2 **7** **Choose the correct answer.**

1 There's been a *gradual / dramatic* fall in unemployment figures. They dropped by over half a million in only one month.
2 His condition has remained *stable / sudden* overnight, so the doctors are feeling happier.
3 Share prices remained *steady / dramatic* recently, with prices staying the same.
4 Life expectancy is set to *rise / remain* sharply over the next century, with many more of us living until we're well over 100.
5 There's been a *big / slight* fall in the number of car owners, but nothing significant.
6 Sales have *declined / grown* recently, so shop owners are very worried.

Language reference

G1 Reported speech

Use reported speech to report someone's words.

'I want to become a famous singer.'

She said **she wanted to become a famous singer**.

'I always hoped to become an actor.'

He said **he'd always hoped to become an actor**.

When we use reported speech, we makes changes to the tense of the verb, to pronouns and to time adverbs. The table shows the most common changes:

Direct speech	Reported speech
tenses:	
present simple	past simple
present continuous	past continuous
present perfect	past perfect
past simple	past perfect
will	would
can	could
pronouns:	
I	he/she
we	they
my	his/her
our	their
time adverbs:	
today	then / that day
yesterday	the day before
tomorrow	the next day / the day after
last week	the week before

'**I work** as a teacher.'

He said he worked as a teacher.

'**We left** our bags at the station.'

They said **they had left** their bags at the station.

'**I start my** new job **today**.'

Rita said **she started her** new job **that day**.'

'They **were** with **me yesterday**.'

Laurie said they **had been** with **her the previous day**.

tell and *say*

Use *tell* with an object before the reported speech.

He told **me** that he couldn't come out. ✓

He told that he couldn't come out. ✗

Never use *say* with an object before the reported speech.

She said ~~me~~ that she would be late. ✗

Commands

Use the infinitive with *to* to report a command:

'Leave my house!'

He told the journalist to leave his house.

G2 Reported questions

To report a question, use expressions like *He asked me ...*, *She wanted to know ...* .

For *yes/no* questions (questions which require *yes* or *no* as an answer) use *if*.

'Do you know Peter?'

They asked me **if** I knew Peter.

'Have you worked on a newspaper before?'

He wanted to know **if** I had worked on a newspaper.

For other questions, use the *wh-* word.

'**Why** are you interested in TV?'

He asked me **why** I was interested in TV.

'**What** experience do you have?'

I wanted to know **what** experience she had.

As with reported speech, the verb in the direct question often changes in the reported question by moving back a tense and there are changes to pronouns and time adverbs.

'Is Rachel coming to stay **today**?'

Mum asked me if Rachel was coming to stay **that day**.

In reported questions, use the same word order as a statement.

Sarah asked me ~~did I want~~ to visit her. ✗

Sarah asked me if I wanted to visit her. ✓

! Don't use question marks with a reported question.

KL Comparing and contrasting

different from …

the same as …

similar to …

much better than …

less important than …

a lot worse than …

V1 Adjectives

breathtaking, classic, groundbreaking, gripping, hilarious, incomparable, moving, outstanding

V2 Words about the media

atmosphere, chapter, character, episode, plot, series, novel, page turner

V3 Genres

animation, autobiography, classical music, country music, crime, current affairs, documentary, folk music, hiphop, hospital drama, horror, jazz, opera, reality, reggae, science fiction, sitcom, soap, soul

V4 Films

choreograph (v), dub (v), full-length, genre, hero, heroine, pitch, romantic comedy, sequel, set (n), special effects

G1 **1** **Rewrite the sentences as reported speech.**

1 'I travel 50 miles a day.'
  She said _____.
2 'I don't want to talk about it.'
  He told us that _____.
3 'I've called three times.'
  He said he _____.
4 'Go home!'
  My father told me _____.
5 'Mel is going to Australia.'
  Jemma said that _____.
6 'They lived here from 1863 to 1899.'
  The tour guide said _____.
7 'I'm leaving.'
  She said _____.
8 'Stop talking!'
  The teacher told the class _____.

2 **Read the conversation between two people who work for a music magazine and complete the report of their meeting below.**

PETER: We're having this meeting to decide who we'll feature in the next issue.

BRYAN: I've spoken to James Blunt and he isn't available until next month. I'm also trying to contact Jennifer Lopez but I can only get her agent.

PETER: I spoke to Paul McCartney at a Music Awards show. He said he can do an interview.

BRYAN: We can't do another issue on The Beatles! Try calling the Pussycat Dolls.

> Peter and Bryan had the meeting to decide who they ¹_____ feature in the next issue of the magazine *Music Now*.
> Bryan said he ²_____ to James Blunt but he ³_____ until the following month. He ⁴_____ also _____ to contact Jennifer Lopez but he ⁵_____ only get her agent. Peter said he ⁶_____ to Paul McCartney and he ⁷_____ he ⁸_____ do an interview.
> However, Bryan told Peter they ⁹_____ do another Beatles' issue. He told him ¹⁰_____ the Pussycat Dolls instead.

G2 **3** **Put the words in the correct order to make sentences with reported speech.**

1 Thierry asked me … had I if seen you.
2 Your boss wanted to know … if late were you.
3 They asked me … why didn't take I the job.
4 She wanted to know … hadn't you called why.
5 Your parents asked me … you were where.

4 **Rewrite the questions as reported questions.**

1 'Can I help you?'
  The shop assistant asked _____.
2 'Why are you here?'
  The receptionist wanted to know _____.
3 'Do you live in London?'
  The tourist asked _____.
4 'Is it your car?'
  The policeman wanted to know _____.

KL **5** **Match the sentence halves.**

1 For some reason the sequel was a lot worse
2 All his films are similar
3 The sequel is very different
4 Special effects are less important
5 Isn't there something better
6 It's the same plot as

a) the first one.
b) than the first one.
c) than a good plot.
d) from the other one.
e) to that other one we saw.
f) than that on TV?

V1,2,3,4 **6** **Choose the correct answer.**

1 The *plot / genre* of this film is so complicated I can't understand who is who.
2 I hate it when they *pitch / dub* movies. I prefer to hear the original language.
3 Episode one of that new detective *sequel / series* is on tonight.
4 There's this *hilarious / gripping* comedy series set in a hotel.
5 The lead actress gave a *moving / full-length* performance. She deserves an Oscar.
6 The *soap / documentary* follows the lives of three real-life policemen in New York.
7 The *special / romantic* effects in that film set in space are breathtaking.
8 The *sets / characters* in Shakespeare are never just as simple as good and evil.

V2,3 **7** **Complete the table with the words in the box.**

chapter   documentary   folk   novel
reggae   page turner   reality   sitcom   soap
hiphop   soul   autobiography   episode

Music	Books	TV programmes

GRAMMAR

G1   Third conditional

Form the third conditional in the following way:

if-clause	+	main clause
if		*would/could/might* + *have*
+ past perfect		+ past participle

If Sarah **had asked** me, I **would have helped her**.

Use the third conditional to talk about unreal situations in the past, i.e. situations that are contrary to the facts.

> If he hadn't driven so quickly, the police **could have caught** him. (He drove quickly, the police didn't catch him)

> If she'd been a little nicer, I **might have gone** to her party. (She wasn't nice, I didn't go to the party.)

We often use the third conditional to:

- talk about regrets.
  If I'd worked harder, I might have got better results.
- criticise.
  If you'd listened to me, you wouldn't have got into trouble with the police.
- make excuses.
  Sorry, but if the plane had left on time, I wouldn't have been so late!

As with the first and second conditional, we can put the main clause first.

G2   Modals for past deduction

Use modal perfects to make guesses (deductions) about things in the past. The modal perfect is formed with a modal verb (e.g. *must, can, should*) + *have* + past participle.

> They **must have climbed** in through the back window.

> They **should have checked** the car before they left.

Use *should have* to say something was a good idea, but it didn't happen.

> To finish the job more quickly they **should have asked** more people to help.

Use *shouldn't have* to say something wasn't a good idea, but it happened.

> He **shouldn't have driven** over the speed limit.

Use *might have* to say that it is possible, but not certain, that something happened.

> He **might have decided** to ask the police for help.

Use *must have* to say it is logically certain that something happened.

> There's a broken window at the back so the robber **must have climbed** in there.

Use *couldn't have* to say that it is not possible that something happened.

> The judge **couldn't have given** any other sentence but 20 years in prison for a crime like this.

See page 146 for present deduction.

KEY LANGUAGE

KL   Discussing court cases

The evidence clearly shows …
I am sure that you will find my client innocent.
The facts of the case are clear.
I'm not certain he's guilty because …
There should be no doubt in your minds that this man is guilty.
I am confident that you will find the defendant guilty.
You can look at it in two ways.
I will bring witnesses to confirm that …
I believe he's innocent because …
It's clear to me that …

VOCABULARY

V1   Crime

case, charge with, evidence, false pretences, fraud, investigate, juvenile, legal, offender, witness (v)

V2   Word combinations

antisocial behaviour, bad behaviour, career decision, close relationship, criminal behaviour, genetic link, good behaviour, human behaviour, long tradition, vicious circle

V3   People in crime

attorney, bank robber, captor, fingerprint, getaway, hostage, job (crime), kidnapping, lawyer, prosecutor, ransom, robbery, suspect (n/v), thief

Extra practice

G1 **1 There is one mistake in each sentence. Correct it.**

1 If Dmitry has asked me to help, I would have.
2 If he hadn't left so much evidence, the police wouldn't caught him.
3 I might have become a solicitor if I would worked harder at school.
4 If you'd had listened to me, you wouldn't have taken the job.
5 Sorry, but if the plane would had left on time, I wouldn't have been so late!
6 You could come if you had wanted to.
7 We wouldn't have missed the deadline if everyone had been done what they promised.
8 If I hadn't have heard the news, I wouldn't have known.

G2 **2 Complete the second sentence so that it has a similar meaning to the first, using a modal perfect form.**

1 The lock was smashed. I'm certain the thief did it.
   The thief _____ smashed the lock.
2 It's possible that the owner forgot where he parked the car.
   The car owner _____ forgotten where he parked the car.
3 The lights weren't on at the house. I'm certain they were still out.
   They _____ been home because the lights weren't on.
4 It's possible that they left a message on your voicemail.
   They _____ left a message on your voicemail.
5 The kids ate everything – they were really hungry.
   The kids _____ been really hungry because they ate everything.
6 There isn't a door at the back. It wasn't possible for the burglars to get in from there.
   They _____ got in from the back because there isn't a door there.
7 It was wrong of them to take the book without asking me.
   They _____ taken the book without asking me.
8 The project went completely wrong. It wasn't planned properly.
   They _____ planned the project properly because it went completely wrong.
9 We didn't take out insurance when we went on holiday and we had a car accident.
   We _____ taken out insurance when we went on holiday.

KL **3 Complete the sentences with the pairs of words in the box.**

> facts + case   look + ways   evidence + shows
> find + client   doubt + minds   you + defendant
> believe + innocent   certain + guilty

1 The _____ clearly _____ that you were at the scene of the crime.
2 The _____ of the _____ are clear.
3 I'm sure you will _____ my _____ innocent.
4 There should be no _____ in your _____ that this man is guilty.
5 I am confident that _____ will find the _____ innocent.
6 You can _____ at it in two _____.
7 I'm not _____ she is _____.
8 I _____ he's _____ because the witness said he was in a different city at the time.

V1,2 **4 Match the words to make phrases.**

1 career   a) relationship
2 long   b) link
3 false   c) circle
4 antisocial   d) behaviour
5 close   e) pretences
6 genetic   f) tradition
7 vicious   g) decision

V1,3 **5 Complete the sentences with the words in the box.**

> fingerprints   getaway   kidnapping
> lawyer   suspect   investigate   witness

1 You are accused of _____ a ten-year-old boy.
2 The police are holding the _____ for more questions.
3 The _____ car was waiting outside for the robbers.
4 I'd like to speak to my _____ before I speak to the police.
5 The detective is trying to _____ the disappearance of the jewels.
6 My first _____ is a woman who was walking past the park at the time of the murder.
7 The police found the thief's _____ left on the window.

COMMUNICATION

INFORMATION FOR STUDENT A

Lesson 1.2 Exercise 8 (p. 8)

> ^{1}_____ was born on 6th May 1856 in Freiberg, Moravia. He went to the University of ^{2}_____ and studied medicine. He graduated in ^{3}_____ as a Doctor of Medicine. He lived in Vienna for 47 years. In 1907 the psychiatrist Carl Jung was introduced to Freud and together they formed the International Psychoanalytical Association. ^{4}_____ was its first president. Most of Freud's family emigrated to London. ^{5}_____ lost all his property when he left Vienna. Freud lived in a house in Hampstead, London. He died in ^{6}_____.

Lesson 2.3 Exercise 11 (p. 21)

Read about jobs 1 and 2 below and tell Student B a little about them. Ask questions about your partner's experience to find out if he/she is suitable for either of the jobs.

Have you ever done any voluntary work?

– Yes, I have.

Oh, when did you do that?

– Well, I worked for Save the Children last summer.

1
Vacancies for speakers of two languages to accompany small groups of 14-year-old students to major European cities such as Paris, London and Rome.
The ideal person will:

- ■ *have experience of looking after groups of children*
- ■ *have knowledge of at least two major European cities*
- ■ *be reliable and well-organised*

2
We require four active, strong and enthusiastic young adults to accompany a trip for older people to the foothills of the Himalayas. The ideal person will:
- have experience of working with or looking after old people
- be physically fit
- be responsible and reliable

Answer Student B's questions about jobs 3 and 4.

Lesson 3.2 Exercise 8b (p. 29)

Listen and correct Student B, using the prompts below. Repeat the whole sentences.

1 Poland   2 for nine months   3 Spanish

Say the sentences below. Your partner will correct you.

1 So you've been working from home for two years.

2 So, you've been studying computing since January.

3 So, you've been driving for six years.

Lesson 3.4 Exercise 8a (p. 33)

1 Think about what key qualities you are looking for in the candidate.

2 Write out the six questions below to ask at the interview.
   a) Why / want this job?
   b) What / sort / person / you?
   c) What / strengths / weaknesses?
   d) What / think / can bring / this job?
   e) What / interests / have / outside work?
   f) Where / see yourself / five years' time?

3 Add three more questions to ask at the interview. Include one killer question.

Lesson 4.3 Exercise 8 (p. 43)

Discuss the motion and prepare your arguments. Use these ideas to help you.

- Lose a language – lose a lot of knowledge.
- Like losing an animal.
- Language is linked to identity.
- Huge cultural contribution (e.g. music, film).
- Helps a community.
- Can teach you about other languages.

Choose a spokesperson to present your basic views, then decide who will say what to support the views.

Lesson 4.4 Exercise 5 (p. 45)

You think that the best option is to send as many staff as possible to the language school near the head office. Try to persuade the other members to accept your idea. Use the ideas below and your ideas from Exercise 2b.

- Staff will be away from their offices, so they can focus on learning English, without interruptions.
- The courses are not expensive.
- The teachers will be well trained and professional.
- You do not want to have English classes in the office because staff will not attend classes regularly. You think online language programmes are a waste of time and money.

Lesson 5.1 Exercise 7 (p. 49)

Lesson 5.3 Exercise 8a (p. 53)

Father

You understand that your son wants a cool, fast bike but you don't want to pay a lot of money. But you think that the smallest, cheapest bike is too small.

Lesson 6.4 Exercise 6 (p. 65)

Read the information below and prepare for the negotiation. When there are options, make a decision about what are the most important points for you. Try to get a good deal for your company.

You want:

- **Quantity**: 50,000 units.

- **Designs**: Oasis – 10,000 units; Mirage – 15,000 units; Horizon – 25,000 units; you make a much bigger profit on the Mirage and Horizon designs.

- **Delivery**: August 7, August 21 or end of August; best date is August 7 – important because retailers will start selling the winter range in September.

- **Payment**: after 60 days (best time), after 30 days, or on delivery

- **Discount**: 10% (high), 5% (usual discount for wholesalers), 3% (low)

Lesson 7.4 Exercise 5 (p. 77)

Spotlight CD player
Description: A touch lamp. You touch the lamp to get three different beams – dim, medium, bright. The lamp hangs from the ceiling; its height can be adjusted. It has an internal CD player, which is controlled by voice commands. It would appeal to anyone who likes modern design.
Qualities: Simple, stylish design, advanced technology, elegant.
Suggested price: $600

Lesson 8.2 Exercise 9b (p. 83)

1 Read the definitions of the words below. Invent two more definitions using relative clauses. Read out your three definitions of the first word to Team B. They try to guess the correct definition.

2 Try to guess the correct definition of Team B's first word.

3 Go to the next word on your list.

Definitions:

thesaurus – a book which includes groups of words that have similar meanings
pachyderm – an animal which has thick skin, such as an elephant
roustabout – a labourer who is unskilled
thimble – a small metal or plastic cap which is used to protect your finger when you sew
ninon – a type of material which is made in France

Lesson 8.3 Exercise 7a (p. 85)

Read your first fact to Student B, who will try to find a fact to match it. Then listen to Student B's first fact and try to find a fact below to match it. If you are not sure, guess. Finally, match each pair of facts with one of the universities on page 85.

A: It is the oldest university in the English-speaking world.

B: It allowed women to graduate in 1920.

It is the oldest university in the English-speaking world.
It was founded in 1209.
It is one of the most famous universities in Germany.
It is situated in the south-west of Moscow.
It was founded in 1701.
It is best known for its faculties of law and literature.

Lesson 8.3 Exercise 9a (p. 85)

Education in Vietnam
Vietnam's education system has five categories:

- pre-primary
- primary (Year 1–5)
- secondary (Year 6–9)
- high school (Year 10–12)
- higher education (four years for undergraduate level and two years for master level)

Recently, nearly one million Vietnamese students took the university entrance exam (considered a pass-or-fail test), but the entire higher education system had space for only 200,000 students (20 percent).
The law states that students only have to go to school between the ages of six and ten.

Make notes about ages of students at secondary school, percentage of students in higher education, length of compulsory education, private universities and other interesting information.

INFORMATION FOR STUDENT A

Lesson 10.4 Exercise 6a (p. 109)

Prepare for the meeting by discussing the list of problems on page 109 and suggesting ways of solving them. You do not have a lot of money to spend on big new projects, so you want to:

- keep charging people to use the beaches – they are an important source of income for the council.
- sell the town's aquarium because it is losing money and is in poor condition. You want to use the money to build a new sports and swimming pool centre.
- charge more for parking permits and parking areas so that people will have to use the excellent bus service more.
- make residents happier without spending too much money.

Decide which one of you is the Mayor. Listen to the residents' ideas for solving the town's problems. Try to agree on the best solutions.

Lesson 12.3 Exercise 8 (p. 127)

Rex Peterson, an army veteran, has been hacking into the victim's computer and monitoring the victim's whereabouts for the last year. He has many photos of the victim, and the victim has complained about him to the police.

Lesson 12.4 Exercise 5 (p. 129)

Case 1 – case for the prosecution
Woman got angry and lost control.
Man already unconscious and no danger.
Burglar had no weapon.
Woman gave no warning.
Burglar was small and light.

INFORMATION FOR STUDENT B

Lesson 1.2 Exercise 8 (p. 8)

Sigmund Freud was born on 6th May 1856 in ^{1}_____. He went to the university of Vienna and studied ^{2}_____. He graduated in 1881 as a Doctor of Medicine. He lived in Vienna for ^{3}_____ years. In 1907 the psychiatrist ^{4}_____ was introduced to Freud and together they formed the International Psychoanalytical Association. Jung was its first president. ^{5}_____ emigrated to London. His brother lost all his property when he left Vienna. Freud lived in a house in ^{6}_____. He died in 1939.

Lesson 1.4 Exercise 5 (p. 13)

Richard: British, aged 22
Quiet, calm personality. Seemed very serious at first, but relaxed later in the interview.
Highly intelligent (high IQ) and has strong opinions on many subjects.
Your three best qualities? 'organised, reliable and creative'
Your worst quality? 'I can be very impatient with people if they perform poorly.'
Your ideal boss? 'He or she should show respect to staff and care about them.'
Why choose him? 'People say I'm strong-willed and that I work very hard.'
Non-smoker.
Dressed in rather unfashionable, grey suit.
Interests: mountaineering, deep sea diving, collecting antiques.

Anil: Indian, aged 24
Easy-going, polite, friendly, sociable.
Your three best qualities? 'even-tempered, helpful, sensible'
Your worst quality? 'I get very angry if people are not polite to me. Also I dislike people who are not generous.'
Your ideal boss? 'Someone who knows their job well and is sensitive and understanding.'
Why choose him? 'I am very ambitious, I want to get to the top as fast as possible.'
Smokes small cigars.
Dressed in a smart black suit and white silk shirt.
Interests: rides a motorbike (at weekends), dances the tango, reads books on philosophy.

Lesson 2.3 Exercise 11 (p. 21)

Read about jobs 1 and 2 below and tell Student A a little about them. Ask questions about your partner's experience to find out if he/she is suitable for either of the jobs.

Have you ever done any voluntary work?

– Yes, I have.

Oh, when did you do that?

– Well, I worked for Save the Children last summer.

---

3 We are looking for five people to accompany scientists on a trip to the Amazon Forests of Brazil. The ideal person will:

- have experience of working in a scientific environment
- have an interest in animals
- be young, fit and enthusiastic

---

4 Assistant travel agent required for work in one of our branches helping visitors with their enquiries about foreign travel. The ideal person should:

- *have some experience of travelling to a variety of places*
- *have good communication skills*
- *have a knowledge of computers*

Answer Student A's questions about jobs 1 and 2.

Lesson 3.2 Exercise 8b (p. 29)

Say the sentences below. Your partner will correct you.

1 So, you've been working in Germany since graduating.
2 So, you've been living in Brazil for six months.
3 So, you've been studying French for a year.

Listen and correct Student A, using the prompts below. Repeat the whole sentences.

1 for four years
2 teaching
3 for two years

Lesson 3.4 Exercise 8a (p. 33)

1 Think about what sort of person the club is looking for.
2 Think about how you would describe yourself in 30 words.
3 Think of six to ten questions you think they will ask at your interview.
4 Think of a killer question. Think about how you would answer it in an interview.
5 Think about your answers to the questions in 3. You may use information from your own life and experience or you may invent any information you wish.

Lesson 4.3 Exercise 8 (p. 43)

Discuss the motion and prepare your arguments. Use these ideas to help you:

- Costs a lot of money to keep a language alive (schools, teachers, books, road signs, festivals).
- If very few people speak the language, why bother keeping it?
- A lot of effort for little use.
- If English continues to be dominant, people will never become bilingual in their minority language.
- Will continue to decline if language community is not economically viable.
- Already too much in curriculum for schoolchildren to learn without learning a useless language.

Choose a spokesperson to present your basic views, then decide who will say what to support the views.

Lesson 4.4 Exercise 5 (p. 45)

You think that the best option is to hire English language instructors to give courses in the office. Try to persuade the other members to accept your idea. Use the ideas below and your ideas from Exercise 2b.

- The teachers will teach British English and American English.
- You will be able to control closely the language training they provide.
- Staff will attend classes when it is convenient for them.
- You do not want to use the nearby English language school because the courses will be in General English with no specialist language. You also think that courses in the US or the UK will be too expensive.

Lesson 5.1 Exercise 7 (p. 49)

Lesson 5.3 Exercise 8a (p. 53)
Mother
You feel very strongly that your son should have a bike that is very safe, not too big and not too fast. You have heard stories about terrible accidents with quad bikes. You also don't want a big engine.

Lesson 6.3 Exercise 2 (p. 62)

3 Mark McCormack

Mark Hume McCormack, sports agent, died on May 16th, aged 72. Mark McCormack started the industry of sports marketing. He was the first person to realise that sports personalities could earn extra money from endorsements and sponsorship. The company which he founded, International Management Group (IMG), represents many of the most famous sports people in the world such as Tiger Woods, Pete Sampras, the Williams sisters and Michael Schumacher.

McCormack had been a promising college golfer. However, after graduating from Yale Law School he worked as a lawyer. Later, he realised that sports marketing had great potential. His first client, in 1960, was Arnold Palmer, the famous golfer. Thanks to his energy and entrepreneurial skills, he built up a highly profitable business. By 1990 he had become the most powerful person in sport.

IMG expanded to include a television production company, sports academies and a branch representing top models such as Kate Moss.

By the end of his life he had also published several books, including the best-selling *What they don't teach you at Harvard Business School*.

He will be remembered for his ability to negotiate huge contracts for a wide range of sports personalities and celebrities.

He leaves three children from his first marriage and one from his second to former tennis professional, Betty Nagelson.

Mark McCormack, 6 November 1930 – 16 May 2003

4 Akio Morita

AKIO MORITA, co founder of the Sony Corporation – died on October 3rd in Tokyo.

He created one of the first truly global companies. His strategy was so successful that Sony was recently voted the number one brand name by American consumers, ahead of Coca-Cola and General Electric.

Morita had a comfortable childhood. He was the eldest son of a wealthy family from Nagoya. He trained as a physicist. Before he celebrated his 26th birthday, he had started his own company with a partner Masaru Ibuka. In 1949 the company developed recording tape and in 1950 sold the first tape recorder in Japan. In 1957 it produced a pocket-sized radio and a year later renamed itself Sony. For the new name Mr Morita combined the Latin word for sound, *sonus*, with the English expression 'sonny boy' to give an impression of a company full of energy and youth. In 1960 it produced the first transistor television in the world.

He moved his family to the USA in 1963. This helped him to understand Americans, their market and customs. Many people believe this was the key reason for his global success.

Sony launched the Walkman in 1979 after Morita had noticed young people's love of music.

Morita was a workaholic, but he was also a playaholic. He loved art and music, and was a sports fanatic.

He also wrote a book in the 1960s called *Never Mind School Records* which argued that academic achievements are not important for success in business.

He is survived by his wife Yoshiko, two sons and a daughter.

Akia Morita, 26 January 1921 – 3 October 1999

INFORMATION FOR STUDENT B

Lesson 6.4 Exercise 6 (p. 65)

Read the information below and prepare for the negotiation. When there are options, make a decision about what are the most important points for you. Try to get a good deal for your company.

You want to sell:

- **Quantity**: 50,000 units.
- **Designs**: Oasis – 25,000; Mirage – 15,000; Horizon: 10,000; you make a much bigger profit on the Oasis and Mirage designs.
- **Delivery**: September 14 (best time), September 7, or by the end of August (bad time)
- **Payment**: on delivery, after 30 days, or after 60 days; important to get your money quickly because you need to pay interest on a large bank loan.
- **Discount**: 0% (best), 2% (for cash on delivery), 8% (for orders over 60,000)

Lesson 7.4 Exercise 5 (p. 77)

Exercise bicycle
Description: A lightweight exercise bicycle. It has a comfortable seat. You can adjust it vertically and horizontally. A training computer gives ten different exercise programmes. The LCD (Liquid Crystal Display) shows your speed, time, distance, calories burned, etc. The bicycle has specially-designed ergonomic handles. Special features include: exercise music, bottle holder, voice instructions from a virtual trainer.
Qualities: Innovative, ergonomic design, very durable
Suggested price: $280

Lesson 8.2 Exercise 9b (p.83)

1 Read the definitions of the words below. Invent two more definitions using relative clauses.

2 Listen to Team A's first word and try to guess the correct definition.

3 Read out your three definitions of the first word to Team A. They try to guess the correct definition.

4 Listen to Team A's second word before going to the next word on your list.

Definitions:
horticulturalist – someone who grows flowers, fruit and vegetables
jackdaw – a black bird that sometimes steals small bright objects
facilitator – someone who helps a group of people discuss things with each other
Nilometer – an instrument which is used to measure the depth of the River Nile in Egypt.
stapes – a small bone in your ear

Lesson 8.3 Exercise 7a (p. 85)

Listen to Student A's first fact and try to find a fact below to match it. If you are not sure, guess. Then, read your first fact to Student A, who will try to find a fact to match it. Finally, match each pair of facts with one of the universities on page 85.

A: It is the oldest university in the English-speaking world.
B: It allowed women to graduate in 1920.

It was established in 1386.
It has produced many Japanese politicians.
It allowed women to graduate in 1920.
It is well-known for producing famous scientists and mathematicians.
It is a private university in Connecticut.
It is the oldest and largest university in Russia.

Lesson 8.3 Exercise 9a (p. 85)

Education in France
Since 1967, school attendance has been compulsory for those from six to 16 years of age.
Secondary schooling is divided into two stages:

- Stage 1 – from 11 to 15 years; almost all children now attend a *collège*
- Stage 2 – from 15 to 18 years they study in a general, technical or vocational *lycée*

13.3 percent of all students are in higher education. French higher education institutions are small but with a large variety.
The *Grandes Ecoles* ('big schools') are very famous, well-respected higher education establishments outside the framework of the public universities. They are generally focused on a single subject area. Higher education is paid by the French taxpayers so fees are very low.

Make notes about ages of students at secondary school, percentage of students in higher education, length of compulsory education, private universities and any other interesting information.

Lesson 10.4 Exercise 6a (p. 109)

Prepare for the meeting by discussing the list of problems on page 109 and suggesting ways of solving them. You are happy in Belleview. You want to:

- use the beaches without paying fees.
- persuade the Council to sell the aquarium. It is in poor condition and fewer people go there nowadays. The Council can use the money to build a new sports and swimming centre.
- have a new venue for visits by pop singers.
- have free travel on buses for people under the age of 21.

Choose one person to lead your group. Present your ideas at the meeting. Try to persuade the Council to accept your suggestions.

Lesson 11.2 Exercise 2a (p. 114)

2

J.D. Salinger
(1919–)

The American writer J.D. Salinger is known for his reclusive nature. He has not given an interview since 1974, nor published any new work since 1965. Salinger's entire published works consist of one novel and 13 short stories, all written in the period 1948-59. In 1997, a rumour started that Salinger was going to bring out the first book version of his last published story. Fans became very excited. However, because of the publicity, Salinger quickly withdrew from the arrangement.

Ironically for a future writer, when he was at college one of his professors insisted he was the worst English student in the history of the college. Before writing his famous book, he had only published a few short stories in magazines.

Salinger established his reputation with a single novel, *The Catcher in the Rye* (1951), an immediate bestseller which still sells 250,000 copies per year. It is also famously the book Mark Chapman was obsessed with, and calmly reading, when he was arrested for the murder of John Lennon in New York in 1980. The main character, Holden Caulfield, is a sensitive, rebellious teenager experiencing the growing pains of high school and college students.

Salinger did not do much to help publicise his masterpiece and asked that his photograph should not be used in connection with it. The public attention which followed the success of the book led him to move from New York to the remote hills of Cornish, New Hampshire. Since the late 1960s he has tried to escape publicity. In 1974 he told a reporter that he liked to write but that he wrote for himself and his own pleasure.

Later, he tried to stop publication of a biography which included letters he had written to other authors and friends. In 2000 his daughter published a biography. In it she claimed her father was not a recluse. She said he travelled often and had friends all over the world. She added that he enjoyed being with people and was friendly except where publicity and celebrity are concerned.

Salinger refuses to sell the movie rights to any of his stories to Hollywood and will not allow any of his works to be involved with film.

Lesson 12.3 Exercise 2a (p. 126)

Read the report then answer the questions on page 126.

The Big Dig By Monte Reel

The hostage crisis inside a Buenos Aires bank had lasted for seven hours, with hundreds of police officers surrounding the building. After negotiating an exchange – four hostages for some pizzas and sodas – the captors inside seemed suspiciously quiet. So police stormed the building.

They found the 19 remaining hostages safe and sound, but the captors had vanished. A hole in the basement wall was covered with an iron lid. Someone had locked the lid from the other side. Later, police discovered that the hole led to a secret tunnel, which joined a drain that emptied into the Plata River. It was a clean getaway.

'Until now, in the history of Argentina there has never been a band of thieves that's had the preparation and the luck that this group of criminals had,' a Buenos Aires provincial police investigator, Osvaldo Seisdedos, told reporters after the robbery.

The subterranean thieves in Argentina got away with cash and safe-deposit box contents worth an estimated $25 million to $70 million, according to police and lawyers representing bank customers. If those estimates are accurate, the robbery will be among the biggest bank robberies in history.

News reports of the Argentine robbery suggest almost everything went as the thieves had planned: before the exchange was negotiated, the hostages were allowed to talk to relatives on cell phones, and the robbers even sang 'Happy Birthday' to one of them. What the thieves really wanted, it seemed, was time to get more than 140 safe-deposit boxes loaded into the tunnel.

'Everyone I know is talking about it and saying the same thing – that the people who did it are geniuses,' said Salvador Peluso, 37, who works at a water-sports store across the street from the bank. 'They robbed a bank without a single gunshot being fired and got away with everything. It's like a good movie.'

According to bank officials, only about $200,000 of the millions stolen was bank cash. However, the vast majority of the money and property came from the privately held boxes.

'Safe-deposit boxes seem to be an Argentine habit because people understand that banks are very insecure here,' said Nydia Zingman, an attorney representing dozens of the robbery victims. 'But the bank is ultimately responsible.'

Similar robberies have allowed Zingman to build a legal career for herself in Argentina; she has represented hundreds of clients who have lost safe-deposit boxes to tunnelling robbers.

© 2006 The Washington Post Company

Lesson 12.3 Exercise 8 (p. 127)

Julie Barriskell used to be a school friend of the victim but became jealous of her success. Julie was the last known person to see the victim. She sent a text message to the victim and invited her to the lake at 5 p.m. Police have a record of the text message. She is a friend of Dr Drake Ramorey. She has an alibi from 8 p.m.

INFORMATION FOR STUDENT B

Lesson 11.5 Exercise 4 (p. 120)

You are the organiser of an International Food Festival. Using the notes below, give a short talk about the festival to your partner. He/she should ask questions at the end of your talk and you should answer them.

> Location: in a park in the suburbs
>
> History of the festival: has been held for the last four years. Not successful last year because of poor weather and not enough publicity. Aimed mainly at adults and food lovers of all ages.
>
> Dates: July 1-4
>
> Times 10 a.m. - 4 p.m.
>
> Activities: opportunities to buy and sample foods from all over the world.
>
> Special Event: celebrity chefs doing cookery demonstrations. Gala evening on first day with special guests.
>
> Advertising: local press, leaflets, local T.V. and radio advertising.
>
> Advantages to sponsors: high number of visitors if weather is good. A lot of press interest this year as famous Jamie Sullivan will be attending each day.
>
> Other information? Other events? Security?

Lesson 12.3 Exercise 3 (p. 126)

a) The robbers sang 'Happy Birthday' to a hostage. ☐
b) The robbers built a secret tunnel. ☐
c) Lots of police officers surrounded the bank. ☐
d) The police stormed the building. ☐
e) The police negotiated an exchange. ☐
f) The police discovered a hole connected to a tunnel. ☐
g) The police found the hostages. ☐

Lesson 12.4 Exercise 5 (p. 129)

Case 1 – case for the defence

The woman was extremely frightened.
Felt that she was in great danger in her own home.
Didn't know how many burglars there were.
There had been several burglaries with violence in the area recently.
The defendant had no confidence in the police.

Case 2 – case for the prosecution

The woman is making the man's life impossible.
He is stressed and receiving medical treatment.
He is in danger of losing his job.
He feels like a prisoner in his own home.
He is worried about what she might do next.

INFORMATION FOR STUDENT C

Lesson 11.2 Exercise 2a (p. 114)

3

Stanley Kubrick
(1928–1999)

Stanley Kubrick is often described as a perfectionist genius, and is admired as one of cinema's greatest talents. As a director he made only 13 feature films in a career of over 40 years, but many of them are regarded as masterpieces, and he earned nine Oscars. Kubrick once said that a film was more like music than fiction, although all his films were adapted from novels.

He directed the Hollywood epic *Spartacus* in 1960, the most expensive film of its day, and the only all-Hollywood movie he ever made. Soon after finishing this film, unhappy with the pressure of Hollywood, he moved from America to Britain.

Kubrick spent five years developing his film *2001: A Space Odyssey* (1969). This is probably his most famous and influential film. It was a science fiction blockbuster which was popular with both the critics and the public. Often described as a masterpiece, its special effects techniques won an Academy award and were a big influence on George Lucas when he came to make the *Star Wars* films. His final film was *Eyes Wide Shut* (1999), starring Tom Cruise and Nicole Kidman.

The film *A Clockwork Orange* (1971) was withdrawn in the UK after Kubrick felt it had been misinterpreted, and it was only shown again in cinemas after his death.

He valued his privacy, and worried about security. He certainly disliked travel after he moved to England, and he also had a well-known fear of flying. He once told a friend that he travelled to London four or five times per year, only for appointments with his dentist.

Kubrick was frequently unwilling to discuss personal matters publicly, and this gave rise to his reputation as an eccentric, reclusive genius. This image of him was denied by his family after his death. It was often reported that Kubrick was rude and tactless to the people he worked with. For example, he had a good friendship with the actor Malcolm McDowell during the making of *A Clockwork Orange*. However, after the filming ended Kubrick never contacted him again.

Kubrick had little contact with the media, so few people knew what he looked like. Kubrick once told a reporter who came to his door that Stanley Kubrick wasn't at home.

Lesson 4.4 Exercise 5 (p. 45)

You think that the best option is to set up English language courses online for all staff. Try to persuade the other members to accept your idea. Use the ideas below and your ideas from Exercise 2b.

- Online courses are a cheap way of teaching large numbers of learners.

- You will be able to work with the language expert on the content of the courses.

- Online courses enable staff to learn English at a time which suits them.

- You do not want to have classes in the office as there are no suitable rooms for teaching English. You also think that one-to-one courses are very expensive and likely to be unpopular with senior staff.

Lesson 5.3 Exercise 8a (p. 53)

Son
You want the biggest, fastest bike with the biggest engine. Your friends will think you are silly if you have a bike that 12 year olds can ride. You think you are responsible and will drive safely.

Lesson 7.4 Exercise 5 (p. 77)

Commuter jacket
Description: A stylish, elegant jacket for men. A very eye-catching design. The jacket is offered in black and grey. It has a built-in inflatable cushion in the neck, and a heater that gently warms the whole jacket.
Qualities: a smart, 'about town' look, modern style, excellent for travelling.
Suggested price: $190

Lesson 8.3 Exercise 9a (p. 85)

Education in Argentina
Argentina has nine years of compulsory schooling. However, children from poor families drop out of school before completing their basic education. In 1998:

- only 20 percent completed the secondary level of education.

- 64 percent of the population between 25 and 34 had not completed the secondary level.

There are plenty of public, free universities in Argentina. There are also many fee-paying private universities for the rich.
Recently, universities have become very poor because of economic and commercial failures in the country. There is also high unemployment among graduates (some qualified doctors have to drive taxis to feed their families) and many are dissatisfied with the quality of the universities.

Make notes about ages of students at secondary school, percentage of students in higher education, legth of compulsory education, private universities and any other interesting information.

Lesson 10.4 Exercise 6a (p. 109)

Prepare for the meeting by discussing the list of problems and suggesting ways of solving them. You are unhappy in Belleview. You want to:

- persuade the Council not to sell the 80-year-old aquarium. They should spend a lot of money on the aquarium to bring it up to standard.

- have more facilities in the town for older people (give some examples).

- have free parking for all resident car owners.

- propose stricter penalties for bad behaviour by young people.

Choose one person to lead your group. Present your ideas at the meeting. Try to persuade the Council to accept your suggestions.

Lesson 12.3 Exercise 8 (p. 127)

Martha Smith is 75 years old and walks her dog by the lake every morning. She found the body and police have not been able to find any connection between her and the victim. She was a judge before she retired and is a well-respected member of the community.

Lesson 12.4 Exercise 5 (p. 129)

Case 2 – case for the defence
It's a free country and she is doing nothing wrong.
He is exaggerating her behaviour.
It is a small town so they go to the same places.
She is just being friendly.
Photography is her hobby.

Case 3 – case for the prosecution
A car is a weapon.
A driver must concentrate on the road at all times.
He shouldn't have given sweets to the children.
None of the people in the car were wearing seatbelts.
The driver should have stopped before helping the child.

INFORMATION FOR STUDENT D

Lesson 4.4 Exercise 5 (p. 45)

You think that the best option is to send senior and middle managers to the UK and the US for crash courses, and to provide as much one-to-one teaching as possible. Try to persuade the other members to accept your ideas. Use the ideas below and your ideas from Exercise 2b:

- Managers will learn English quickly.

- Crash courses in the UK / the US are the most effective way of learning English.

- One-to-one teaching means that managers can learn English when the time is convenient for them.

- You do not want to have online courses. In your opinion, they are not effective. You need face-to-face contact with a teacher.

Lesson 7.4 Exercise 5 (p. 77)

iPod speakers
Description: Speakers for an iPod. The speakers allow you to use your iPod inside or outside your home. The sound quality is excellent. They are stylish and compact, so they are easy to carry and do not take up too much space. They have a carry case, remote control and adaptors for other countries. They can get power from a mains source or from four AA batteries. They can be used at barbecues, picnics, parties, etc.
Qualities: Excellent sound quality, good treble and bass, very good value for money, portable.
Suggested price: $100–$120.

Lesson 8.3 Exercise 9a (p. 85)

Education in Germany
In all 16 of Germany's states, the starting point is elementary school for a period of four years. But afterwards, each state is responsible for its education system. This means there are many different school systems. If families want to move from one state to another there can be problems for the children because the syllabus and textbook for each subject will be different.

- The federal government cannot say what must be studied or how it should be studied. However, federal standards on the quality of teaching are being established.

- The former East Germany had a different school system from West Germany so when the two merged there were further problems.

- English is studied in all secondary schools.

- Universities in Germany are part of the free state education system, which means that there are very few private universities and colleges. Unlike other countries, e.g. the USA, private universities and colleges in Germany are generally not as famous as public universities.

Make notes about ages of students at secondary school, percentage of students in higher education, length of compulsory education, private universities and any other interesting information.

Lesson 12.3 Exercise 8 (p. 127)

Professor Ewan Shapiro is the father of the victim. He has a water-tight alibi. He hosted a large dinner party from 6 p.m. till 11 p.m. last night and was seen by 14 people. He will inherit a small amount (one quarter) of his daughter's money.

Lesson 12.4 Exercise 5 (p. 129)

Case 3 – case for the defence
It was an accident.
He was not speeding.
The car was in good condition.
The road was narrow and needed repairs.
The people outside the café were sitting in a dangerous position.

SUPPLEMENTARY INFORMATION

Lesson 12.3 Exercise 8 (p. 127)

Student E rolecard:
Dr Drake Ramorey was engaged to marry the victim. Surprisingly, he was already in the victim's will. He will inherit most (three quarters) of the victim's money. He is an expert on chest and lungs. He has a history of violence with his previous girlfriend.

Lesson 3.4 Exercise 9 (p. 33)

For candidates:

NAME OF INTERVIEWER _____
[For each category, write a number from 1 to 5.
1 = excellent, 5 = poor]
1 Did the interviewer make you feel relaxed?
2 How good / fair were the interviewer's questions?
3 Did the interviewer give you enough time to answer the questions?
4 How carefully did the interviewer listen to your answers?
5 How appropriate were the follow-up questions?
6 Did the interviewer give you the opportunity to ask any questions?
7 How effective was the interview?
OVERALL QUALITY OF INTERVIEWER _____

For interviewers:

NAME OF CANDIDATE _____
[For each category, write a number from 1 to 5.
1 = excellent, 5 = poor]
1 Education/qualifications
2 Experience
3 Appearance
4 Communication skills
5 Enthusiasm
6 Leadership skills
7 Personality
OVERALL SUITABILITY OF CANDIDATE _____

Lesson 5.3 Exercise 8b (p. 53)

Name	Dolphin x100	Barracuda x300	Shark x400	Dirt Monster x700
length	1,100 mm	1,600 mm	1,700 mm	2,300 mm
width	760 mm	900 mm	1,200 mm	1,200 mm
height	740 mm	850 mm	1,200 mm	1,200 mm
engine size	50 cc	125 cc	250 cc	300 cc
top speed	22 kph	28 kph	75 kph	80 kph
minimum age	12	14	16	16
price	€300	€550	€3,000	€3,200
safety rating	*****	*****	****	**

SUPPLEMENTARY INFORMATION

Lesson 12.3 Exercise 8 (p. 127)
Student F rolecard
Encourage people to talk about how the crime was committed. Do not reveal this information till near the end: ice melts.

Lesson 8.4 Exercise 4 (p. 87)
List of problems:
1 Teaching staff
Some lecturers are very boring. They read their lectures and do not ask students any questions. Many lecturers do not use visual aids or provide good reading lists. Tutorials are not useful. The lecturers talk most of the time and the students say nothing.
2 Attendance
Attendance of classes and lectures is poor: few students attend 80 percent of their lectures. Most students miss the early morning lectures from 9 to 11 a.m. As a result, teachers do not prepare their lectures properly. Many students fail their degree because of poor attendance. Some students spend too much time downtown instead of attending lectures.
3 Facilities
Some of the sports facilities are in very poor condition, for example, the swimming pool, tennis courts and gym. New equipment is urgently needed, so a bigger budget to buy equipment is essential.
4 Bullying
A first-year student, Lisa, is being bullied by a senior member of the staff. He makes fun of her in tutorials, asks her very difficult questions, and is not interested in her answers. She is so unhappy that she wishes to leave the college at the end of the semester. Other students, in previous years, have complained of this teacher's attitude and behaviour.
5 Cheating and plagiarism
Cheating and plagiarism have increased during the past few years. It is believed that students pass information to each other in examinations. Many students consider cheating at examinations to be a kind of game. Lecturers complain that students often copy directly from internet sources without giving references. Plagiarism is common at the university. It is said that some rich students buy essays from poorer colleagues.

Review 7–19, Exercise 1b (p. 100)

Lesson 9.2 Exercise 1 (p. 92)
Statement 3 is false. Asteroids are mainly rocky bodies that orbit the sun.

Lesson 9.2 Exercise 8a (p. 93)
Make as many present or past simple passive sentences from the table as you can. Make guesses if necessary. You have ten minutes. (You will need to add prepositions, e.g. *by*, *in* or *to*.)

1 The Taj Mahal	set up	Tim Berners-Lee
2 The ballpoint pen		Gianni Agnelli in 1899
3 Nokia mobile phones	invent	South Africa
4 Diamonds	build	around 1640
5 The first computer	make	Laszlo Jose Biro
6 The World Wide Web	use	Finland
7 The motor company Fiat	develop	Alan Turing
8 The telephone		Alexander Bell
9 Microsoft	mine	William Coolidge
10 The X-ray tube	refine	Bill Gates
11 The Nobel Prize for Physics	found	Sri Lanka
12 Tea	grow	Guglielmo Marconi in 1909
13 Toyota cars		in the 18th century
14 The first steam ship	award	Japan
15 The first motor car	manufacture	Carl Benz in 1884

Lesson 9.4 Exercise 6a (p. 97)
1 What is the best name for the new city?
2 Which material should be mainly used to construct the city? Glass? Concrete? Steel? Other?
3 Who should the new city be for? Poor people? Rich and poor people? Anyone who can afford it?
4 What style would be suitable for the apartments? Classical? Modern? Futuristic? Other?
5 Should there be many or few restaurants?
6 Should the new city have closed circuit television? Where?
7 What should transport inside the building mainly consist of? Lifts? A monorail and minibuses? Bicycles? Other?
8 How can the builders protect the city against fire, hurricanes and very hot weather?

Lesson 1.1. Track 1.3

Christina, Helen, George

C: Oh, Helen, come on! You can tell a lot from a person's appearance. I mean, when people meet me for the first time, they can see I'm quite a sociable person – I love parties, going out, enjoying myself, that sort of thing. I always try and have a good time and not take life too seriously.

H: I don't know, Christina. It's certainly not the same for me. Look, I've got quite a lot of friends, but most of them say they thought I was really quiet and serious when they first met me. Maybe it's the way I dress. But you know me, I think I'm quite energetic. And I'm interested in everything.

G: Mmm.

H: Maybe people think I'm strange because of my sense of humour, I don't know, or because I don't care what people think. I like to do things my way. Anyway, you always laugh at my jokes, George.

G: Yes, I think you're really funny.

H: What about you, George? You're very different from how you look.

G: How do you mean?

H: Well … you've got a really good job, running your Internet company. You're hard-working, very focused on your career. You seem to know exactly what your aims are. People would never guess, just looking at you – they'd probably think you're an out-of-work actor or something.

G: Yeah, you're right, Helen. I suppose I am a bit strange because I don't dress like a typical manager or businessman. I think I'm a pretty serious person and people don't always realise that when they first meet me. I like to be in control, I plan everything very carefully and I don't like too much change in my life. That's the way I am.

C: I suppose you are very different from your appearance, George, and you are a bit strange …

H: Christina!

C: … but you're a good friend, that's the important thing.

H: She's right. You're very reliable and you have high standards. I think you're a person with real principles, and there aren't too many people like that these days.

G: Thanks, Helen. I think that's a good description of me – you know me well, don't you?

Lesson 1.2. Track 1.4

Anchor, Presenter, Frank Partridge

A: And now at 11 o'clock it's over to Jenny Mason and today's edition of 'Changing World'.

P: Good evening everyone. Our guest tonight is Dr Frank Partridge, an expert on personality. Dr Partridge – our listeners are very interested in personality tests, so can I ask a few questions about those before we talk about your current research?

F: Yes, certainly, and good evening everyone.

P: OK, my first question. What exactly does psychometrics mean?

F: Well, psychometrics is really related to the measurement of intelligence and personal qualities. It measures four things: the measurement of knowledge, the measurement of abilities, the measurement of attitudes and personality traits. It's really about the differences between individuals.

P: I see. How did psychometric testing start? I mean, who designed the early tests?

F: Well, the first psychometric tests were designed to measure intelligence. I think the first usable intelligence test was the Stanford-Binet test. The test was developed originally by a French psychologist called Alfred Binet.

P: Mmm, interesting. So, how useful are the tests? Are they reliable? That's what most people want to know.

F: Well, that's a good question. All tests must have reliability and validity. Let me explain what I mean. When you use a reliable test, you get the same results each time. If the test is valid, it measures what it's supposed to measure … and not something else.

P: Mmm. I wonder if you could you give us an example of what exactly you mean by validity?

F: An example? Well … if you test a teacher on how many books they can carry, that's not a valid measure of their ability as a teacher.

P: Right, I see. Well, what can personality tests tell you about a person?

F: Well, there's one test, called the Myers-Briggs test, which is widely used all over the world. It's based on an Internet study of more than 20,000 people. Organisations think it's useful when you want to work out people's roles in a team. Some people say it's useful to decide your personality type. You can, for example, find out how organised, reliable and sociable you are. I think the questions are quite interesting and people seem to enjoy doing them. There are questions like: 'Can you stay calm under pressure?' 'Are you a good team player?' 'How motivated are you?' And so on.

P: Have you taken any of these tests yourself?

F: Yes, I have. The results were very interesting.

P: OK, thanks for that. Now, let's get on to your research. What are you working on at the moment, Dr Partridge?

F: I'm currently carrying out research into personalities of identical twins. I'm looking at the similarities and differences of their personalities and I can tell you it's …

Lesson 1.4. Track 1.5

Ben, Sylvia

B: I can't understand it, Sylvia, two assistants leaving us in the last three months. It's not our fault, is it?

S: I don't know, Ben, maybe it is. Let's face it, we're not easy people to work with. You're very intelligent and ambitious, but you seem to forget other people don't have those qualities. I think you probably expect too much from them. And then you get angry if they don't do their job properly.

B: Hmm, I suppose I am a bit bad-tempered sometimes. I shout if things go wrong. But Barbara didn't seem to mind.

S: I don't know, I think it really upset her. What did she say about you? That you were bossy, and, erm … insensitive.

B: OK, but maybe she said that because I wouldn't give her time off to do her shopping. I pay people to work 9.00 to 5.00, Sylvia, not to leave the office whenever they feel like it.

S: Come on, Ben, an hour off, just before Christmas? Not asking for much.

B: OK, maybe Barbara asked at a bad moment, I don't know. Anyway it wasn't just that. She didn't like me smoking in the office – it really bothered her. You know, I like open-minded people, so I was really quite pleased when she left. Anyway, I got on all right with Louise, but she didn't like you or your secretary much, did she?

S: Well, it's true, Louise and I didn't get on. I reckon she didn't like me because I'm very sociable and I'm a bit noisy when I'm enjoying myself. Louise was a very quiet person. Another thing – she was really jealous because Susan and I have a good relationship. Louise didn't like it when Susan made fun of her. She just couldn't take a joke – she was far too serious.

B: I don't agree, Sylvia. Actually I thought Louise was quite nice, but she was a little sensitive, I agree. She told me you were really moody – one minute nice to her, the next unpleasant. I think she was afraid of you in the end.

S: Really? You surprise me. I know I've got a strong personality – some people don't like that. But moody? I don't think so. Look, Ben, why don't we try and get a man as our assistant this time? To be honest, I think we'd both work better with a man.

B: I don't know – male or female, does it really matter, as long as they have the right personality? We've got to get someone who'll fit in here. The skills are less important – most people seem to have the basic skills we're looking for. It's not a problem. What we need is someone who'll be a good match for us. I suggest we contact the agency again. Let's see what they can come up with this time. We'll give them a good briefing so they know exactly what we want.

S: Great idea. Let's do it.

Lesson 2.1. Track 1.6

Nadia, Lisa, Armando, Jacques, Tom

N: OK, so that's my experience. Have you got any questions?

L: Hi, Nadia, my name's Lisa.

N: Hi, Lisa.

L: Nadia, what's the furthest you've travelled from home?

N: Mmm, let me think … well, I suppose the answer is Indonesia.

L: Indonesia? Did you enjoy it?

N: Yeah, it was fascinating. I went with a friend and we got on really well. And she's still a good friend, I'm pleased to tell you. The country's got thousands of islands and we visited quite a few of them. I must say, I'll never forget Komodo – they have the largest lizards in the world there, Komodo Dragons, and one of them chased us across the beach. It was absolutely terrifying, I can tell you!

L: Wow! What an experience!

N: Mmm, not to be forgotten. Who's next?

A: Hi, I'm Armando

N: Hi, Armando.

A: What's the longest journey you've been on?

N: You mean, in time?

A: Yeah, in time.

N: Well, I've travelled for four months, three times. During those trips, I visited, erm … Mexico, Indonesia, India and many other south-east Asian countries, like Thailand and Vietnam. I loved Vietnam – the people were so friendly, and the food was wonderful. But it was a bit noisy in the streets – you know, a lot of people travel on motorbikes, and you hear them everywhere.

J: Hi, I'm Jacques. Erm … what are the most popular destinations for people from your country?

N: Depends a lot on the group, Jacques, but I'd say older people, say the over-fifties, they like to go to the Canary Islands, and young people prefer Thailand, to really get away from it all. Next question?

T: Hello Nadia, I'm Tom. People say that travel broadens the mind. What are the reasons why people travel, in your opinion?

N: Hmm, interesting question, Tom. I suppose there are lots of reasons. Some want to see new sights and explore new places, erm … meet new people and experience different cultures. I certainly wanted to do all those things. But I also wanted to learn new skills, especially social skills. I wanted to become more self-confident. Oh, yes, and I was also interested in learning a new language, or at least getting some knowledge of an Asian language. Now my friend, Joanne, she just wanted to earn some money while she was abroad, to finance her studies. But there are lots of other reasons why people travel.

T: How do you mean, exactly?

N: Well, how can I put it, erm … some people travel to, erm … find themselves, I mean, to learn more about themselves and perhaps become more independent, and just generally to broaden their horizons. One thing's for sure, Tom, if you travel a long way from home, for a long time, you're a different person when you return. It makes you into a …

Lesson 2.3. Track 1.8

Interviewer, Alice

I: Alice Harker? Come in. Have a seat.

A: Thank you.

I: Thanks for coming in today. Can I get you a coffee?

A: No thanks. I've had two cups this morning.

I: OK. Did you have a good journey here?

A: Yes, thanks. I travelled up by train yesterday and I stayed in a hotel last night. I'm catching a train back at half past eleven.

I: Oh, right, we'd better begin then. You've applied for a place on the 'Sherpa Tensing' expedition. Why do you want to go on this expedition?

A: Well, I've visited nearly every continent in the world, and I've done a lot of climbing, but I've never done anything for charity before.

I: I see. Have you ever been on an expedition like this before? I mean, this challenging?

A: Oh yes. I've climbed extensively in the Alps and I've already taken part in six Himalayan expeditions, but I haven't climbed to the summit of Everest yet.

I: Well, you've had the right mountaineering experience, Ms Harker. So that's not a problem at all. Now, tell me something about your last job.

A: Mmm, well … I worked as a consultant last year, for a management consultancy firm, running team-building courses.

I: So why did you leave that job?

A: That isn't really what I want to do. I thought I'd try it, but really, I want to spend more time climbing. I've been on two expeditions so far this year.

I: OK, that's all very useful. Now, …

Lesson 2.4. Track 1.10.

Harry, Ingrid

H: We need to think about the problems on the last trip so we don't have the same ones this year.

I: I agree with you, Hans, a lot went wrong. The group never became a team, did it? They just didn't get on with each other at all.

H: Yeah, some of them ended up hating each other. The problem was that they didn't know each other well enough before they left.

I: Yeah, I agree, it was a big problem throughout the trip.

H: Definitely. You know, another thing, they didn't know what to do if anything went wrong, like, erm … remember when they lost their cameras?

H: Hold on, Harry, they didn't lose their cameras, they were robbed. But why didn't they go immediately to the police and report the matter? We only heard about it a couple of days later, when it was too late. So, they got no money from the insurance company because they didn't report the matter.

H: Well, they said they were afraid to go to the police – they didn't think the police would speak English.

I: That was pretty stupid, surely. Lots of people speak English there now. You know, the students got on my nerves at times – they were always complaining. The accommodation was no good, the hotels were for business people, not students. I mean, it was rubbish. The hotels were fine, in my opinion. And you know what really upset me, Harry?

H: Yeah?

I: They said we tried to do too much during the trip. They didn't have enough free time.

H: Well, we talked about that before we went, how much free time to give them. There are arguments for and against, aren't there? On the one hand, giving them a lot of free time is good – they have a chance to explore places they visit. On the other hand, if they have too much time, they say we haven't organised enough trips. You can't win, can you?

I: True, and don't forget Hans, another disadvantage of giving them a lot of free time is that they get into trouble. You know, they do stupid things. Look what happened last time – remember those students who slept all night in the park?

H: Don't remind me! Actually I've got a few suggestions for this next trip.

I: Me too.

H: Good. Well I think we should have more meetings with the students before they leave. An advantage of this is they'd get to know each other a lot better.

I: Yeah. That's true. Also, it'd be a good idea to give the students maps of the cities they visit. I suggest we write to the tourist boards and ask them to send us some.

H: Yeah, why not? And how about asking the students where they want to stay? Do they want to share a room in a cheap hotel, or stay in a youth hostel? There are lots of possibilities.

I: Yeah, let's do that, Hans, let's ask them and then they won't be able to complain later.

Lesson 2.5. Track 1.11.

Good morning. The subject of today's talk is the explorer Thor Heyerdahl. First of all I'll give you some background information, before going on to look at his career, achievements and finally, his main publications and awards.

Heyerdahl was born in Larvik in Southern Norway in 1914. He studied Zoology and Geography at the University of Oslo and then made his first expedition to Polynesia from 1937 to 1938. While he was staying in Polynesia, Heyerdahl became interested in how the islands were first inhabited. He had the idea that humans came with the ocean currents from the west.

Now I'd like to look at his career. After giving up his study of Geography, he set out to prove his theories. How did he attempt to test his theories? Well, to begin with, in 1947 he built a raft named the *Kon-Tiki*, and then with five companions crossed from Peru to Polynesia in 101 days. The main idea he wanted to prove was that the cultures of the ancient world were linked by sailors who could cross oceans. After the success of the Kon-Tiki expedition, Heyerdahl continued to travel. He organised the Norwegian archaeological expedition to the Galapagos Islands in 1952, before leading an expedition to Easter Island from 1955 to 1956. In addition to this, during 1969 and 1970 he sailed two more rafts, *Ra 1* and *Ra 2*, across the Atlantic to show that ancient Egyptians had contact with South America.

What will Heyerdahl be remembered for? Well, most people believe his greatest achievement was the Kon-Tiki Expedition. However, all his expeditions and ideas had a great influence on anthropology and archaeology. Moving on to his publications, the most famous were *The Kon-Tiki Expedition*, in 1948, *The Ra Expeditions*, in 1970 and *The Tigris Expedition*, in 1980.

Finally, I'd like to turn to his awards. He received many awards during his lifetime – two of the most important were his election to the Norwegian Academy of Sciences in 1958 and then the American Academy of Science in 1960. Furthermore, his film of the *Kon-Tiki* expedition won an Oscar in 1951 for best documentary feature.

Thor Heyerdahl died in 2002 at his home in Italy.

Lesson 3.1. Track 1.12.

1

Well, the hours are very long and I have to work shifts, but I like my colleagues and I enjoy the variety of the work. You know, every day's different. I suppose the main reason I like the job is the contact with patients. I like to feel that I'm helping people, and my colleagues are great, so that makes the job very rewarding. It's certainly not the pay – that's terrible!

2

I really enjoy my job, although there can be a lot of routine paperwork and I have to attend a lot of meetings. Preparing cases takes up a lot of my time, and can be very challenging. The best parts of the job are meeting clients and going to court. I work for a big international firm so there are good opportunities for promotion and I get to travel quite a lot, which is nice.

3

Some people would say it's a glamorous job, and I suppose it is sometimes, but actually it's very hard work as well. There's also not much job security. The pay's good, but sometimes I don't work for a few weeks, so that can be a worry. I suppose I enjoy the travel – there's a lot of that – but sometimes there's a lot of waiting around for photographers and stylists, which can be really boring.

4

Some parts of the job are not very interesting, like filling shelves. Also, changing the window displays gets a bit repetitive. Really, it's dealing with people I like, on the phone and face to face. My boss is a lovely person but he's so badly organised. He usually gets me to deal with problem customers who want refunds, that kind of thing. Some people think I'm a workaholic, and it's true I do a lot of overtime, but I like to do a job well and I'm proud of my work. It's a big chain so I hope I'll become assistant manager next year if I move to another branch.

5

What I particularly like is that it's a very flexible job. I can work from home some of the time. I find it exciting, meeting and interviewing different people. It's also satisfying when you finish a long article and it's published. I've got a book coming out next year as well. One thing about working on a monthly magazine is that I have a lot of tight deadlines. That makes the job very stressful.

Lesson 3.2. Track 1.13.

1

I'm a language graduate and I've been translating from Italian to English for most of my career. We've been in Milan for nearly 20 years and I've been working from home for 12 years, since my first child was born. I've found that my work-life balance has been easier to manage since I started working from home – and it needs to be easy to manage when you've got children!

2

I'm a writer and I've been working from home for the last 18 months. I must say it's been pretty tough. For one thing I've been paying a lot more for heating. And I've missed the office gossip. To be honest, it's quite lonely. I almost wish I could go back to my old job.

3

Working from home has really changed my life. I love it. I love being my own boss. I've been working from home as a website designer since I left my last job in 2004. I have a bit more time these days. I've bought myself a new guitar and I've been taking guitar lessons for the last six months.

4

It's not for everybody, but I like working from home. I do contract work in design. The best thing is that I don't have to commute to work on crowded trains. I've had lots more time and I've been learning a new language since I started working at home in January. I've always wanted to learn Spanish.

5

I'm German but I've been living abroad for five years. I've been working in marketing for a pharmaceutical company near London and I've been working from home part of the time since January. I work from home three days a week and commute in to the office twice a week. I was very lucky to get this opportunity. When I work from home I get up late and work late in the evenings. I've never been a morning person.

Lesson 3.4. Track 1.16.

Harry, Marta

H: I think you're right, Marta, educational qualifications and experience are not really so important – we've got to find someone with the right skills and personal qualities.

M: Exactly. The person we choose will get six months' training in New York, so that'll prepare them well for the job. As you say, it's the personal qualities which are so important. It'll be pretty stressful, building up the club here. They'll have to work long hours and be very flexible. OK, we're offering a competitive salary, good perks, a nice working environment – that should attract some good candidates. But the job's not as glamorous as it sounds. We'll need someone who's very dynamic, energetic, erm … enthusiastic, and with lots of ideas.

H: Absolutely. And I think the best candidate will be very determined, someone who has a real desire to succeed, because it won't be easy. We need an outgoing

person, I'd say, who can work with people from different cultures. Don't forget – a lot of our customers won't be English. All the candidates must also have an interest in health and fitness, don't you think?

M: Definitely. And I agree – we need a fairly extroverted person, with really good communication skills. If possible, they'll be fluent in another language – French, German, Japanese, whatever.

H: Yeah, I like the sound of that. But most important of all, we want someone who's looking for a long term career with us, someone who'll stay with us and build up the club. There's tremendous potential here for a health club, we know that, and the right manager can make a lot of money for us.

M: OK, I've made a note of the points we mentioned. Now let's write the advertisement.

Lesson 3.4. Track 1.17.

Interviewer, Candidate

1

I: Now, looking at your C.V. I'd like to know what you feel you learned in your last job.

C: I'm glad you asked me that because I developed some important skills while I was there.

2

I: I'm also interested in knowing your reasons for leaving the job.

C: That's a very good question. Basically, it was no longer challenging enough.

3

I: Now, a question we like to ask all our candidates. What are your strong points?

C: Well, without going into too much detail, I have very good people skills.

4

I: I was wondering what you feel you can bring to this job?

C: Let me just think about that for a moment. Well, my sales and marketing experience should be very useful to you.

5

I: OK. Thank you. A question now about your computer skills. What software are you familiar with?

C: I thought you might ask me something about that. Well, what I can say is, I have a good knowledge of Excel and Word, and can prepare excellent Powerpoint presentations.

6

I: Let me follow that up with another question. How do you feel about working abroad?

C: I haven't really thought about that, to be honest, but I think it'd be really interesting.

7

I: Right, thank you. Moving on, could you tell me what you think the growth areas in the leisure industry are?

C: Well, I'm not an expert, but I think the boom in fitness centres will continue in the next few years.

8

I: OK. Just one final question. Where do you think you'll be in five years' time?

c: I'm afraid I don't know the answer to that, but I hope to be working for your company in a senior position.

Lesson 3.5. Track 1.18.
Student, Counsellor

s: I know you usually send a covering letter with a CV. But, what is it exactly?

c: Well, really it's a letter telling an employer why you're interested in their company or organisation. You can tell them about your special skills and qualities and why you want to work with them. It gives you an opportunity to sell yourself to the employer.

s: I see. Erm … how long should it be?

c: It depends. But generally I'd say a covering letter should be short, perhaps one side of an A4 sheet of paper. And the tone should be enthusiastic and professional.

s: Right. Could you give me a little more detail about what to put in each paragraph?

c: OK, I'll suggest a structure, a way to organise the paragraphs, if you like.

s: Thank you.

c: Right. The first paragraph is your introduction. You say who you are, why you're writing and where you saw the position advertised.

s: OK, I've got that.

c: In paragraph two, tell the employer why you want the job – in other words, say what attracted you to the organisation. Show that you're enthusiastic and motivated.

s: Right.

c: The third paragraph is really important. This is where you sell yourself. Here you mention your qualities, erm … skills and experience that match what they are probably looking for. You tell them what you can contribute to their organisation. OK? Now we come to the final paragraph. Say when you're available for interview. And end on a positive note. For example, say you look forward to hearing from them soon, or something like that. OK, that's about it.

s: Thanks, that's really helpful.

Lesson 3.5. Track 1.19.

1

I think you should put as much as possible in a CV so the employer gets a complete picture of your qualities and skills and qualifications. If you don't do that, they may not call you for an interview.

2

It's essential to write a personal profile at the beginning of your CV. Everyone's doing it these days. It helps to focus your reader's attention on what you really have to offer their organisation. It's where you can sell yourself as a candidate.

3

If you're sending out CVs to lots of companies at one time, I mean if you're just seeing if there's any interest, not replying to an ad for a job, then I think your CV should be really short, just one side of an A4 sheet.

4

I try to write as much as possible in the Work Experience section. I start with my first job then put my most recent job last – that's the order I prefer. I had a period of six months when I was unemployed, but I never show that on my CV.

5

I have just one CV which I send out whenever I'm looking for a new job. Of course, I always bring it up to date. That's the advantage of keeping it on my computer – it's easy to bring my employment history up to date.

6

To be honest, I think the covering letter's much more important than your CV. If they like what they read in your letter, they'll look at your CV. But if your letter's no good, they'll throw your CV in the bin right away.

Review 1–3 Track 1.20
Kris, Piotr

k: I think we should head for Greece, Piotr. For one thing it's cheap to fly there.

p: I don't know. It's a bit too hot for me. Besides, what will we do?

k: Well, on the one hand you've got loads of historical sites so that's interesting and on the other hand you can always spend a few days by the sea relaxing.

p: Yes, well it's true about the history and broadening the mind but sitting on the beach isn't my idea of real travelling!

k: What does that mean?

p: Well, we only have four weeks and I can go to a beach any time I want!

k: But we're going to want to have some time doing nothing after our exams, aren't we?

p: Yes, you're right. OK then. It'd be a good idea to go to an island, get a tan and then after about a week we can go to Athens and travel on the mainland.

k: Great idea. Oh, by the way, I was wondering if Pavel could come with us?

p: What? Err, I don't know about that.

k: Why not?

p: Don't get me wrong. Pavel's fine as a person but it'll be easier to book rooms for two than three.

k: Well, if we stay in hostels we'll share rooms with lots of people anyway. I did it last year and it's a really good way to meet other travellers.

p: That's true, but another disadvantage of Pavel coming is that there'll be three of us, which always makes it harder to come to decisions about what to visit – you know, one person wants to do one thing and someone else doesn't want to.

k: OK. He doesn't have to be with us all the time but how about saying to him that he can meet up with us somewhere?

p: Let me just think about that for a minute.

Lesson 4.2. Track 1.21
Howard, Fred

h: Hello.

f: Oh, hi, Howard. It's Fred here.

h: Fred, hi. Have you finished the essay on King Lear yet?

f: No, not yet. I'm going to finish it tonight. What about you?

h: I'm finding it quite tough. I'm not very good with Shakespeare … but I'm definitely going to finish it by tomorrow's class. I want it out of the way!

f: Howard, I'm just phoning to ask – James and I are going to the cinema on Thursday evening, do you want to come?

h: No, I can't. I'm giving my presentation to the language seminar group on Friday, …

f: Oh, of course.

h: … so I have to prepare that. I'm doing it on SMS – you know, text messaging. I read something recently that said that text language will be the English of the future – can you believe that?

f: Yeah, I can. We all use it, don't we? I saw an article about it in the paper the other day. I'll find it for you.

h: Thanks, that'd be great. When's your presentation?

f: It isn't till the end of next week.

h: Do you know what you're doing?

f: Yeah, I'm doing mine on spelling and how important it is.

h: That's interesting. I saw a film a while ago on spelling competitions in America. They're really popular there. Anyway, I'd better get on with the essay. I'll see you at the lecture tomorrow.

f: Great. I'll text you when I find that paper.

h: Thanks. Bye.

f: Bye.

Lesson 4.3. Track 1.22.
Presenter, Bradana

p: Now, for our 'Language now' slot. My guest today is Bradana MacKinnon, spokesperson for the Society for the Promotion of Gaelic. Thank you for being on our radio programme today and, indeed, on our series on different languages.

b: Thank you. It's a pleasure to be here.

p: Bradana, I'd like to begin with your name. It's quite unusual. Is it a Celtic word?

b: Yes, it is, and it's not common. It's a Gaelic word meaning 'salmon'. Just a small point here – Celtic usually refers to the culture; Gaelic is the language.

p: Thank you, Bradana, I'll remember that. If you don't mind, I'll get straight to the point. Should we fight to keep a dying language alive, even if few people will ever use it or hear it?

b: Mmm, that is something to consider, I suppose, but I'm not sure it's a relevant question here. It's true that in the last 100 years or so, the number of Gaelic-only speakers in Scotland, and I mean people speaking just Gaelic and no English, well, that number has fallen from nearly 44,000 to zero. And yes … Gaelic has declined throughout the 20th century. But it's also true to say that since the 1970s there has been a revival in the Celtic culture and Gaelic language.

p: I see. So where do you find that revival – in schools?

b: Yes, definitely in schools, and that's important. If we have Gaelic-medium education at all levels, more people will speak Gaelic. There has been a huge increase in the number of young children being educated in Gaelic in primary schools … and nurseries. So, if Gaelic is a dying language, then why are more and more Gaelic schools starting in Scotland?

P: Good point, but if it's only schools …

B: Yes, I agree. We need more. If we have more TV and radio programmes in Gaelic, more people may listen to the language. Also, if the economy in the Gaelic-speaking heartland improves, then Gaelic will not die out. Opinion polls show that people are more confident in the Gaelic-speaking communities – they feel that the economy is improving. If young people return to live and work in those communities after university, then things will improve.

P: Well, that all sounds very promising. So, what is the Society for the Promotion of Gaelic doing now?

B: Oh, we have lots going on. Unless we all continue to promote Gaelic, there might not be a significant increase in speakers of Gaelic. But, to answer your question … at the moment we're trying to raise our profile, and we have a new fund-raising campaign. When we reach our targets, we'll invest in more Gaelic books in public libraries. And as soon as we get more Gaelic speakers involved, we'll run more Gaelic language classes. But unless we recruit and train more Gaelic-medium teachers, we won't make a big difference in schools. Basically our fund-raising supports all of that.

P: To go back to my first question, Bradana, why should we fight to keep Gaelic alive?

B: Well, I believe that every language provides us with knowledge about human thinking and behaviour. And every language, like every species of animal, is unique and worth protecting. When we lose a language, we lose a lot of knowledge.

P: Bradana MacKinnon, thank you very much.

Lesson 4.4. Track 1.23.
Sven, Don, Delphine

S: As I see it, we can't do much with such a small budget … so I think we should focus, first of all, on the directors and senior staff. How about sending some of them on crash courses to Britain? It's a quick way to improve their English. What do you think, Don?

DO: Mmm, I don't know about that. I can see a problem right away. If we send them to England, it will have a bad effect on our work. We don't want to lose half our top people just like that. I mean, who'd run the charity?

S: Yeah, I think you're right. That would create problems for us. Well, how about this? Why don't we send just one or two directors and a few senior staff to England and offer the rest one-to-one classes when they have free time?

DO: Yes, I think that would work. Good idea, Sven. What do you think, Delphine?

DE: Well, I'm afraid I don't like the idea. If we do that, what will happen?

Just when we need to talk to one of them, they won't be here, they'll be in Britain. We've got so many projects going on at the moment, we need everyone here to deal with the work. You know, I'd like to discuss another problem if that's OK with you.

DO, S: OK.

DE: I wonder, should we teach British or American English? Some of our staff might prefer to learn American English, you know.

S: I think you're right, Delphine – some staff will want to learn American English. What do you suggest?

DE: Well, we could hire two teachers to run courses at our head office. One could be British and the other American. I think that would solve the problem.

S: Mmm, good idea, Delphine.

DO: Yeah, I like that idea. It's definitely worth considering. Another thing I'd like to talk about Sven …

S: Oh, yes?

DO: We've talked mostly about the directors and senior staff. What about the other staff? They'll need to improve their English too. And we'll need to set up a programme very soon.

S: I'm not sure about that, Don. The volunteers will need to improve their English, it's true, but other staff will have to have priority. Don't forget, our budget for language training is limited this year and we can't afford to …

Lesson 5.1. Track 1.24.

A: OK, let's brainstorm how we're going to promote this product.

B: Well, we could get a famous celebrity like David Beckham to endorse it.

A: I think that would be much too expensive. Sponsorship of a TV programme would also cost a lot. And a TV commercial is out for the same reason. I've seen some great TV shots which are visually beautiful and really eye-catching, often set in romantic or exotic locations. But I don't think they've been very effective as people can't remember the product they're advertising.

B: I agree, but we don't want something dull and boring. How about advertising on the radio – would the budget run to that?

A: Yes we could stretch to that.

B: And would you like something witty and catchy?

A: Maybe. I want something new and original. But most importantly, it must be persuasive. It must get people to buy the product.

Lesson 5.1. Track 1.25.

1

I remember a really eye-catching advert for a Ford car. It showed the car starting, then being driven out of a car park and through the city. And it started all the lights in the surrounding buildings. In the country it powered the overhead power lines and the electricity seemed to follow the car along the road. It really was an attention-grabbing ad. It is difficult to be original with car adverts but I thought this was quite creative. It also

had a catchy slogan: 'Feel the power. Ford. We have ignition.' You could also see the recognisable Ford 'blue oval' logo. It must have been an effective ad because I've actually remembered that it was a Ford car. It was also quite persuasive as I would consider buying a Ford next time.

2

I normally like humorous ads. But the ad that sticks in my mind was really inspirational. The music was really lively and it was set in different exotic locations. Everyone was drinking this soft drink, but I can't remember which one it was, and the camerawork was really creative. It made you want to be there, drinking that soft drink, having fun.

3

I saw this really dull advert for washing powder on the television recently that I'd really like to forget. But it had this really catchy tune that I can't get out of my head. It's so irritating. It was informative – it gave you lots of information about the product but I can't even remember what the brand was.

Lesson 5.2. Track 1.26.
JP, Roberta

JP: We both know it won't be easy to advertise the Raymond Jacquet Classique range. Our problem is money. If we had a bigger budget, we'd get someone well known to endorse the product. There are plenty of performers in the movie industry who'd do it, but they're very expensive. We couldn't afford it.

R: OK. Well, if I were you, I'd look for a cheaper way of doing it. You don't always have to pay a fortune to get good publicity. An endorsement by someone famous isn't the only solution …

JP: Mmm, what exactly do you mean?

R: Well, you want to reach younger people with the Classique range, right? If you did that, you'd achieve your objective, to sell to a new group of consumers.

JP: Yes. That's true.

R: How about this then? If you ran a series of short TV commercials, you could reach a younger audience and it'd be a lot cheaper than using a film star or whatever.

JP: OK, but what sort of commercials should we run? We haven't really thought about that.

R: Well, I have. Why don't you contact some people who are really good at their job, let's say, at the top of their profession, and use them in your commercials? I don't mean stars or famous people, who cost the earth, I mean, for example, a young concert pianist, erm … a young lawyer or professional tennis player – no one famous, but they'd all be young, attractive and good at their job. The sort of successful people a young person would identify with. A role model, if you like.

JP: Mmm, interesting. Yes, if we got the right people, it might be a lot cheaper than using a film star. We'd be able to afford them, probably.

R: Exactly. In each commercial, you could show them briefly at work, with no mention of Raymond Jacquet, and then in the final shot, the camera could zoom in and focus for a few seconds on their wrist. They'd be wearing the Classique model, of course. Some nice modern music would play in the background.

JP: Mmm, good idea. It's clever, very subtle, in fact. Just right for a stylish range of watches aimed at young people.

R: Yeah, and if you got a young director to do the films, you wouldn't have to pay them too much. I'd say that's the solution to your problem.

JP: Mmm, it's worth considering. Definitely. I'll put it to everyone at our next meeting and let you know what they think.

Lesson 5.4. Track 1.27.

Amy, Larissa

A: There are several points I'd like your team to cover in their presentation.

L: OK.

A: Well, for a start, we can't agree on a name for the drink. We've had lots of suggestions but none of them have been very exciting, so could you come up with some new ideas for names, please?

L: Certainly, no problem.

A: We need a good slogan too, something that's easy to remember and original. One of our staff wanted to call the drink 'Krakkle' – she came up with the slogan 'Kool kids drink Krakkle', but no one really liked that one. We'd also like your ideas for the design of the packaging. Should it be a can or bottle, or something different? Nothing too detailed, just … oh I don't know, design, colour, shape – that sort of thing.

L: OK, erm … what else do you want us to look at?

A: Well, we've talked quite a lot about the kind of advertising we should use. Should we have a TV commercial during children's TV in the afternoon? Or maybe early in the evening? How about advertising in children's magazines? Should we use the Internet as well? Another question is, do we want just one TV commercial, with different languages for the various markets, or should we have a different TV commercial for each country?

L: Interesting. What about radio spots?

A: Ah yes, I forgot to mention that. Do you think we should advertise on radio? If you do, what time of the day should we choose for a radio spot, and what sort of programmes could we sponsor?

L: Is that everything?

A: I think so … Oh yes, one other thing, if your team have any interesting ideas for special promotions, let us have them. I mean, would it be a good idea to give out free cans in schools? Or offer cheap T-shirts with the logo on them? That sort of thing.

L: Fine. I'm sure we can come up with some good ideas for you. We'd certainly like to be your agency for the campaign.

A: Well, if we like your presentation, you'll have a good chance of winning the contract.

L: That's good enough for me.

Lesson 5.4. Track 1.28.

Good morning, I'm Larissa Klein, head of Klein Benson Advertising. I'd like to introduce my colleagues, Emilio Sanchez on my left, and next to him, Karl Reiner.

Our purpose today is to present some ideas for your new product. We'll also suggest how to advertise and promote it. Our presentation is divided into three parts. First, I'll talk to you about our ideas for the name of the soft drink and a suitable slogan. After that, Emilio will give you our ideas about the can – he's an expert on packaging – and finally Karl will tell you our ideas about how to advertise and promote the drink. If you have any questions, we'll be pleased to answer them at the end of our presentation.]

Lesson 5.4. Track 1.29.

Moving on now to the design of the can. We asked a group of young people about this. We showed them ten different designs. Please look at the screen. As you see, we've numbered the designs one to ten. If we now look at the table of results, it's very clear. Over 80 percent of the group preferred design six, the blue can with the yellow stripe …

Lesson 5.4. Track 1.30.

Well I've given you our ideas for advertising and promoting the drink. I hope you've found them interesting. Now, let me summarise our main points. Larissa gave you three possible names and mentioned the one we prefer. She told you what slogan we liked, with her reasons.

Emilio showed you the design for the can that we recommend. Finally, I talked about ways of advertising the drink and told you about our ideas for special promotions.

Thank you very much, everyone, for your attention. Are there any questions?

Lesson 5.5. Track 1.31.

Presenter, Eric, Lisa, Rebecca

P: Tonight we're focusing on road safety. Before we talk to the experts, we've invited three members of the public to give their opinion about a new television advert. Good evening, Eric, Lisa and Rebecca.

E/L/R: Good evening.

P: Let me start with you, Eric – I know you have strong feelings. You've seen the television advertisement. A teenager is knocked down in the street because the driver is going too fast. You see the boy lying on the road. Dead. How do you feel about this?

E: I think it's awful and it shouldn't be on our screens. You see the boy lying there with blood coming from his ears. It's a terrible commercial. I saw it last night and couldn't sleep all night thinking about it. I'm really worried by this advertising trend. Why on earth do they show such shocking things? It's just not right!

P: Thank you, Eric. Lisa, what's your opinion? Do you agree with Eric that the advert shouldn't be on our screens?

L: No. I agree that it's shocking, but that's the point, isn't it? Too many teenagers

are killed or injured on our roads. We've got to do something about it. It's true, the advertisement is hard-hitting, but it has to be. You've got to shock drivers, so that they change their behaviour and drive more slowly. That way, accidents will decrease. And that's what we all want, isn't it?

P: Thanks, Lisa. Now Rebecca, how do you feel about this?

R: It's difficult really. I think the adverts are really shocking and that's not good for some people, like people who are sensitive, or people who have heart problems. On the other hand, if the advertisements reduce the number of deaths of teenagers, it's worth showing them, isn't it? Actually, I think we need more research into the effects of this type of advertising. I mean, will shock advertisements result in fewer deaths of young people? I'm not sure about that.

P: Thanks Rebecca. I agree – more data about the effects would be very useful. Now let's turn to the experts … *[fade]*

Lesson 6.1. Track 1.32.

Interviewer, Allan

I: Tonight, we're focusing on starting your own business. I have with me Allan Smith, an accountant and business adviser. Good evening, Allan – thanks for joining us.

A: Good evening, John – it's a pleasure.

I: Allan, could I start by asking you to give us the most important tips for someone setting up a business?

A: Certainly. First of all, I'd say you must understand you'll never know everything there is to running a business – it's as simple as that. So, you'll need help in certain areas – maybe with finances and tax, or perhaps with selling and marketing. Once you know the areas where you need help, you can train yourself, or bring in an employee who has the skill you need. Another way is to get advice from an expert or a friend who has their own business. OK?

I: Right, very useful. Anything else?

A: Yes, my second tip is all about marketing. You need to be sure that your product will sell in sufficient numbers, at a price that covers your costs. In other words, it must give you a return on your money; it's got to make a profit. To do this you must be clear about how you price your product – for example, are you going to price it above, the same as or below your competitors? Then, you must also think about how you'll promote it. I mean, how are you going to let people know about the product, so they become aware of it? That's important. And, you know, you may have to market it in a different way to different people. That could be the key to success.

I: OK, so good marketing is essential when you start your own business.

A: Exactly.

Lesson 6.1. Track 1.33.

Interviewer, Allan

I: You spent many years, Allan, working in accountancy firms with businesses that failed, that went bankrupt. Why did most of them fail?

A: Erm … I think there were three reasons really. Firstly, some failed because the market had moved on, and the business was left behind. It was using old equipment that just wasn't up to date, wasn't efficient – the printing trade is a good example of that. Another reason was that some of them depended too much on one main customer, and then if the customer decides they don't need you any more … And the third reason, well … it could be a number of things, poor planning, cash flow problems, bad debts, erm … not dealing with tax properly, that sort of thing – just not managing the business properly.

Lesson 6.1. Track 1.34.

Interviewer, Allan

I: A final question – what do you think about business plans?

A: Oh, they're vital. You should think of them as a map which'll take you from today to how the business will be in a few years' time. The business plan will set out your objectives, how you are going to get there, to achieve them, and how you are going to measure your progress. Too many people say their plan is in their head. But when that happens, they often can't deal with unexpected things, like, erm … sales that are lower than they hoped, or rising costs. You should get your forecasts down in writing.
Check how you are getting on and use your plan to help you succeed in the business. Oh, yes, one other thing – don't expect to get the forecasts right straight away. You'll improve later when you have more experience.

I: Thanks very much, Allan. Some good advice there for people starting up a business.

Lesson 6.1. Track 1.35.

A: I think a car washing business is a good idea. We'll need to research the market a bit first. Maybe the supermarkets will allow us to wash customers' cars in the car park?

B: Yes, good idea.

A: Also, how about contacting a local taxi firm? They have a lot of cars which always seem to be dirty. There could be a cleaning service for the inside of the cars as well. We wouldn't need much equipment, but we should have a good name – how about something like Kar Klean, with a K – you know, K–A–R K–L–E–A–N?

B: Yeah, good idea. We could give people a discount to start with and print a few leaflets to advertise the business.

A: Yes, I don't think it'd cost much to set up the business and we could make quite a lot of money.

Lesson 6.4. Track 1.37.

Vanessa, Bob

V: Could I speak to Bob, please?

B: Yes, speaking. How can I help you?

V: Hi Bob, it's Vanessa from Domino in Italy here.

B: Hi Vanessa. How are things?

V: Fine. Did you get my email?

B: Yes, I did, but I've been really busy – sorry I haven't replied. You want to order some sunglasses from us.

V: Well, yes … maybe. Thanks for the samples you sent us, Bob, they certainly look good.

B: They sure are Vanessa, they're selling really well. OK, how many would you like to order?

V: Mmm, well, we're thinking of placing quite a large order, about 50,000, at the price you gave us in the email.

B: Great!

V: Yeah, but it's really important that you can deliver to us in August.

B: Oh, I'm afraid that would be a bit difficult, Vanessa, we've already still got quite a few summer orders to deal with. Maybe in September – that should be OK.

V: What about if we pay earlier? Will you be able to deliver in August?

B: Vanessa, let me check if I understand you, do you mean payment on delivery, in August? Well, that would be good …

V: No, we couldn't pay that soon. I was thinking of paying after 60 days. How do you feel about that?

B: Sorry Vanessa, I don't think we can wait that long. How about 30?

V: I'm not sure about that. OK, Bob, look … I'll think it over and maybe get back to you.

B: That sounds fine. Well … I hope to hear from you soon.

V: Right, Bob, thanks a lot. Bye for now.

B: Bye.

Review 4–6 Track 1.38.

A: Hello. Can I help?

B: Yes, we're thinking of placing quite a large order of mobile phones. I run a company and some of my staff need them.

A: Right. How many would you like to order?

B: Well, about twenty I think. Five of them are going to a conference this weekend so we'd need them straight away.

A: I'm afraid that would be a bit difficult for us. We don't have a lot in stock. But I could probably get you five today and the rest in one week. It depends a bit on the model.

B: That sounds fine.

A: So when you say you want the phones, are you saying you also want an account with us? We have some good company rates. For example, you can pay a flat monthly fee for all phones.

B: Let me check if I understand you. We'd pay one fee every month. But how much would the phones be?

A: You don't pay for the phones. Just the calls.

B: So that's even if my sales people are on the phone all the time, is it?

A: Well, it doesn't include overseas calls of course.

B: Oh. I'm afraid I don't like that idea. What about if we included that as well? What would it cost?

A: You mean include the overseas calls in a flat monthly fee?

B: That's right.

A: Yes, I think that would work. Look. Let's go through some of the options.

Lesson 7.2. Track 1.40.

A: Let's brainstorm some ideas for our new project, the folding chair. So, first, who exactly is our target consumer?

B: Well, the chair could be useful for all kinds of people, you know, people going camping or fishing, or even going to outdoor concerts. In fact, it could be suitable for anyone who has to sit outside for a long time.

A: OK, what about the materials for making it?

B: Well, it must be light and easy to carry if we want to gain market share. We can't use steel – that's too heavy. We can use aluminium for the frame, and canvas for the seat. And to keep down costs, maybe we should make it in just three colours.

A: Yes, that's important. Also, it must be cheap if we want to be competitive. There are one or two chairs on the market that sell at under €50. We can produce something similar – it doesn't have to be very different for this market. But we can have a second, more expensive model too, if that's what people want.

B: Mmm. Good point. OK, another thing, and this is very important, it has to be safe because the regulations are very strict now. The rules also say it has to be strong enough to support a heavy person.

A: Absolutely. OK, in terms of timing, we could launch it just before the summer – there'll be a big demand for it then. In fact, we really mustn't miss this opportunity.

B: You're right, but we shouldn't launch it until we're really ready. Look, I think we should wait for the results of our market research before making any decisions. But I can do some designs before we meet again, so we can continue with the development.

A: Right, and I can get more information about our competitors' products. I mustn't forget to do that.

Lesson 7.3. Track 1.41.

Anna, Barbara

1

A: Wow, look at that. What is it?

B: It's a drawing. I think it's a sort of flying machine.

A: Yes, it could be that. Who do you think it's by?

B: Mmm, it might be by da Vinci, I believe he did that sort of thing. Have a look at the sign. What does it say?

A: Erm … yes, you're right, it is da Vinci.

B: Goodness! It's in very good condition … it says here he was born in 1452, so it must be over 500 years old.

A: Yes, and it's an amazing drawing.

B: Yeah, I read somewhere he was fascinated by birds and flying. Perhaps that's where he got his ideas for the drawing.

A: Yeah, you're probably right.

2

Elias, Freddie

E: Freddie, I want to see the racing cars. Where are they?

F: I haven't got a guide, but I'm sure they're in that large space at the back. Let's go there first.

E: Here they are. Look at that one over there. It must be a Ferrari, surely.

F: Yes, it can't be anything else. It's so red and stylish. But it's a pretty old one – look, it's quite high off the ground. What year do you think it is?

E: It could date back to the 1930s.

F: That's impossible. It can't be that old. Look, here it says it was made in the 1940s.

E: You're right. It's amazing they were able to go so fast at that time.

3

George, Sally

G: What's that?

S: I've no idea. What could it be?

G: It might be a spaceship. Well, a toy spaceship. It's the right shape.

S: No, I'm certain that it's not that. It wouldn't really be in a museum of design.

G: Mmm, I see what you mean. And maybe it's too heavy to be a toy. What else could it be?

S: Mmm, I don't know really. What does it say on the notice?

G: It says it's a lemon squeezer. Apparently it's the designer Philippe Starck's best-known design.

S: Ok I see it now. Would you like something like that?

G: No way! It just doesn't look practical.

Lesson 7.4. Track 2.2.

OK, everyone, I think we agree now on the qualities we'll be considering when we choose the winning design. Let me summarise.

The winning design will be innovative and will look different from other products in its category. It'll be stylish too – in other words, attractive and fashionable. But it'll also be functional and easy to use. It'll be really useful and also good value for money. It shouldn't be too expensive for what the designer is offering. One last thing, we expect the winning design to be well made, so it's got to be durable.

Lesson 7.4. Track 2.3.

I think this is by far the best entry. It's a desk designed by Vanessa Pironi. She's working in a studio in Milan. As you can see, the desk looks very stylish. It's got a very modern design; we haven't seen anything quite like it before. It's made of solid oak, so it's obviously very durable. There are several features I really like. For example, there's a well-designed stand for your keyboard. There's also a secure section for a laptop. You can hide the computer when you're not using it. I like that design feature. And there's a drink holder – you pull it out – and you can put your cup of coffee, soft drink or whatever in it. I also like the big file drawers – there are two and they have good locks on them. One of the best points is that the desk's functional. I'd say it's aimed at home computer use. It would appeal especially to a business person, working from home. It's really got everything we're looking for. It's excellent value for money too. The designer thinks the price will be about $1,200. Not a

lot for a desk of this quality. In my opinion, we have a winner here.

Lesson 7.5. Track 2.4.

Teacher, Erika

T: So you'd like me to give you some advice on editing your work, Erika?

E: Yes, if you could give me a few tips, it would be very helpful. I know I need to check my written work more carefully.

T: OK, I'll try to keep it simple. What are the most common mistakes students make when they write? These are the sort of things you should be looking for. And everyone should think about them when they check their written work.

E: Exactly.

T: OK. I'll give you five or six points to think about. First of all, check your spelling and punctuation carefully. If you've typed your work, don't forget to use a spellchecker.

E: Oh, yes. Good idea.

T: Of course, you'll make mistakes with difficult words, like, oh, erm … 'accommodation' or 'receive', but students often make mistakes with simple words, like spelling 'writing' with two Ts! And of course you need to punctuate your work correctly. Many students seem to forget that we use full stops when we write English!

E: I know what you mean. My teacher is always telling me to use a full stop instead of a comma!

T: Right. And don't forget about capitals. Check your written work to make sure that you have used capital letters where they're appropriate.

E: OK. Got that.

T: My next tip is to check your work for grammatical errors. In particular, check your verb tenses and verb forms. Make sure you've used the right tense or form. You have problems using the present perfect tense. Think carefully before you use the tense. It's easy to make a mistake with a verb form, especially with the past tenses of irregular verbs. Don't use 'gone' when you mean 'went' and don't use 'catched' when it should be 'caught'. OK?

E: Right, I often make mistakes with irregular verbs – they're very difficult to learn and then I write the wrong form in an essay.

T: Yes, they're difficult and so are prepositions. Check that you've written the correct preposition after an adjective or verb. For example, don't write 'depend of' when it should be 'depend on'. So many students make that error, you wouldn't believe it.

E: OK, be careful with prepositions. I'll check them in a dictionary if I'm not sure.

T: Good. Word order is important too. Check that you've used the right word order in your sentences. That's especially important for you.

E: Yes, it's true – I often make mistakes with word order. It's a real problem for me.

T: My final piece of advice is, after you've written something, always ask yourself the questions 'Is my meaning clear?' and 'Will someone reading my work understand what I'm trying to say?' That's it, really, I hope my tips will help you.

E: I'm sure they will. I'll put them into practice when I write my next essay.

Lesson 8.2. Track 2.5.

We had a teacher called Mr Rojas and he taught us chemistry. He was an excellent teacher, but we couldn't say that we actually liked him. He wasn't friendly, or easy-going – the opposite in fact. He was different from the teachers we normally liked. In fact, he often criticised us. He treated us all equally – well, criticised all of us equally. He didn't treat us like unique individuals so it was funny that we all respected him. He was very strict, and always punctual – and I don't think he was ever late, and neither were we! He gave us lots of tests and lots of homework, and his formal approach to teaching seemed to work. He explained things very clearly and was very good at answering all our questions. He was always very well prepared and his lessons were always interesting. He always varied things, changed the pace of the lesson, and used different methods to teach us. The chemistry laboratory was a strange environment to be in but we all enjoyed the classes. In the end, we all passed the chemistry exam and chemistry became my favourite subject on the curriculum.

Lesson 8.2. Track 2.6.

Quizmaster, Barry, Felicity, Keira, Michael, Anna, Frank

Q: Team A, now, it's your turn and the next word is *ammeter*. Barry, would you like to start with Definition 1?

B: Erm … yes, OK. Ammeter. An ammeter is what it says – it's a meter, and we use the meter for measuring electricity, electric current actually. So, it's an instrument which is used to measure electric currents.

Q: Felicity – Definition 2, please.

F: Well, Barry's completely wrong – it's nothing to do with electricity. An ammeter is a tiny little animal, so I suppose the word is related to 'ant'. This animal is so small that it only has one cell – we can't see it. So, an ammeter is a very small creature that only has one cell.

Q: Thank you, Felicity. Now, Keira, Definition 3.

K: Felicity is sooo wrong! Barry is almost correct – an ammeter is a machine, a meter in fact, but it isn't a machine that measures electric current. It's a meter that measures temperature – but only in stables. It's important that horses have the correct temperature, so we need a special machine, and that's it. An ammeter is a machine which is used to measure the temperature in a stable.

Q: OK. Now, over to you, Team B. Is an ammeter a meter that is used to measure electric current, a creature that has only one cell, or a machine that measures temperature in a stable? Do you want to start, Michael?

M: Mmm, I suppose so. Well, I think Felicity is wrong – an ammeter isn't an animal. It must have something to do with measuring, because of the word *meter*. I don't think Felicity really believed her definition anyway. I think the correct definition is Barry's – a meter for measuring electricity. Anna, what do you think?

A: I agree with you, Michael. Barry really seemed confident, and it has to be a meter. So, yes, Barry's right.

M: Do you agree, Frank?

F: I don't know. I think it could be Keira's definition – a meter for measuring temperature. But I think I'm going to go for Barry, too.

Q: So you all agree that the correct definition is number 1 – an instrument which is used to measure electricity?

M: Yes.

Q: Team A, who had the correct definition?

B: They're right – it's me – Definition 1!

Q: Well done, Team B – that's six points to you as you all agreed. So, on to the next word …

Lesson 8.3. Track 2.7.

1

I'm an American, and I can tell you, a college degree in the US puts you way ahead of people who don't have one. If you want to work in cities like Boston, New York or San Francisco, your starting salary will be much higher than guys who don't have a degree, and you certainly need a good salary to afford an apartment in those cities. I think I'll get about $50,000 as a starting salary once I graduate, and I'll get a lot of fringe benefits too, like life insurance and a retirement plan.

2

I'm from Argentina and everyone I talked to said 'go to university' – careers advisers, teachers, family, friends. Why did I listen to them? I've got massive debts now, and no chance of getting a good job. For the last five years, I've been in a dead-end job, with no security, no prospects, and low pay. Most of my friends left school at 16 and they're doing really well now. They got promoted while I slaved away to get a degree, and it isn't worth the paper it's written on. Of course I feel bitter.

3

I did my degree at Cambridge University – it was a three-year course. I don't like the idea that you study for a degree for what it gets you later in life. You should go to university because you're really interested in the subject you choose. I don't think my degree helped me to get a job. OK, it may have given me an edge over non-graduates for getting interviews, I suppose. But I really enjoyed studying French literature, and don't regret it at all. When I left, I applied for lots of jobs, and I think employers liked the fact that I was confident and had good people skills. I'm now a computer programmer, nothing to do with literature.

4

I graduated in 2006, when Germany hosted the World Cup. I did enjoy my time at university, and maybe that's the problem. I did well at school, so it was logical to go to university. I guess I just enjoyed myself too much. Without the discipline of school, I didn't study as hard as I should, so I only just got a degree. A lot of my friends got

jobs straight from school and are now doing really well. There are a lot of unemployed graduates around these days. I don't regret my time at university – I learned quite a lot about people, and I did a lot of sport. I'm not sure it really helped my career though.

Lesson 8.4. Track 2.8.

Marie, Eva, Koichi

M: OK, I accept what you're saying about the library and the equipment, and some of the staff. I'll raise those issues with the Board of Governors. Now, you want to discuss late-night parties in the halls of residence, right?

E: Yes, they're a problem. A lot of students have complained about them. There seem to be more and more parties in people's rooms these days, and they're really noisy, you know, loud music, everyone talking at the top of their voices, dancing. They often go on for hours, and nobody else can do any work. That's the problem.

M: Mmm, that's not fair, is it? A lot of students study in the evenings in their room. They need some peace and quiet.

E/K: Exactly./Right.

M: Let's see, there are several ways to deal with this. Erm … we could agree to ban parties in rooms, or we could only allow parties after the exams. What do you think, Koichi?

K: Well, the good thing is that it's fair to everyone, but the bad thing is that it wouldn't be very popular. I mean, everyone likes parties, don't they? It's part of our education.

E: Could I make a suggestion, Marie?

M: Sure, go ahead.

E: Supposing we let each floor of the hall have one party each semester. That'd reduce the number of parties a lot.

M: Maybe, but there would still be quite a lot of noise when each floor had their party. No, to be honest, I don't think that's the right thing to do. Let's see, what other things can we do?

K: I've got an idea. How about letting the students book a room in the main building for parties? You could charge a small fee, and tell them that they have to book, say, four weeks in advance. I think most people would accept that.

M: Yes, good idea. That's the best solution, I think. Happy with that idea, Eva?

E: Yeah, I think so. You have to do something about the parties, it can't go on.

M: OK, so the next thing to do is for me to talk to everyone. How about if I attend your next student union meeting? I could explain the proposal there.

E/L: Fine/Great.

M: OK then, we seem to have solved that one. Now, there was also the issue of …

Lesson 8.5. Track 2.9.

Manfred, Louise

M: That was a nice letter Jane Goodman sent me, Louise. I'd like to attend the course – it sounds interesting.

L: Yeah, I read the brochure. I must say, I liked the topics they're covering. Professor Dawson's good. I've seen him give lectures

in London – he's well worth seeing. I saw his book in a store the other day – you know, it looked really interesting. Why don't you get it before the course begins?

M: Good idea, I'll do that. But Louise, there are some points in the letter I'm not clear about.

L: Oh yes?

M: Well, for one thing, I'd like to know what sort of people attend the course. I mean, are they teachers, or students, young or old? And where do they come from, mainly? I don't want to spend the time with a group of people from Germany. I'd prefer an international group, so I can practise my English.

L: Mmm, I can understand that. Why don't you check? Also, have you thought about accommodation? I noticed there was a bit about home-stay possibilities in the brochure, but not much else. What about accommodation in halls of residence? They're often cheaper and a lot better than hotels.

M: OK, I'll check that out too when I write to Jane Goodman. You know, I couldn't see anything about methods of payment for the course. The prices were all there, but nothing about how to pay. I'd like to pay by cheque if possible, when I arrive. I hope they accept that.

L: I'm sure they will. Another thing – when you write, why don't you find out how the course will be organised? I mean, what sort of methods will they use? Will it just be lectures, or will you have to make presentations, individually or in groups? And, erm … will there be a lot of discussion, videos, cassettes, that sort of thing? I don't think you can get as much from just lectures.

M: Good point. One other thing – do you think I'll get a certificate or something if I complete the course? That'd be useful. And are there any examinations? Oral or in writing? Actually, there are a lot of questions I need to ask.

Lesson 9.1. Track 2.10.

Interviewer, Lindsey

I: For our next guest on 'A Woman's World', I'd like to welcome to the programme Lindsey Barone, head of engineering at Swift Aerospace – a very good example of a woman in a man's world.

L: Good morning everyone.

I: Lindsey, you're an engineer, but why did you become one? What got you interested?

L: Well, from a young age I was always interested in how things work. I chose engineering as a career because I wanted to make things better. Engineering isn't just about testing theories and building models. It's about designing new products and finding new uses for old products. I want to improve the way the world works.

I: Mmm, interesting. And could you tell me a bit about your training?

L: Well, I studied engineering at university. I was the only woman in the mechanical engineering department!

I: So, how was that?

L: Well at first I felt a bit uncomfortable, but after a while it didn't bother me. People got used to me and I was treated like anyone else. In fact sometimes it was a bit of an advantage because people liked to have me in their team!

I: You're head of engineering now. How did you get to where you are today?

L: Well, I started in a test lab for aeroplanes. I did stress and fatigue tests there. Basically, I broke things! Doing that sort of research is very important as it tells you what loads the structures can carry. Then I went into aeroplane design. I worked on all areas of commercial planes before moving into project management in the aircraft industry.

I: Could you tell me a bit more about what you do now?

L: Sure. These days I mainly work in project management. I take ideas for projects and investigate their feasibility – that means I see if the projects are possible. Next, I develop the objectives and estimate the cost of the project. Then I help the people working on the project to meet their deadlines. I have to make sure projects come in on budget and on schedule.

I: Now you're head of department and I guess in charge of a lot of men. How do you find that?

L: Well, it wasn't too easy at first. I had to prove myself. When they could see that I had good practical experience and ability, everything was fine.

I: I suppose that's true of anyone who's in charge. OK, Lindsey, finally – what's the best thing about being an engineer?

L: That's an easy one to answer. I love the challenge of finding solutions to problems. I hope that what I do improves people's lives. For me, engineering is fun, exciting and satisfying. So let's have more women in engineering in the future!

I: Thanks very much, Lindsey. Now, our next guest is someone who …

Lesson 9.4. Track 2.11.

Some exciting news now from the Minister of the Environment, Susan Lau, which should please all the engineers in our country.

The Government has announced that it is considering the possibility of building the tallest city in the world – a vertical city located just on the edge of our capital, which would bring new life to the city, as well as boosting tourism. It will be over 1,500 metres high – at least that's the idea – with a width of about 500 metres at its base. The idea is that about 40,000 people will live there, and over 100,000 will work in the city during the day. The vertical city, which will be called the Sky-High Project, will have apartments, a hotel, an international conference centre, offices, food outlets, entertainment and leisure facilities. And just like any other city, there'll be green spaces, fountains, parks and gardens.

At the moment, it's just an idea, but an exciting one – it would really put the country on the map, no doubt about that. The Minister plans to contact engineering

departments in universities and invite new angles and discussion of the idea.

Lesson 9.4. Track 2.12.

A: Hey, did you see on the news last night about the vertical city? What do you think about it?

B: I think the idea's really good – building the tallest city in the world. It'd be great publicity for the country, everyone would talk about it, and it'd attract a lot of tourists.

A: I agree – it's the best idea the government's had for a long time. It'd help with the over-population problem, and might help with the crime problem in that area. You could have lots of closed-circuit TVs on all the floors – that'd cut down crime.

B: Yeah, I think so. And it'd be good too for working people – much less stress, probably, as they wouldn't have to commute long distances to get to work. There'd be plenty of jobs in the new city, wouldn't there?

A: I suppose so. And fewer traffic jams as well because people wouldn't have to drive to work. They could walk there or take some kind of internal transport.

B: Yeah, true. There's another benefit, come to think of it – it's a very good way of using the land in the city. It's putting a lot of people in a small space. And that's an efficient use of resources.

A: Yes, good point.

B: So, let's hope the Sky-High Project gets off the ground.

A: Well, it depends on a lot of things, I think. Will it be popular with the public? And if it is, will it be feasible?

Lesson 9.4. Track 2.13.

1

– What do you think about the present name, the Sky-High Project? It's easy to remember.

– I'm not too sure about that. Another possibility is Tower City. It's short and easy to pronounce.

2

– I think Hope is a good name for the city. It'll give accommodation for a lot of poor and homeless people.

– That's a possible solution.

3

– Tower City? Yes, I think that's the best name. Why don't we suggest it to the Minister?

– Yes, let's do that. It's the best solution, I think.

4

– We all agree then. We'll call it Sky-High City.

– OK, let's put the name in our report to the Minister.

Lesson 9.5. Track 2.14.

… So, when you give any talk, you need to plan it carefully. First of all, think about your audience – who they are, what they know about the subject and what they expect from

you. You want to match your presentation to the needs and interests of your audience.

The next stage is to think about how you will structure your talk, how you'll organise it. A good way is to divide your talk into sections, and tell your audience what the sections are. For example, you may say, 'I've divided my talk into three parts', then introduce each section with words like *firstly*, *secondly*, *finally* – that's a common way of giving the plan, the map of your talk.

Following that, prepare your material by dividing it into essential points you want to make, and extra points that you'll make if you have time. Of course, think carefully about what your overall message will be. Most people use notes when giving a talk. One way is to give each section of your talk a heading, then put the headings on small cards. You may like to add a few words to each heading to remind you of what you want to say. Then, number the cards in the order you present your points. Cards will give you confidence, and help you structure your talk.

Next, you'll need some kind of visual aid. If you have to give a very formal talk, you'll probably use software such as Powerpoint. But for less formal talks, posters or diagrams may be enough. A word of warning – don't overuse computers. People come to listen to you, not to look at computer screens all the time.

Also, think about the beginning of your talk very carefully. You need to think of a 'hook' – that's something to attract the attention of the audience. Some people use a famous quotation or an amazing statistic, or ask the audience a question. A lot of presenters like to start with a joke, or tell a short story, maybe something from their experience.

Finally, you need to end strongly. Prepare some sentences which will really impress the audience and make a strong impact on them. It's good to end the talk with a bang, so say something that will stay in the audience's mind after they've left you.

Review 7–9 Track 2.15

A: OK. Thank you all for coming. We have a number of options but I'd like us to look at this one in particular. There are several features I really like. For example, when the passenger in front moves the seat back the TV screen part stays where it is. The good thing about this is that the passenger feels they have more space. This is especially interesting because in reality the seat takes up less room than normal seats. What do you think about it?

B: I'm sure it's good but it looks very similar to any other airline seat.

A: Supposing we made it look more stylish or different so passengers feel they are sitting in something completely new – would that help?

B: Yes, that's a possible solution. And it would appeal to low-fare airlines with lots of economy class passengers. But the other bad thing is that the head rest doesn't move – sometimes you want to change the position without moving the whole seat.

We need to ask the designers what they can do about it.

A: Yes, let's do that.

Lesson 10.2. Track 2.17.
Manager, Chloe

M: Hello Chloe, good to see you. We've got a little time before my next meeting, so … how are things going?

C: Very well, thanks. I've really enjoyed my first week here. I've talked to a lot of the trainees and served a few customers.

M: No problems, I hope?

C: Not really. There were just a couple of customers who were a bit difficult, but they were OK in the end.

M: Good. Let me give you one or two tips while I have the time. First of all, many trainees think they don't need to know anything about the rest of the store, but we've found the best sales staff are not just fashion specialists, they also find out about the rest of the store so they can help customers when they're looking for other sections. So don't forget, you'll need to answer questions about other departments, especially cosmetics and jewellery.

C: Right, that's good advice. By the way, I've noticed no one wears any kind of uniform in this department. Most of the assistants seem to be wearing designer labels. Is that your policy then?

M: Yes. We have no rules about uniforms. Staff can wear some of our fashions. You see, you and your colleagues are models for our fashions as well as advisers. We picked up this idea last year in Milan during their fashion show. We visited a few of the top stores in Milan and learned a lot from them.

C: So you travel abroad?

M: Yes. I used to do all the trips on my own with no help but last year I took some of the assistants along with me. It's good training for them.

C: Wow! I didn't realise you did that. No wonder you keep your staff for years!

M: [laughs] We believe in treating staff well, it's very important. Actually, we need to start thinking about next year's fashion shows – but we've got plenty of ideas and we'll get some information from the organisers soon.

C: Do you have any other tips for me, like how to approach customers? I don't have a lot of sales experience.

M: I know, but you've got the right personality. Look, the best piece of advice I can give you is to give customers enough time to make up their minds without any pressure. Give them a lot of attention and plenty of advice, but only when they need it. It's your job to judge the right moment. OK? Never oversell or put too much pressure on a customer. We have enough sales assistants to do the job properly.

C: Thanks very much. That's very helpful.

M: Good, well Chloe, I must be off to my meeting. I've enjoyed chatting to you. Well done, you've had a very good first week.

Lesson 10.4. Track 2.19.
Mayor, Councillor 1, Councillor 2

M: Let's talk about the quality of life here. In my opinion, the situation's getting serious. I get letters every day from people complaining about one thing or another. There seems to be a feeling that Belleview isn't a very nice place to live in anymore.

C1: I don't know about that. Older people aren't very happy, but young people enjoy living here. But there are some worrying trends, I must admit – things we need to sort out.

M: Oh yes?

C1: Well, parking, for instance. More and more people have cars – so, what do we do? We employ an army of parking attendants to put tickets on cars. Car owners have to pay big fines, they aren't happy, and visitors complain because parking's so difficult and expensive. I hear car owners are going to demonstrate to draw attention to the problem.

M: Hmm, parking is a huge problem, I agree. An attendant even tried to put a ticket on my car the other day! What else do you think people are unhappy about?

C1: Well, they certainly don't like paying to go on some of our beaches. I think we made a big mistake following the American trend, charging people to use beaches. It's been very unpopular with everyone. People feel a beach is public land, so why should they pay to go on it?

M: OK, but they don't seem to understand – the money is used to improve the beaches' facilities and keep them clean.

C2: Sorry, could I just say something, please?

M: Of course, go ahead.

C2: I'd like to mention something else which is annoying people – bad behaviour by young people. It's getting worse every year. You know what I mean. They stand around on the pavements and don't get out of the way if older people want to pass. And in the buses, they never offer their seat to women with young children. It's so impolite. And what about late at night! They're so noisy and badly behaved. People can't stand this kind of behaviour – it creates a really bad image for the town. We've got to do something about it. The situation's getting out of control.

Lesson 10.4. Track 2.20.
Councillor, Resident 1, Resident 2

C: Good morning everyone. Thanks for coming. We're here to discuss the parking problem in your area. First of all, tell me what the problem is, exactly, and then we'll look at solutions. Yes, Mrs … erm … go ahead please.

R1: Thank you, I'm Ingrid Oberman. To be honest, I'm very unhappy with the present situation. I've been waiting for over a year for a parking permit. I contacted your office and they tell me there's a long queue, and that I have to wait my turn. It's not fair.

C: Mmm, I understand how you feel – it's a long time to wait, I must say. But you must understand our position. There

are more and more cars for the spaces available. Frankly, I'm not sure I can do anything to help.

R1: I don't agree. For one thing, you could tell parking attendants not to issue so many fines. If you park in the wrong space for just two minutes, a parking attendant rushes up, puts a ticket on your car, and you get a £40 fine. Ridiculous! It's not acceptable – I'm sure you understand that.

C: Mmm, I see how you feel. Look, I'll look into the matter and talk to the parking department. That might help …

R2: Sorry, could I just say something, please.

C: Yes, Mr Ashley, please make your point.

R2: Well, I strongly believe there are not enough car parks in the town. Why not build more car parks? If you did that, there'd be more spaces for parking outside our house or apartment. At the moment I'm spending £400 a month to rent a garage. I can't afford to do it much longer.

C: Thank you for your comment. But there's no easy answer. As you know, car parks cost a lot of money, and take time to build. We have other big projects that need finance, and our budget is limited. But I note your suggestion.

C: Well, to sum up, I'll talk to the parking attendants and explain the situation to them, that you feel they're doing their job a little too efficiently, and I'll ask the council to look into the possibility of building more car parks. Thanks very much everyone. Have a good day.

Lesson 10.5. Track 2.21.

1

I like to test myself by putting new vocabulary I want to learn onto cards. I put an example sentence with the word or phrase missing on one side of the card. On the other side I put the word or phrase. I often test myself when I'm on the train.

2

I like to organise new vocabulary under topic areas, for example, verbs, nouns and idioms connected to a subject, like crime, so I can concentrate on learning vocabulary on the same theme.

3

I like to have word families in my vocabulary book. I test myself by starting with a verb or noun and then try to remember adverbs or adjectives, and synonyms and opposites.

4

For difficult vocabulary I try to make a link with my own language, so I try to think of a word that sounds the same, and I remember the new word that way.

5

I like to record new vocabulary onto a tape and listen and repeat when I'm driving my car. I think pronunciation is really important.

6

I try to note down five new words each day and learn their meaning. What I do is write them on post-it notes and stick them on a board in my office.

Lesson 11.1. Track 2.22.

4

Good morning listeners. Last night, I attended the first live recording of the new comedy series *It's a Laugh*, which is going out on Radio Comedy Channel 1. It'll be on every Monday evening for six weeks. I'm pleased to report that the series lives up to its name. It's hilarious. Some of the jokes don't always work but overall I really recommend it. You'll enjoy yourselves.

5

Even though you're probably fans of his, I'm sorry to tell you all that there's no real plot. It's meant to be a gripping thriller but nobody seems to have a reason for doing anything. I couldn't relate to any of the characters. This is the worst novel I have read recently. I found the first few chapters very heavy going. I know his first novel was excellent but this was a huge disappointment.

6

Good evening, viewers. The first of the old films we're discussing tonight is *Dracula*, the 1931 version. It's a classic example of the horror genre and I'm sure it'll keep you on the edge of your seats. It made Bela Lugosi an international star and its dark atmosphere is truly frightening.

Lesson 11.3. Track 2.23.

Nura, Richard

N: Hi, Richard. How did you get on in the interview? Did it go well?

R: I don't know really. I think so.

N: So … what kind of questions did they ask you?

R: Well, the editor of the newspaper did most of the talking. She asked me why I wanted to be a foreign correspondent and obviously I was expecting that. I said that I'd travelled a lot when I was a student, that I enjoyed travelling and that now I was a journalist, I wanted it to be part of my job. Then she wanted to know what parts of the world I was interested in.

N: Mmm, what did you say?

R: Well, all the Arab countries, and South America. I told her that I also knew Brazil and Argentina well, so they would be interesting to report on.

N: I see. What else did she ask you? Those questions don't sound too difficult.

R: No, they weren't really. Well, the subject of languages came up. She asked if I spoke any foreign languages.

N: Ha! That was an easy one for you!

R: Yeah, I told her I was bilingual in English and Arabic and that I spoke Spanish and Portuguese fluently. She seemed pretty impressed.

N: I'm sure she was. Did she offer you the job on the spot?

R: Not quite. She wanted to know where I'd gone to university and if I'd taken any further qualifications. She also wanted to know what articles I'd written and so on. There was only one difficult question really …

N: Oh yeah?

R: Mmm, she asked me what qualities a journalist needed to be a foreign correspondent. I wasn't sure how to answer that one.

N: How did you handle it?

R: Well, I said, obviously, I'd never done the job, but I had thought about it. I said that foreign correspondents had to be able to make decisions without waiting for people to tell you what to do. So, they needed to show initiative when they were reporting in a foreign country.

N: I think that's a really good answer. Was she pleased?

R: She seemed to be. Anyway, there were a few more questions, then at the end, she asked if I was physically fit.

N: Funny question, but I suppose it's important if you travel a lot in your job.

R: Yes, true. Anyway, I said that I went to the gym three times a week so I should be.

N: Good answer. Do you think you'll get the job?

R: I've got a good chance, I think, but I wasn't the only candidate. I'll just keep my fingers crossed and hope for the best.

Lesson 11.4. Track 2.24.

Dan, Bob

D: Well Bob, you know I think that this is a great opportunity for the company, but it's very different from the kind of things we've done in the past. We could make a lot of money, but we could also lose a lot.

B: Dan, don't worry too much. It's the same as TV really, just everything's bigger.

D: I hope you're right. I just want a safe investment, something which is quite similar to the sort of stuff we usually make. I think some kind of mystery is the sort of thing most people really like.

B: Now, that's where we disagree again. I think this is a great opportunity to do something very different – you know, a proper big-budget film, something which will really sell around the world and something much better than what we've been doing recently. You know, those rather sad mini-series about unhappy housewives. I don't think the genre is that important really. It could be action, adventure, or even a musical. It just has to be different!

D: I see your point Bob, but we need to be sure exactly what we want. What are our main criteria for investing?

B: Well, for me it has to be down to the originality of the idea. That's what'll get people interested and help sell it.

D: Yes, I understand that, but I also think the experience of the director is important. They can make or break a film and they make a difference to its sales.

B: True. Actually, I think the director is less important than the location, though. I think we need plenty of locations around the world so people see places they've been to or would like to visit. So the film becomes aspirational.

D: Mmm, good point, and a variety of locations will help to sell the film in different places. It'll have more international appeal, but if we choose a film like that it'll be more expensive, don't forget. We have to think about cost.

B: Yes, we do, but if we want a big hit, we'll need to spend more.

D: Maybe I'm being too careful, but I don't want to spend millions and find we have something a lot worse than our usual TV series.

B: Yes, you are a careful person Dan. Maybe that's why you're successful. But film-making is always a big risk, whether for TV or cinema.

Lesson 11.4. Track 2.25.

1

What can I say – who doesn't enjoy this sort of film? Look how successful *Star Wars* was. I know a lot of people in the business and I don't think I'll have problems casting for the film. There are a couple of big stars I might be able to get. I promised not to mention their names until I get finance for the project, but they're very interested. Also, the special feature of the film will be the special effects – they'll be out of this world! I know it's really important to get a good special effects guy. The top man in Hollywood is Jack O'Brien and he's a personal friend of mine.

As you know, I've done a few films in my time, some good, some bad. But this one's looking real good to me. I like the script. It's not just an action film – it doesn't just depend on special effects. There's a lot of interest in how the group of survivors work together to save the planet. The ending will be uncertain so we could make a sequel. We won't need to spend money on a lot of locations as we can make the whole film in the studio. The budget will be about $60–80 million, but a lot of that is for the special effects. We'll have hundreds of spaceships flying across the screen.

2

I jumped at the chance to buy this script. It's written by a young writer called Mark Fulton, who's becoming very popular. The script is based on his first book – it was a bestseller and it introduces Fulton's main character, Melanie Drake. This is really the special feature – the character of Melanie Drake. She's a great character – beautiful, mysterious and cool – and she always manages to get out of dangerous situations by using her intelligence and charm. She'll make money for you for years to come. I don't know exactly who'll play her yet, but it'll be one of the biggest female stars in Hollywood. I know the budget is big, probably about $100–120 million, but as well as a big star, there'll be locations all over the world – the USA, Switzerland, Australia and Brazil. There'll be a lot of twists and turns in the story and the ending will be a big surprise. I realise we could easily go over budget if we're not careful. But the return on your money could be fantastic. Remember, if you don't back me, you may regret it for the rest of your lives.

3

The simple stories are always the best in this business. The film will appeal to people all over the world. Asian filmgoers love this type of film, and now cinema fans in other countries are becoming really interested.

People nowadays want films to have a good story line, a real hero and heroine – someone they can admire. I have in mind a young, unknown actor who wants to play the main role. He's very good looking and charismatic – I think he'll become an international star, like Bruce Lee. The leading female role will also be played by an unknown actress. The fight scenes are of course the special feature – one lasts over ten minutes. They will be choreographed by the best in the business. Almost all of the action will take place in Japan and the Philippines. There won't be a lot of dialogue in the film, so it'll be easy to dub and distribute worldwide. It's a very moral story with a happy ending, so audiences will go away satisfied. The budget will be about $50–70 million. I've made this sort of film before, when I worked in Hong Kong.

4

I really hope you'll support this project – I'm confident it'll make a lot of money for all of us. We've got a top camera crew who'll do most of the filming. The special feature is the terrific script. Very well written, funny situations and clever dialogue. Everyone who's read it thinks it's great.

The action takes place mainly in Venice – it's such a romantic location – and also Moscow. We'll use unknown actors for the main parts because we need real twins. We'll save money here, so a lot of the money will go on finding really good locations for the big scenes – you know, smart, luxurious hotels, magnificent villas and country houses and so on. The sets will look fantastic – audiences love that sort of thing. The budget will need to be between $40 and $50 million. The ending will be sad because there are too many films with happy endings these days. I think audiences want something different.

I know this'll be my first full-length film and I'm really excited about it. I just know it'll make my reputation and lead to other big projects.

Lesson 11.5. Track 2.26.

1

Good morning, everyone. I want to talk about our plans for the music and dance festival in September. It was a pity about the rain last year, wasn't it? It rained so much and people got really fed up. Only a few people attended each day and the festival was a total disaster. We were all so disappointed – the sponsors weren't very happy, I can tell you. OK, let me get back to the subject. We plan this year to invite local dance groups and musicians as well as performers from abroad. I've divided my talk into three parts, so first, I'll tell you what arrangement we've made regarding bookings …

2

Hi everyone, I'm going to talk about our plans for the music and dance festival in September. I'm sorry, I'm a bit nervous, but I'll do my best to tell you how we're going to arrange things. My talk is divided into three parts. First, I'll talk about how the performers make bookings – in other words, how much they have to pay – where they can get forms

and so on. Then I'll talk about how we're advertising the festival. Finally, I'll explain why this will be a very good festival for you to sponsor. If you have any questions, please interrupt me at any time. Is that all right everyone?

3

Good morning, everyone. It's nice to see you all. Thank you for giving up your time to listen to me. I'm going to talk to you about our plans for the music and dance festival in September. Let me tell you about how I'd like to organise my talk. First, I want to talk about our booking system – where performers can get the application forms, what the entrance fee is, and so on. After that I'll talk about how we'll advertise the festival. Finally, I'll explain why you should sponsor the festival.

4

Hi everyone. Well, I'd like to talk about our music and dance festival, which takes place in September. I was thinking of telling you about the overseas performers we've invited, but maybe I'll do that later on. How about this? Why don't you ask me some questions and I'll try to answer them. Oh right. OK then, as you don't seem to have any questions, let me think about some points I can cover. Well … you're probably interested to know how the dancers and singers can apply for the festival. OK, we've produced an application form, erm … they put down some details about themselves and enclose the fee …

Lesson 11.5. Track 2.27.

Good morning, everyone. Thank you for coming to my talk. I'm going to tell you about our plans for the music and dance festival in September. I've divided my talk into three parts. I'll start by telling you about the kind of performers we're trying to attract and I'll mention some well-known people who'll attend the festival. Next, I'll discuss how we're advertising the event – what plans we have for that. I know that's of interest to you. Finally, I'll explain why this will be the ideal festival for you to sponsor. I'll be pleased to answer any questions at the end of my talk. Is that OK, everyone? Good. Right, let me tell you about the performers we hope to …

Lesson 12.2. Track 2.28.

1

It's no surprise I'm in prison. I'm just like my dad. He was a big man, and he had a very quick temper. He was violent at home, always hitting me and my mum, and he was violent outside the home, always picking arguments and fighting with people, so he was in and out of prison all the time. I'm the same. That's why I'm in jail at the moment. Me and some mates, we went to a club, someone said something I didn't like and I hit him. Really hard, so he was badly injured. The police came and took me off to the station. In the corridor of the police station, I did something really stupid. I lost my temper with a police officer and attacked him. I'm sorry now, of course. If I had learned to control my temper when I was a

kid, I wouldn't have hit the police officer. You just can't do that. In prison, I attend a class on how to control your anger. I'm learning a lot from the instructor and the other people in the class. I think it'll be useful when I come out of prison – I'll be able to control my temper better. Actually, all I want to do now is keep out of trouble, settle down and lead a normal life.

2

The newspapers called me 'Mr Big'. I liked that, but I didn't like the sentence I got – 20 years in prison. I didn't expect to be caught. You see, I plan crimes, but I don't actually commit them. I get other people to do that. I know I'm very intelligent – everyone says so. If I had wanted to, I could have become a top businessman or maybe a lawyer. But early on, I decided to follow a life of crime. It was an easy way to make money. And later, I started planning really big robberies. That's what I really enjoyed. I organised some big robberies and we made lots of money. But then I planned a robbery at the airport – gold bullion, worth over £10 million. Unfortunately, my team of robbers made a mistake. They stayed at the airport too long. If they had done the job more quickly, they would have left in time, and the police wouldn't have caught them. One of my gang gave my name to the police and I was arrested. I'm 51 now. When I get out of prison, I'll buy a villa in Spain and retire there. Plenty of my friends are already over there.

3

My parents didn't have much money but they were good to me. We lived in a poor area in Glasgow. A lot of people were unemployed and the crime rate was high. When I was about eight years old, I joined a gang of girls and we used to go shoplifting – you know, stealing things from shops and stores. It was great fun, until we got caught. I'll never forget my mum's face when the police officer came to our door.

Then, when I was a teenager, I started stealing from houses and when they caught me, I was sent to reform school – that's where they put young people who commit crimes. When I came out, I couldn't get a job and I was unemployed for over a year. So what choice did I have? If I hadn't been unemployed, I wouldn't have started robbing cash machines. I was sent to prison for two years. I'm 21 now, and I don't want to go back to prison. I think I've been so unlucky in my life. If I had lived in a different area, I wouldn't have become a criminal. And, I might have tried harder if I hadn't been unemployed. So, my life would have been totally different. I would have studied at night school if I had found a good job, and got some qualifications. Anyway, now I'm going to move out of the area and make a new start somewhere else.

Lesson 12.3. Track 2.29.

1

They took so much money that everyone in this country and in Europe will be aware of it, and they might have wanted to use the money in Europe.

2

They shouln't have stolen such a large amount of money. Someone found a huge bag of cash the other day and the first thing they thought was, 'Could it have come from that Tonbridge job?'

3

Basically, they can't have planned it properly. They should have involved fewer people. And you know, the more people involved, the greater the chance a friend or relative will tell the police. Mind you – some friend.

4

The £2 million reward might have got some informers and other criminals interested. The culture of not informing on other criminals no longer exists. People will do anything to get their hands on that much money.

5

Banks have become much better at tracking bank notes, so there is a possibility that they might have traced some of the cash.

6

The police think someone with inside knowledge could have been involved – someone who works there – and if so that person will be the most likely one to offer up information when they are questioned by the police. They won't be used to police questioning and they could be the weakest link.

7

The security people must have been very careless. The robbers could have been caught easily if the security people were doing their jobs properly.

8

Well in one sense it couldn't have been more successful. They got away with £50 million.

Lesson 12.4. Track 2.30.

1

Members of the jury, the facts of this case are simple. You have a poor, homeless man who faced a lonely night in a cold station. To keep warm, he went into a bookshop, read a book for a while and then decided to go out, probably to get a cup of tea. And then he thought, 'Why don't I take a few books with me to have a look at while I sit on a bench? I'll put them back later when I've finished my tea.' The evidence clearly shows that the manager of the bookshop acted too quickly. He accused my client of being a thief in front of other customers. I will bring witnesses to confirm that he is an honest man who has fallen on hard times. I am sure that you will find my client innocent.

2

The facts of the case are clear. Let me summarise the events for you. A homeless man goes into a bookstore early in the evening. He has no money, so he slips three books into the inside pockets of his overcoat, hoping that nobody will see him, then leaves the shop without paying. I suggest to you that this man probably goes into stores quite

often to steal books and then sells them to local second-hand bookshops. He does not deserve your sympathy. He is simply a common thief. There should be no doubt in your minds that this man is guilty of theft. A witness will claim that she noticed the man looking around to make sure that no one saw him stealing the books. Unfortunately for him, this man forgot that the store has security cameras. I am confident that you will find the defendant guilty.

3

J1: You can look at it in two ways, I think. Do you believe the witness who said he was definitely stealing the books, or do you believe the man himself? He said he was just borrowing the books for half an hour to read on the bench outside the store. Then he was going to return them. But he didn't get the chance to do it. I believe he's innocent because the manager didn't give him a chance to explain before calling the police. He seems an honest person to me. What do the rest of you think?

J2: Mmm, it's a difficult one. On the one hand, he had some good character witnesses, but on the other hand, one witness is sure he was stealing the books. Personally, I'm not certain he's guilty because I think he acted on impulse, without really thinking. What does anyone else think?

J3: Well, I've made up my mind. I'm certain he's guilty. He didn't look honest to me. No, he didn't fool me for one minute.

J2: I don't think it's a case of trying to fool us. It's clear to me that he's not guilty.

Lesson 12.5. Track 2.31.

Good morning. I'm Police Constable Martin Wilkes and today I am going to talk to you about simple home security. How can we improve security in the home and how can we protect ourselves? In the first part of my talk I'm going to mention simple precautions that don't cost anything. In the second part, I'll talk about devices you can buy to help with home security.

You might think I'm stating the obvious, but in my experience failing to follow these simple steps leads to most security problems. First, always remember to close the doors and windows at the front of your house or apartment when you are at the back of the building or in the garden, especially in warm weather. Leaving your windows open creates a target and an opportunity for burglars. Second, don't leave signs that you are not at home, such as leaving a note on the front door saying you've just gone to the shops and you'll be back soon. Another simple precaution is to ask for identification from any visitors who claim they are from the gas, electricity or water companies.

Now for the second part of my advice. An easy way of improving security is to buy and fit locks for your windows. Window locks are cheap to buy and easy to fit. A further simple and cheap device is a safety chain. This allows you to open the front door just a little. You can then see who is calling and talk to them. The advantage of the safety chain is that no one can push the door open and

come into the house. You mightn't believe it but many people who have safety chains forget to put them on when opening the door to strangers. A more expensive security method is to fit improved locks to all your doors. These locks are difficult to force open so they keep your property safe. An even more expensive method is to fit a burglar alarm for when you're away from home. Alarms are very effective ways of deterring burglars. If you use all these methods you'll find that you can make it very difficult for thieves to burgle your home.

Lesson 12.5. Track 2.32.

Good morning. Today I'm going to talk about two main topics. The first is car security. That means keeping your car secure. The second is security in the car. That means keeping yourself safe and secure in the car.

If you have a car or if you're a passenger in a car there are some simple tips that will help you to protect your goods. The first tip is always to lock the car, even if you're just going to be away from it for a few moments. Secondly, never leave anything valuable where it can be seen, even if the car is locked. If you can't take your valuable goods with you, make sure they are locked in the boot of the car. Radios, DVD players and satellite navigation systems are expensive. Remove them from the car when you park. Nowadays, a lot of drivers use car immobilisers, which prevents thieves from starting the car, and tracking devices that help the police track the position of your stolen car. Finally, if your car is old and doesn't have an alarm, put one in.

Now, let's switch to security in the car – your personal security. The first thing to do is to lock your car doors as soon as you get in. A common trick for thieves is to wait for a driver to get in the car, then to open the passenger door and steal a bag on the passenger seat, for example. But there is one point to always remember – release the locks when travelling at high speed. This helps you get out of the car quickly in case of an accident.

My next point concerns protecting yourself when you are stationary. If you see any crowds or if someone on the street shouts at you, lock all the doors and close all the windows. This is a simple precaution to prevent theft from the car. My mother once nearly had her bag snatched as she sat in the car at some traffic lights on a busy street. Fortunately, she was very quick-thinking and managed to hold the thief's fingers, bending them backwards and forcing him to drop the bag in the car. She then closed the windows, checked that the doors were locked and drove away. She was lucky. But unless you follow my advice you mightn't be so lucky. Of course, you shouldn't really leave your bag or briefcase in the front with you – it's much safer in the back, with the doors locked.

Finally, worse than this is carjacking – someone jumping in at traffic lights and stealing your car with you in it. This is less likely to happen if your doors are locked.

So, remember, car security is not only the security of your car and of things in it, but also your security in the car. Follow my advice and stay safe. Thank you.

Review 10–12 Track 2.33

A: OK. Thank you all for coming. We're here to discuss the new space the university has given us for a coffee bar. Firstly, I'd like to say that it's clear to me that the new area is much better than what we had before so I'd like us to be positive about it.

B: I agree. I was very unhappy with the appearance of the old coffee bar. It had lots of bad paintings on the wall and really uncomfortable seats. I think this new area could be a much nicer place to relax.

A: Thank you for your comment – I think we'd all agree with you. This is very different from the old recreation area. For a start, the room is in a completely new building and nearer the lecture rooms.

C: Sorry, could I just say something please? I think the university could give us something much better than this area. After all, we pay fees …

A: I understand that but you can look at it in two ways. Yes, it's not perfect, but it's better than what we had.

Intermediate and Upper Intermediate levels

David Falvey studied Politics, Philosophy and Economics at the University of Oxford and did his MA in TEFL at the University of Birmingham. He has lived in Africa and the Middle East and has teaching, training and managerial experience in the UK and Asia, including working as a teacher trainer at the British Council in Tokyo. He is now Head of the English Language Centre at London Metropolitan University. David is co-author of the successful business English course *Market Leader*.

Simon Kent studied History at the University of Sheffield. He has 20 years' teaching experience including three years in Berlin at the time of German reunification. Simon is co-author of the successful business English course *Market Leader*. He is currently Senior Lecturer in English as a Foreign Language at London Metropolitan University.

David Cotton studied Economics at the University of Reading and French Language and Literature at the University of Toronto. He has over 30 years teaching and training experience, and is co-author of the successful *Market Leader* and *Business Class* coursebooks. He has taught in Canada, France and England, and been visiting lecturer in many universities overseas. He is currently visiting lecturer at London Metropolitan University.

Elementary and Pre-intermediate levels

Ian Lebeau studied Modern Languages at the University of Cambridge and Applied Linguistics at the University of Reading. He has nearly 30 years' experience in ELT – mainly in higher education – and has taught in Spain, Italy and Japan. He is currently Senior Lecturer in English as a Foreign Language at London Metropolitan University.

Gareth Rees studied Natural Sciences at the University of Cambridge. Having taught in Spain and China, he currently teaches at London Metropolitan University and University of the Arts. He also develops English language materials for the BBC World Service Learning English section and he makes films which appear in festivals and on British television.

Far left: Simon Kent
Centre left: David Falvey
Centre: Gareth Rees
Centre right: Ian Lebeau
Far right: David Cotton